PRAISE FOR THIS BOOK

This book is a wonderful resource for anyone who cares about the spread of Christ's church. It is thorough, biblically faithful, full of hard-won wisdom, and practical without being overly prescriptive. I found my thinking about church planting was sharpened and my zeal for church planting was kindled. I intend to implement many of the things I've learned and hope to read this with as many church leaders as I can.

Mike McKinley

Senior Pastor, Sterling Park Baptist Church, Sterling, VA
Author of *Am I Really a Christian?*

If someone asked you what it means to plant a church, would you know how to answer? (Hint: It's not about gardening.) *Churches Planting Churches* combines biblical depth with field-tested strategies to help you prepare, send, and sustain healthy churches. Drawing from seasoned practitioners and rooted in rich biblical theology, this book offers both the "why" and the "how" of multiplication—starting with a robust vision of the church as Christ's beloved Bride and body, then moving into clear, field-tested strategies for preparing, sending, and sustaining church plants. This book will inspire your heart, sharpen your convictions, and equip you to join God's mission of making disciples to the ends of the earth.

Eric Bancroft

Lead Pastor, Grace Church, Miami, FL

I believe that the multiplication of healthy local churches is the primary means by which the Great Commission goes forth. The reflective practitioners who offer us this book, *Churches Planting Churches*, have done an outstanding service to the Church. In each chapter, we are given wisdom from faithful and experienced pastors, all undergirded by a robust biblical ecclesiology. If you are partnering with a church plant, praying to plant a church, or planting a church, this is an invaluable resource to have on your bookshelf. I pray this book finds a wide audience with sending churches and planting teams.

Matt Capps

Lead Pastor, Fairview Baptist Church, Apex,
Author of *Drawn by Beauty:
Awe and Wonder in the Christian Life*

This incredible volume kicks off with a foreword by a friend who has taught me to treasure Christ every time we talk and ends with a postscript for a friend who absolutely exudes pastoral care in every conversation we have. Each one of these chapters offers practical advice for those aspiring to church plant. I've learned much by watching the ministries of many of these authors so I'm thrilled that a generation of church planters can gain from their wisdom as well. Written by Baptists who are committed to biblical ecclesiology—please pick this up and read it!

Ryan Robertson

President of Reaching & Teaching

Congratulations to the Pillar Network for putting together this thoughtfully conceived resource for those interested in, involved with, and called to the important work of church planting! This volume answers foundational questions about the church and church planting and then proceeds to offer extensive guidance on almost every phase and facet of church planting, including the challenges that can be anticipated. More than a how-to handbook, this volume, authored by a geographically and demographically diverse group of contributors and shaped by the capable editorial hands of Matt Rogers and Phil Newton, points the way toward healthy church starts, which can be nurtured, sustained, and multiplied, with the enablement of God's Spirit, for the advancement of the gospel and the glory of God.

David S. Dockery, Ph.D.

President and Distinguished Professor of Theology,
Southwestern Baptist Theological Seminary

Jesus' plan A is healthy local churches. As healthy families nurture and send out their children, so healthy churches ask God to help them spread and reproduce. Yet church planting is hard and painful. Like parenting, it can be a remarkable joy when done well. I am eager to put this sober and wise handbook in the hands of both planters and those sending them.

John Erickson

Director of Care and Advance-Treasuring
Christ Together Network

Church Planting Churches consistently highlights a crucial partnership: the bond between the sending church and the church plant. In the realm of church planting, the importance of this relationship is undeniable. Church planting is inherently challenging, even under the best conditions. That's why the unwavering support of a gospel-preaching, Spirit-led sending church is vital for nurturing and establishing vibrant new Christ communities. This partnership is not just beneficial; it is essential for success. Well done!

Michael A Proud, Jr., D.Min.
Executive Director,
Colorado Baptist General Convention

Biblically faithful, theologically anchored, and intensely practical, this guidebook feels like a full-on training camp hosted by an elite roster of player-coaches who know the game because they've lived it. They're not celebrity strategists, but ordinary planters and pastors (and a pastor's wife!) who have modeled extraordinary faithfulness. For sending churches ready to take the next step in planting and multiplying churches but unsure where to begin: start here.

Sam Martyn
Church planter and church planting
team leader among Muslims in Europe

Churches Planting Churches is a comprehensive resource designed to equip churches both theologically and practically, enabling them to multiply healthy congregations. The book is a gift to pastors and congregations longing to fulfill the

Great Commission, of which church planting is a vital part. As a guide for multiplying churches, it prioritizes spiritual vitality over pragmatic success, rejecting secular models in favor of reliance on biblical theology and the work of the Spirit. As Nathan Knight notes, the volume is not a "handbook," but rather an "invitation" to form Christ-centered communities, prioritizing spiritual formation. The authors prioritize planting enduring, biblically faithful churches in an era of transient, ever-changing church models.

David E. Prince, Ph.D.
Pastor, Ashland Avenue Baptist Church, Lexington, Kentucky
Author of *Preaching the Truth as it is in Jesus:*
An Andrew Fuller Reader

Fall in love with the church all over again and you'll want to see more churches planted. *Churches Planting Churches* is no dry manual or pragmatic how-to on developing new churches. It is a book written by saints in the trenches of healthy church ministry, sharing their story, inspiring all of us to impact the world through new churches. A one-stop shop for church planting, the host of voices hit everything—from how to find a planter to the role of women in church planting. But what I love most about it — it begins with a compelling vision of who the church is and why she is needed. Listen to these voices and join in the work of multiplying churches.

Joel Kurtz
Lead Pastor, The Garden Church, Baltimore
Director of One Hope

What a wonderful resource this is! We are indebted to Matt Rogers and Phil Newton for assembling this valuable collection of essays beautifully wedding the theological and practical. Too many church planting discussions are long on planting but short on church. Some then end up long on ecclesiology but short on real practice. These essays provide a robust ecclesiological vision to guide the whole process and then they speak to vital, day-to-day issues which churches must consider in order to faithfully and partially carry out that vision. I am excited for this book to be available to my students.

Ray Van Neste, Ph.D.
Dean, School of Theology & Missions,
Union University, Jackson, TN
Professor of Biblical Studies; Vice President,
University Ministries

Whether you're aspiring to pastor a church plant or a church hoping to plant, you'll want to read this "playbook" from cover to cover! It's packed with wisdom, practical advice, and Biblical foundations from a host of practitioners that will equip every leader who's laboring to see churches multiplied for the glory of Christ.

Brian Parks
Senior Pastor, Covenant Hope Church, Dubai, UAE

The local church is God's primary instrument for the accomplishment of the Great Commission. This timely book from the Pillar Network reminds us of the necessity and critical role of church planting in Great Commission work. *Churches Planting Churches* helpfully guides pastors and churches in both the theological and practical aspects of church planting. This book addresses the foundational issues related to the nature and essence of the church and is full of wisdom from those who have experience planting churches across North America and beyond. Excited to see how this book will be used to encourage and equip future church planters and church plants.

Paul Akin, Ph.D.

Provost and Associate Professor of Christian Missions,
The Southern Baptist Theological Seminary, Louisville, KY

I've never planted a church, but I hang out with guys all the time who want to one day. So I'm regularly looking for resources to help them. *Churches Planting Churches* has quickly jumped near the top of the list. Sure, it's theologically faithful. But it's also chock-full of practical counsel. Rare is the book that offers both. I recommend this book not only to the aspiring church planter—that's obvious—but also to the established church that needs a little nudge to risk their resources to obey the Great Commission.

Alex Duke

Director of Training & Sending at
Third Avenue Baptist Church, Louisville, KY;
Editor for 9Marks

This is an excellent book that I will be quick to commend for those interested. In planting biblically faithful and sustainable churches. It is comprehensive and in depth. It is thorough and readable. It is helpful and enjoyable. Few books can check all these boxes, but this book does!

Daniel L. Akin, Ph. D.

President, Senior Professor of Preaching & Theology,
Southeastern Baptist Theological Seminary

I have always been worried about people planting churches out of a cool wave in the evangelical world. This book roots you in the scriptures as a motive, walks you in the process as a mentor, and reminds you of those sent as a pastor. Highly grateful for this amazing resource.

Juan Hernández

Pastor, Iglesia Cristiana Rescue Mission Church,
Barranquilla, Colombia

CHURCHES
PLANTING
CHURCHES

CHURCHES
PLANTING
CHURCHES

*A Guide for
Multiplying
Churches*

EDITED BY
MATT ROGERS &
PHIL A. NEWTON

Churches Planting Churches: A Guide for Multiplying Churches
Edited by Matt Rogers and Phil A. Newton

ISBN 978-1-955295-69-7

Cover design and typesetting by
Rachel Rosales, Orange Peel Design

 **COURIER** PUBLISHING

100 Manly Street
Greenville, South Carolina 29601

Printed in the United States of America

TABLE OF CONTENTS

PART 5: CARING FOR A CHURCH PLANT

FOREWORD

Just think about the courage it took for the "woman of the city, who was a sinner" to show up at the dinner party of a Pharisee unannounced (Luke 7:36–39). It'd be like a mouse willingly showing up at a cat's house.

Yet she went.

Why?

Because she couldn't help herself.

She had to be with Jesus.

By the end, it was clear she made the right decision. She left his presence not as one used, but as one forgiven, loved, and at peace—not used and taken advantage of as she'd been so many times before.

This story pictures the motive behind faithful church planting.

The Body of Christ

The church *visualizes* Jesus. The church makes the spiritual tangible. As the "body of Christ," the church invites sinners to show up to the house of the Redeemed so they too can go in peace, just as the woman did.

When the beloved sons and daughters of God gather each Lord's Day to hear the Word preached, sinners hear the words of Jesus. When the beloved sons and daughters of God gather each Lord's Day to sing, they hear the voice of Jesus. When the beloved sons and daughters of God gather each Lord's Day to pray, they pray to the Father through Jesus. When the beloved sons and daughters of God gather each Lord's Day to take the Lord's Supper, they come to Jesus' Table. When the beloved sons and daughters of God serve in joy or pain, they serve Jesus. When the beloved sons and daughters proclaim the gospel, they invite people to trust in Jesus.

The local church does all this and more. That's why we don't see church planting as a fad but a necessity. We need more and more healthy churches in every city around the world so that the world can see the beauty of Jesus and treasure Him.

An Invitation (Not a Handbook)

What you hold in your hands is an invitation to form communities of Christ. The authors believe the local church is God's plan for how saints grow in treasuring Christ on planet Earth. They believe that the local church is the gospel made visible. They want to help you start local churches so that sinners can find peace and wholeness in Jesus Christ until He returns and calls the Redeemed home forever. Our local churches are a foretaste of this heavenly reality.

Churches Planting Churches starts with robust ecclesiology because nothing else can undergird our planting efforts. From there, you will read chapters on funding models, picking the right locations, and even associationalism. These topics are full of hard-won, practical wisdom, and these chapters are full of counsel that help people tangibly meet with and treasure Jesus.

Tested

Not only is this not a handbook, but this is also not just another church planting resource. It's different because it uniquely commends Christ with a view toward His tangible presence through His tested people.

I've received members from the church Matt Rogers serves. They've walked in the door with these principles already at work. I sat in a small office a little under 20 years ago and heard Nate Akin articulate these principles. He's practiced what he has been preaching since then. While Dave Kiehn and I are bitter baseball rivals (go Cardinals!), this brother has worked against a formidable tide of toxic "cultural Christianity" in South Carolina and cultivated a counter-cultural witness that has stood the test of time. As a young seminarian, I heard Dwayne Milioni not only teach these things, but some of my dearest friends in the faith were sent out of the church he pastors.

And Phil Newton. My goodness, what a model. This brother has pastored for more than four decades! You might know someone that has served the church that long, but I doubt you know someone that did that and still gushes humility, joy, service, and passion for Christ.

These are just a few of the authors that you will learn from. There's more Christ-exalting wisdom from others here that have walked through the fires of what they write about. Don't just read them—*listen* to them.

Castles, Not Tents

In a world that drags us down in every crevice and ditch, Christ is the only one who can lift us up. Our local churches should be able where people can confidently go, like that sinful woman, to meet Jesus and find forgiveness and healing. Even more, may we go to them with the gospel!

As we gather and go, may we form the kinds of churches that are more like castles, not tents. Windy days flatten tents. Castles last. This book proposes castles, not tents, through strong and meaningful membership, biblically qualified elders, and an interest in multiplying more churches that practice these things. These works must characterize us if we are not going to build in vain.

Be strong and courageous. Be saturated with the love of Christ. Be informed and inspired. Be Christ to communities. The words that follow will orient you in all these things and more.

For the glory of Christ and the good of His church,

Nathan Knight
Pastor, Restoration Church DC, Washington, DC
Author, *Planting by Pastoring:*
A Vision for Starting a Healthy Church

PREFACE

Matt Rogers

The Bible echoes. Words or ideas presented at the start of the Bible echo from beginning to end. As God's story develops, we see that it's not so much new ideas that are presented, but prior concepts are clarified, refined, and directed. Unlike human words that lose potency and volume as they echo, God's words get louder and clearer.

"Be fruitful and multiply" (Gen. 1:28). These are the first words God speaks to His image-bearers. These four words echo throughout the Bible's story and even into the present. God intended for the first couple, Adam and Eve, to fill the earth with worshipers of the one true God.

As we fast forward to the New Testament, this work of multiplication remains primary. Jesus famously tells his disciples to go and make disciples of all nations—in other words, He tells the disciples to multiply themselves by going, baptizing, and teaching the nations (Matt. 28:19–20). The echo is heard again at the start of the book of Acts: "You will be my witnesses in Jerusalem, in all Judea and Samaria, and to the ends of the earth" (Acts 1:8). Once again, Jesus commands His first followers to multiply themselves by witnessing to the resurrected Christ so that the entire earth would be filled with those who love and follow Jesus.

Throughout the book of Acts and beyond, this work of multiplication is closely tied to the multiplication of healthy churches. The disciples are faithful to the work of multiplication, and through their witness to Jesus, God births local churches of the redeemed (Acts 2:42–47). As the mission expands, so grows the church, both in terms of its size in any one location and in terms of its reach to new locations. These churches then step into God's created pattern by being fruitful and multiplying (see Acts 13:1–3). Healthy churches multiplying other healthy churches—that's how the Great Commission gets fulfilled according to God's design.

Most church leaders understand the need for healthy churches. The overwhelming secularity of our day makes it clear that virtually any city around the world needs more and more healthy churches. But focusing on church planting alone isn't enough. Consider parenting. Everyone agrees we need healthy teenagers—guys and girls who are wise, free from addiction, in healthy relationships, and so on. To get healthy teens, however, you must equip parents *and* you must disciple kids long before the teenage years. You won't get a mature teen if you only begin the year before he turns thirteen.

The same holds true for churches. We need more healthy churches, but we don't get them by hyper-focusing on coaching and training existing church plants. We get them by equipping potential sending churches to step into their God-given mandate to multiply other healthy churches. That's the goal of this book.

You might think of this book like a playbook. There are two times to draw up a play. You can do so in the huddle in the final timeout before the last play of the game. Everything's on the line. The crowd is screaming. The players are nervous. In just a few seconds the outcome will be clear. Or you could draw up a play at practice. There you have the luxury of doodling on a whiteboard, trying out the play with real players, making the various positions and movements better after evaluating it in action. If you draw up a play in practice, then when it comes to the end of the game, you simply have to remember what you did in practice. When it comes to church planting, it's far better to work on the play in practice by reading a book like this. Don't wait until the final buzzer and try to figure it out as you go along.

We've assembled some of the best church planting practitioners—or coaches—and asked them to design a guide for churches who want to multiply. Our aim is to equip churches to understand and address the practical dynamics of raising up, sending, and supporting new churches. These brothers and sisters have been doodling on church-planting white boards for decades, and now have agreed to bring you into the huddle so you can learn from their successes and failures. Just as a team studies a playbook so that its players accomplish their goal, we're trying to provide a unified playbook to keep a planting team together and focused.

Hopefully after reading this book you will have confidence that God can use your church, regardless of its size or location, on this glorious mission of planting churches.

In Part 1, we will unpack God's design for His church. Before we launch into practices, it's important that we first have a robust understanding of the definition and purpose of the church. From there, starting in Part 2, we'll consider what's necessary to prepare a church to be a sending church. Part 3 then looks at a series of key questions that sending churches tend to get stuck on. In Part 4, we dip into some of the nitty-gritty of developing a church plant. In Part 5, we want to show you how to shepherd those you've sent.

Who would find this book helpful? Elder teams, church staff members, aspiring church planters, and everyday church members seeking to understand how they can multiply. As the sending congregations understand the foundation, practice, and process for planting, the more enthused they will be in supporting the work. And some who've never thought of being part of a planting team might be eager to join. God is continuing to say to His people, "Be fruitful and multiply." We want to help you listen and obey.

CONTRIBUTORS

Nate Akin is the Executive Director of The Pillar Network. He is also a founder of Baptist21. Nate is married to Kelsey and father to Ada and Ryland. He is pursuing a PhD in Pastoral Theology at Southeastern Baptist Theological Seminary. He's the author of *Convictional, Confessional, Cheerful Baptists*.

Nathan Baumgartner serves as the Director of Finance and Development at The Pillar Network. Prior to transitioning to full-time ministry, Nathan spent sixteen years working in corporate banking. He holds an undergraduate degree from Liberty University and a Master of Business Administration from The University of Chicago, and he is currently enrolled in doctoral studies at The Southern Baptist Theological Seminary. He's married to Rachel, and they have four children.

Clint Darst is the planter and Pastor over Preaching and Vision at King's Cross Church in Greensboro, NC. He previously served on staff with Campus Outreach and as a football chaplain at Page High School, Wingate University, and the Carolina Panthers. He's written for 9Marks, Baptist21, and the Center for Preaching and Pastoral Leadership. He's married to Rachel, and they have three children—Eden, Nias, and Noah.

Liam Garvie serves as Associate Pastor of the historic Charlotte Chapel in Edinburgh, UK, after pastoring for several years in St. Andrews. He also serves The Pillar Network as Director of Ministry: International. He grew up without any knowledge of Christ but after hearing a sermon on Gethsemane while at university, he believed the gospel and committed his life to Christ. He's married to Kathryn, who joins him in coordinating Pillar's International Conference in Edinburgh. Liam and Kathryn have three children.

Dave Kiehn is the Pastor of Park Baptist Church in Rock Hill, SC and Director of Ministry for the Americas for the Pillar Network. He teaches at several seminaries and equips pastors for gospel-centered ministry. As an author, he writes on church leadership, preaching, and revitalization. He's the author of *Pulling the Thread: A Pastoral Theology of Church Revitalization.* He's married to Ellen, and they have three children.

Brandon Langley serves as the Lead Pastor of St. Rose Community Church, a church planting church in the New Orleans Metro Area. He serves on staff at The Pillar Network as Associate Director of Regions, has contributed articles to 9Marks and TGC, and is the author of *Devoted Together: How to Find and Join a Church.* He's married to Anne Marie and they have two children.

Ben McRoy has been in pastoral ministry for almost two decades. He is Pastor of Mobilization at Faith Baptist Church, Youngsville, NC. Ben leads pastors and churches toward church planting and revitalization in multiple venues on local, state, and national levels. He and his wife, Shelby have two children—Rylee and Nathaniel.

Karson Merkel is an Associate Pastor at Midtown Baptist Church in Memphis, TN. He spent the past five years serving at Covenant Hope Church in the United Arab Emirates and is currently finishing his MDiv at the Southern Baptist Theological Seminary. He's married to Kenoa and they have one son, Banks.

Dwayne Milioni has served for decades as Lead Pastor of Open Door Church in Raleigh, NC and as Associate Professor of Preaching at Southeastern Seminary. He also chairs the board of The Pillar Network, which he co-founded to plant and revitalize healthy Baptist churches. He wrote the study notes for the *CSB Jesus Daily Bible.* He's married to Kay and they have four children and three grandchildren.

Phil A. Newton is Director of Pastoral Care and Mentoring for the Pillar Network after serving as a lead pastor for forty-four years. He's Visiting Professor of Pastoral Theology at Southeastern Seminary and Adjunct Professor at Midwestern Seminary. He has contributed to several journals and writes most often about church, pastoral ministry, and the Christian walk. His most recent book is *Unburdening the Soul: Per-*

sonal and Corporate Confession of Sins. He's married to Karen and they have five children and nine grandchildren.

Victor Rodriguez was born in Texas and grew up in Puerto Rico before moving to Charlotte in 2004. He serves as Hispanic Church Coordinator for The Pillar Network. In 2020, his Hispanic church merged with Park Baptist Church in Rock Hill, SC, displaying the beauty of unity and God's glory. After much prayer and discernment, in 2025, Park Baptist Church sent Victor and many members to plant Iglesia Bautista Soli Deo Gloria in Rock Hill, SC, where Victor serves as Pastor. He has a master's degree in Christian Studies from Southeastern Seminary. Victor is married to Eunice and they have three children.

Matt Rogers has served as the Pastor of Christ Fellowship in Greenville, SC for the last sixteen years. In addition to pastoral ministry, Matt resources churches in The Pillar Network and teaches at Southeastern Baptist Theological Seminary. He and his wife Sarah have recently published *Generation to Generation: Fulfilling the Great Commission One Life at a Time.* Matt and Sarah have five children.

Sarah Rogers serves as the Women's Ministry Coordinator with The Pillar Network and aids churches in developing ministry to women. Sarah is married to Matt, and they have five children, all of whom Sarah has homeschooled. She recently published a book on disciple-making with Matt, entitled, *Generation to Generation.*

Steven Wade has been a pastor and professor for over twenty-five years. Since 2017, he has served as Lead Pastor of Faith Baptist Church in Youngsville, NC. He is also Professor of Pastoral Theology at Southeastern Baptist Theological Seminary in Wake Forest, NC where he has been on faculty since 2004. He has contributed chapters to *Entrusted to the Faithful: An Introduction to Pastoral Leadership* and *Equipped to Serve: How Seminary Strengthens Your Ministry.* Steven and his wife, Jenny, have four children— Caleb, Sarah, Lydia, and Anna—and enjoy living on their hobby farm in North Carolina.

PART 1

FOUNDATIONS FOR A CHURCH PLANT

CHAPTER 1

WHY MUST CHURCHES START CHURCHES?

Nate Akin

It's a strange reality. You can attend a church planting conference and hear speakers who slam the church. It's like going
to a fitness seminar where all the presenters dismiss healthy
eating and exercise. These leaders are well-intentioned. They
tend to emphasize God's mission to save people and make
disciples, not merely to "build a church." But the implica-
tion often follows that in church planting, ecclesiology does
not matter. Just reaching people—as if those things were
somehow at odds in God's economy—seems to be the main
appeal. In truth, the sentiment of "reach people and worry
less about ecclesiology" undermines the very means God has
ordained to save and disciple—*the church* herself.

At the end of time, Christ will be presented with His bride that will be a people, not just disconnected individuals. The corporate emphasis on the people of God runs throughout Scripture. The church is indispensable to the Great Commission. In the New Testament, there is no faithful multiplication, no lasting discipleship, and no visible expression of the Kingdom apart from the local church. Even at the end of history, the church is there (Eph. 2–3; Heb. 12:18–24; 1 Pet. 2:4–10; Rev. 21–22).

Many conferences and workshops highlight the priority of making disciples. I applaud and join with that priority. And yet, when disciple-making gets untethered from the church, it risks undercutting and minimizing the very means that God has ordained to make disciples—the church. If the church is incidental to the work of disciple-making and evangelism, then why care about planting churches anyway?

We believe that the church matters both now and into eternity, which is why the present collection of authors in Pillar Network churches want to give serious consideration to the work of church planting and multiplication. We are also fervently committed to Church-Centered Missions.[1] We commit to grow in becoming multiplying churches because we believe the Great Commission is accomplished by the

---

[1] For more on church-centered missions, Alex DiPrima and I have an upcoming book on the subject entitled, *I Will Build My Church: The Priority of the Local Congregation in Christ's Plan for the World* (Nashville: B&H Academic, forthcoming). In addition, 9Marks will be releasing a series of books on this topic. The first has been released. Check out Aaron Menikoff and Harshit Singh's *Prioritizing Missions in the Church* (9Marks Church-Centered Missions; Wheaton, IL: Crossway, 2025).

starting and strengthening of churches since they are both the means and the end for this work.

If this is true, then I want to set up all that follows in this book by arguing that **churches who want to fulfill the Great Commission must start other churches.** The idea that God's mission is just about reaching people apart from the church represents an anemic view of the local church that undermines, rather than enhances, the New Testament pattern to start other churches. This false idea presents the church as almost disposable in the mission. It shockingly implies that the church is an impediment rather than the right means to the desired end. My burden is to encourage us all to be faithful in the present to plant churches. We'll unpack this idea by starting at the end and then working our way back to the beginning of the grand story of Scripture.

I love sports, especially big tournaments like March Madness. The best part of that tournament every year is "One Shining Moment," the final video that highlights all the great moments throughout the tournament. It gets me every time. My coach at Murray State University would start every season showing us the previous season's video. He would end with the exhortation: "Being in that video is our goal." He started at the end to motivate us for the journey to come.

That's what I want to do here. Allow me to paint a picture of the glorious end first, and then map how God ordained for us to get to that end through the starting of churches. My hope is that God will produce in us hope, faith, perseverance, fervency, faithfulness, and partnership in planting churches to the glory of our great King. C. S. Lewis helps us see why future hope is so important for present duty. He writes,

> Hope is one of the theological virtues. This means that a continual looking forward to the eternal world is not (as some modern people think) a form of escapism or wishful thinking, but one of the things a Christian is meant to do. It does not mean that we are to leave the present world as it is. If you read history you will find that the Christians who did most for the present world were just those who thought most of the next . . . because their minds were occupied with Heaven. It is since Christians have largely ceased to think of the other world that they have become so ineffective in this one.[2]

As we think about the next world, I pray we will be those who do the most for the present one. Why do we plant churches? If it's for self-aggrandizing reasons, it has no lasting value. But if it's to follow the New Testament pattern to the glory of God, then it's among the most important endeavors imaginable.

Let me identify eight reasons we labor to plant churches.

The Church Will Be Given to Jesus at the End

At the end of all things, the church in all her splendor will be presented to the King. It is the "One Shining Moment" reel depicted in Revelation 21–22. We begin at the end to give

---

[2] C. S. Lewis, *Mere Christianity* (New York: Harper Collins, 2001), 134.

us all a picture of what our efforts in this life, empowered by the Spirit for the glory of our King, will produce. As Lewis stated, conducting this work with hope of the future world will be of the most good in the present one. John provides us the final picture:

> Then I saw a new heaven and a new earth, for the first heaven and the first earth had passed away, and the sea was no more. And I saw the holy city, new Jerusalem, coming down out of heaven from God, prepared *as a bride adorned for her husband.* And I heard a loud voice from the throne saying, "Behold, *the dwelling place of God is with man.* He will dwell with them, and *they will be his people,* and God himself will be with them as their God. He will wipe away every tear from their eyes, and death shall be no more, neither shall there be mourning, nor crying, nor pain anymore, for the former things have passed away." . . . The one who conquers will have this heritage, and *I will be his God and he will be my son.* . . . Then came one of the seven angels who had the seven bowls full of the seven last plagues and spoke to me, saying, "Come, *I will show you the Bride, the wife of the Lamb.*" And he carried me away in the Spirit to a great, high mountain, and showed me the holy city Jerusalem coming down out of heaven from God, having the glory of God, its radiance like a most rare jewel, like a jasper, clear as crystal. ... And I saw no temple in the city, *for its temple is*

the Lord God the Almighty and the Lamb. And the city has no need of sun or moon to shine on it, for the glory of God gives it light, and its lamp is the Lamb. By its light will the nations walk, and the kings of the earth will bring their glory into it, and its gates will never be shut by day—and there will be no night there. They will bring into it the glory and the honor of the nations. (Rev. 21:1–4, 7, 9–11, 22–26; italics added)

That vision ought to provoke all of God's people—both pastors and church members—to give of themselves through prayer, generosity, and action to the starting and strengthening of churches locally, nationally, and globally. When John speaks of the bride, he's not talking about singular Christians, he's talking about the church. He describes not just the beauty of a glorified saint but the splendor of the glorified people of God, the church. So there is a church in heaven. Not the brick-and-mortar that we all know, but the gathered people who have been redeemed by the Lamb, and they will forever rejoice before the eternal throne (Rev. 5:9–10).

Think back to your own wedding day, or to a wedding you attended. I got married in a beautiful chapel at Southeastern Seminary. The outer adornments were amazing. Yet for me, the best moment was when those doors opened, and I saw my bride smiling (because I knew it meant she had not backed out). Oh, what a day it will be when the door swings open and we behold our King.

We start at the end because it makes it more difficult to have an anemic view of the church now. As we picture what the church will one day be, we are motivated to shape and to grow the church in the present. So we labor to start churches because those churches will be filled with saints who will one day make up that final bride given to her King.

How does God bring us to this final point? Let's consider the grand story as we work our way back from the beginning to this end. God has consistently worked through a people for their good and His glory. From the beginning, God has always had a people He reveals His glory *to* in order to reveal His glory *through*. This revelation began in the Old Testament when God established covenants with His people. God's work culminated when He established the New Covenant through the work of Christ with His people, the church. God revealed His glory *to* the church in the person and work of Jesus Christ in order to reveal His glory *through* the church to the nations.

God has provided a basis and pattern for the church through the promises and requirements of the previous covenants. Each covenant reveals aspects that are only fully realized in the church. We see this, for instance, as God reveals Himself to a people by their selection, salvation, identification, celebration, and proclamation, which takes us back to God's purpose in creation in the first place.

The Church Is the Means of Filling the Earth with Worshipers

God's revelation begins when He selects Adam and Eve (by creating them, Gen. 1:26–28), identifies with them (by naming them image bearers, Gen. 1:26–28), gives them food for celebration (Gen. 1:29), and gives them a mandate that points forward to the Great Commission (Gen. 1:28). They are to fill the earth with worshippers of God who will reflect His image. Some have even argued that this can be called the "Old Testament Great Commission."[3]

God continues this pattern of revelation by establishing the Abrahamic Covenant. God revealed Himself to Abraham through the selection, identification (in circumcision), celebration with food (in Gen. 18:1-8, although Abraham was not ordained as later in the Levitical requirements for such offerings), and corresponding proclamation ("in you all the families of the earth will be blessed," Gen. 12:3). God reveals more of His salvation plan as each covenant expands on previous covenants.[4]

Some take a disjointed approach to God's revelation and purpose, as though He had one idea in the Old Testament and another in the New Testament. But the purpose of filling the earth with worshipers goes beyond the Garden and the Abrahamic Covenant. The glory and honor of the nations worshiping our God will be brought into the New Jerusalem (Rev. 21:24–26), which John identifies with the church, the wife of the Lamb (Rev. 21:9–14). The church remains central to the divine purpose of gospel mission to bring people from every tribe, tongue, people, and nation into the glory

---

[3] Mark Liederbach and Evan Lenow, *Ethics as Worship: The Pursuit of Moral Discipleship* (Phillipsburg, NJ: P&R Publishing, 2021), 79, provides a helpful table pointing out the parallels of the Adamic mandate and the Great Commission, or what they call the "Old Testament Great Commission" and the "New Testament Great Commission."

[4] John Sailhamer, *NIV Compact Bible Commentary* (Grand Rapids: Zondervan, 1999), 25.

of worshiping the Triune God. And that happens due to the redemptive work of Jesus who was slain to purchase eternal worshipers (Rev. 5:9–10).

The Church Is How Abraham's Seed Will Bless the Nations

Next, God's revelation in the Old Testament expands from Abraham's family to include a consecrated nation with a clear mission in the Mosaic Covenant. Moses writes in Exodus 19:5–6, "'Now therefore, if you will indeed obey my voice and keep my covenant, you shall be my treasured possession among all peoples, for all the earth is mine; and you shall be to me a kingdom of priests and a holy nation,' These are the words that you shall speak to the people of Israel." The people of God are to be a distinct people (selection), a holy people (identification), marked by the Passover (celebration), and a kingdom of priests (proclamation). Douglas Stuart unpacks Israel's special role when he explains,

> Israel's assignment from God involved intermediation. They were not to be a people unto themselves, enjoying their special relationship with God and paying no attention to the rest of the world. Rather, they were to represent him to the rest of the world and attempt to bring the rest of the world to him. In other words, the challenge to be "a kingdom of priests and a holy nation" repre-

sented the responsibility inherent in the original promise to Abraham in Gen. 12:2–3.[5]

Finally, God's revelation through the Davidic Covenant establishes the kingdom dimension of His saving plan. We see similar themes in this covenant of selection and identification as the promise is made to "*my people* Israel" (2 Sam. 7:10–11). There is an implicit connection to proclamation as David's name will be among "the great ones of the earth" (2 Sam. 7:9). This verse, when coupled with David's Psalm 2 and Psalm 110, demonstrates that the Old Testament did not have in mind a kingdom that was merely for itself but for the world. This idea is consistent with God's previous covenants and their promises and demands.

These Old Testament precursors culminate in the Son of David who will have a people through selection (salvation), identification (baptism and membership), celebration (Lord's Supper), and proclamation (Great Commission). Peter Gentry and Stephen Wellum helpfully make the point, "The church is *new* in redemptive-history precisely because she is the community of the new covenant. With the coming of our Lord Jesus Christ, all of the previous covenants have reached their fulfilment."[6] And notice how important the new people are by the language used of them in the New

---

[5] Douglas Stuart, *Exodus: An Exegetical and Theological Exposition of Holy Scripture* (NAS; vol. 2; Nashville: Holman Reference, 2006), 423.

[6] Peter Gentry and Stephen Wellum, *Kingdom through Covenant: A Biblical-Theological Understanding through the Covenants* (2nd ed.; Wheaton, IL: Crossway, 2018), 684-685.

Testament. Since these people are so powerful and precious to God, this seems to demand starting churches.

While precursors from the Old Testament provide a developing pattern of how God works through a missional people for His glory, the New Testament highlights the stunning place that the church holds as those people in the New Covenant. The church holds the central place in the fulfillment of God's grand commission. In fact, the metaphors used throughout the Old Testament serve as forerunners for the church in the New Testament.

Just notice the importance of the church based upon staggering descriptions and characteristics assigned to the church from Jesus and the Apostles.

The Church Is Christ's Authoritative Kingdom on Earth

The church is Christ's idea. He originates and establishes it. He gives her status as the holder of His kingdom's keys. Despite the efforts of some to skirt around the church in pursuit of disciple-making, the church is intimately connected to Christ's kingdom because she holds the keys. He did not give these keys to another institution or program, but only to the church. Consider Jesus' words in Matthew 16:18–19: "I tell you, you are Peter, and on this rock I will build my church, and the gates of hell shall not prevail against it. I will give you the keys of the kingdom of heaven, and whatever you bind on earth shall be bound in heaven, and whatever you loose on earth shall be loosed in heaven." The Church is Christ's chosen vehicle to accomplish His kingdom purposes in the world. The church identifies who the kingdom citizens are (identification) and she presses the fight to the very gates of hell (mission).

The Church Is Sacrificially Loved by Christ

Not only does Jesus speak of the special, royal nature of the church, but the Apostles also write in stunning ways about Jesus' love for her. Paul calls the church His "bride" and "body" (Eph. 4–5, Col. 1:18, 1 Cor. 12:12–27). As Christians, our union with Christ remains so strong and undivided that we're called His bride and body. The analogy of marriage powerfully shows the importance of the church. In marriage, we vow, "to have and to hold, for better, for worse, in sickness and in health, to love and to cherish, till death do us part." Christ has done this for His bride. Now all that belongs to Him—His identity, His mission, His future—He shares with us as the church. This reveals the depths of His love, seen supremely at the Cross.

Consider the astounding closeness of this union of the church as the body of Christ, as revealed in Acts 9. When Jesus confronts Saul on the Damascus Road, He doesn't say, "Saul, why did you kill Stephen?" or even, "Why are you persecuting my people?" Instead, He says, "Why are you persecuting *me*?" (Acts 9:4).[7] Jesus was stoned when His brother Stephen got stoned. Staggering! No wonder Paul later tells the Ephesian elders, "Pay careful attention to yourselves and to all the flock . . . to care for the church of God, which he obtained with his own blood" (Acts 20:28).

---

[7] Italics added.

If Christ so identifies with and loves His people, and if He longs for their flourishing, then so should we. The local church, with all its imperfections, is still Christ's body—bound to Him as inseparably as one's own limbs. As His bride, the church shares everything belonging to Jesus. Believer, aren't you thankful He had no hesitation to welcome His bride—better yet, to walk the road to Calvary for her?

That's why Spurgeon marveled, "If I had heard that Christ pitied us, I could understand it . . . that He had mercy on us, I could comprehend. But that He actually loves us—who can grasp such an idea? Who can fully understand it? 'HE loved me, and gave Himself for me.'"[8]

The Church Is God's Family and His Dwelling Place on Earth

By Christ's work, we've been adopted into God's household (Eph. 2, 1 Tim. 3). Your role now is that of a family member living in God's own home. As Tim Keller once tweeted, "The only person who dares wake up a king at 3:00 AM for a glass of water is his child."[9] That is who we are—sons and daughters made so by the work of His Son.

In the prophets, God promised to the Old Covenant people (cf. Ezek. 43; Zech. 8) that He would dwell in their midst. They could dream about this privilege because God had promised it. Now we enjoy a privilege that Old Cov-

---

[8] See *Metropolitan Tabernacle Pulpit*, Vol. 17, Sermon #1000, preached July 9, 1871; accessed 30 July 2025: https://www.romans45.org/spurgeon/sermons/1000.htm

[9] Tweeted on *X* @timkellernyc, 23 February 2015.

enant people only dreamed of: God no longer dwells in a tent or temple, but in His people! Paul unpacks this truth in Ephesians 2. Peter writes in 1 Peter 2:4–5, "As you come to Him, a living stone rejected by men but chosen and precious in God's sight, you also, like living stones, are being built into a spiritual house, to be a holy priesthood, offering spiritual sacrifices acceptable to God through Jesus Christ." Peter paints a richer picture of the church than what we learned in Vacation Bible School. The church is not a building, but a living temple with Christ as the cornerstone. Astonishingly, believers have been fit together as living stones with Him. Peter paints this beautiful picture of the nature and purpose of the church, which includes "proclaiming His excellencies" (1 Pet. 2:9). This is what has happened to us in Christ—this is who we are!

The Church Is the Focus of the Apostles' Work

Not only do we find theological precursors for this work, but the starting of churches as the fulfillment of the Great Commission is the revealed biblical pattern. Once God births His church in Acts 2, the normative pattern is for new churches to be established. Consequently, it is a false dichotomy to pit (or even to underemphasize) the role of the church against discipleship or the advancement of the kingdom. Because not only do we have these powerful metaphors for the church demanding her central role, but this is exactly what Paul and Barnabas intentionally left the church at Antioch to do in Acts 13. Certainly, as they headed out on this journey, they were going to evangelize and make disciples. But ultimately, they sought to establish churches (Acts 14:21–23).

Because of this vital work, churches must start churches. The Apostles established healthy churches; they didn't just send missionaries to evangelize. That pattern sets the groundwork for disciples to be made generation after generation.

Think of the church as both the *means* and the *end* of mission. When Paul and Barnabas go out, they likely do not have John's full and finalized view of the church in mind. But they do get glimpses of God's glory through these cities on a hill. Paul will later call these new churches a "bride" and the "household of God," metaphors that John will pick up in his end-times vision. If the end goal is the eschatological vision of Revelation 21 with a spotless bride, the means to that end goal must include a dogged determination to establish robust pillars of that consummated work now (1 Tim. 3:15).

The New Testament clearly declares the importance of the church and the necessity to start churches. Paul and Barnabas started and strengthened churches. Paul wrote letters to local churches. Paul used glorious metaphors to describe local churches. Peter and John are identified as elders leading local churches. Jesus speaks to local churches. John, who earlier wrote to the "elect lady," gave a final vision of the church. Since this is so, then the best missiology connects to the healthiest ecclesiology because the church is the "pillar and foundation" of the truth (1 Tim. 3:15; CSB). The best missiology in the advancement of the truth must be accomplished through the sturdiest of pillars! Thus, we plant churches because of Christ's affection for them, and because that is how the Apostles accomplished the nation-blessing work of the Great Commission.

The Church Has Multiplied Through History

This biblical story continues through church history to to-day. The book of Acts and the early church set the pattern that persists throughout Christian history. Consider a few historical examples of the eschatological, theological, and biblical foundations for why churches must start churches. For brevity, I will only mention two examples from church history.

John Calvin

Phil Newton explains that Calvin's work in church planting was due to his commitment to raise up faithful men. He writes, "Scores of churches with pastors, elders, and deacons started each year in France, with the Company of Pastors in Geneva sending 120 pastors to French churches between 1555 and 1566."[10] One of the key elements to starting churches, one that will be covered in a subsequent chapter, is to raise up and multiply faithful men who will carry on the work.

---

[10] Phil A. Newton, *The Mentoring Church: How Pastors and Congregations Cultivate Leaders* (Grand Rapids: Kregel Ministry, 2017), 89. See also, C. Scott Dixon, *Protestants: A History from Wittenberg to Pennsylvania 1517–1740* (West Sussex, UK: Wiley-Blackwell, 2010); Williston Walker, *John Calvin: Revolutionary, Theologian, Pastor* (Fern, Tain, Ross-shire, UK: Christian Focus, 2005; from 1906 ed.); and Ray Van Neste, "The Mangled Narrative Of Missions And Evangelism In The Reformation," *Southeastern Theological Review* 08:2 (Fall 2017).

Charles H. Spurgeon

Spurgeon purportedly planted hundreds of churches including 53 of London's 62 new Baptist churches over a 20-year period. Spurgeon said that his Pastors' College was committed to Kingdom work by starting new churches.[11] Furthermore, Spurgeon provides us a piercing quote for why we should be about starting churches. He wrote,

> The Christian church was designed from the first to be aggressive. It was not intended to remain stationary at any period, but to advance onward until its boundaries became commensurate with those of the world. It was to spread from Jerusalem to all Judaea, from Judaea to Samaria, and from Samaria unto the uttermost parts of the earth. It was not intended to radiate from one central point only, but to form numerous centers from which its influence might spread to the surrounding parts.[12]

The Church Is an Offensive Tool for Good

Historically, it hasn't just been prominent churches that started new churches, but also Baptist associations. For instance, the first Baptist Association on American soil, the Philadel-

---

[11] Alex DiPrima details these statistics in chapter 9 of his book *Spurgeon: A Life* (Nashville: B&H Academic, 2023).

[12] April 1865 issue of *The Sword and the Trowel*.

phia Association, started in 1707 with five churches. It grew to 34 churches by 1770.[13]

Across the pond, the Association of Irish Baptist Churches formed in 1895 with 27 Irish Baptist churches. In the successive century, they have multiplied and now are comprised of over 100 cooperating churches.[14]

Our own Pillar Network, through doctrinal alignment, relational connectivity, and missional impulse, has grown from a handful of churches in 2009 to over 650 by 2025. More than a third of those churches were planted since the inception of Pillar.

Finally, consider your own testimony. It is no exaggeration to say you have come to know, believe, and love the gospel because of a church that is connected to the church at Jerusalem. Ultimately, if we see the church as Jesus does, then we will be compelled to start more local churches—just as the Apostles did, as church history confirms, and as is consistent with how God has always worked for His glory.

Exhortations

Given all that has been argued, the exhortation then is to pray, practice, and persist in the very things that will be detailed in the chapters to come. Be aggressive, pray fervently, practice with intentionality, and persist in these means as fo-

---

[13] "The Philadelphia Baptist Association," *The Baptist Encyclopedia*, 1881: https://baptisthistoryhomepage.com/philadelphia.association.html.

[14] I detail more of the importance of cooperation for planting in an article entitled, "Partnering to Plant" from 9Marks Journal Oct. 13, 2023: https://www.9marks.org/article/partnering-together-to-plant/.

cused soldiers, disciplined athletes, and hard-working farmers (2 Tim. 2:3–6). Cooperate with like-minded churches who agree on what the church is and does. Churches can do far more together than they can on their own. This type of cooperation is at the heart of partnerships shared by churches in the Southern Baptist Convention. We are at our best when we work together to plant healthy, baptistic churches.

Finally, keep the future in mind for present faithfulness and fervency. What was predicted in the Old Testament, and began with a bang at Pentecost, will end in a wedding feast celebration at the Eschaton. Interestingly, nearly all the New Testament metaphors mentioned earlier are alluded to in the John's vision of the future. In that passage, we see the kingdom as a glorious, fortified city (Rev. 21:9–14); the bride (Rev. 21:2, 9); those identified as God's family (Rev. 21:7); and God's final dwelling place (Rev. 21:3).

So we press on, realizing that the seven struggling churches of Revelation 2 and 3 will give way to the purified, sanctified, now-glorified bride of Revelation 21. Yes, we are between the times, but that simply means we get to play our part, our jar-of-clay part, looking forward to when that bride, described as a most rare jewel, is presented to Him in full. Thankfully, we are not alone. We have the indwelling Spirit and the church; we serve the slain Lamb who is not dead but standing (Rev. 5:6) ever ready on our behalf. I hope this encourages us all to put our hands to the plow of this eternal work to build churches with the final day in view, a day when Christ will receive the reward of His suffering. On that day, even though He is the One who has made all of this happen, the doors will open and He will behold—not

His Kingdom or His disciples—but "the wife of the Lamb" (Rev. 21:9).

Why start churches? Because when death is in the rear view, what will be left standing will be Christ and His Church. May the Lord give us grace to play our part as we daily anticipate that one shining moment.

CHAPTER 2

WHAT IS THE CHURCH?

Phil A. Newton

My experience in church planting turned out to be backwards. Here's what I mean. I planted in the late 80s before church planting networks or sending churches were prominent. Some may have existed, but I knew nothing of them when I felt the burden to plant. So, a few churches in Alabama where I pastored helped with financial support for the first six months as I moved with my family to Memphis to plant a new church. I had studied church planting methods at Fuller Seminary, read dozens of books on the subject, and had a genuine burden and enthusiasm to plant. Was I ready to plant? Not quite, but I planted anyway.

A major problem arose several years into the plant. I realized that I had presumed upon the church's ecclesiology and polity. We were *a church* in that we had covenanted together and affiliated with other SBC churches, but what did that mean biblically? We functioned with a churchy-type atmosphere, but in what ways did our church have the marks of a New Testament church? We had a structure and governance that existed between my ears, but how did that square with biblical church polity? What did the congregation understand about our polity?

I planted a church with little thought to what a church is, how it functions, what the New Testament demonstrates it should look like, and how it needs to be structured for unity and ministry. This paucity in ecclesiology meant that my discernment became quickly overcome in the face of church pragmatism. I gullibly swallowed practices that ran counter to biblical church life. It took several years to reverse this backward approach and get on solid footing as a local church. I wished that I had experienced life in a healthy church, one that trained and sent me out, one that modeled good ecclesiology and polity and could help me navigate the challenges of planting. Studying and observing healthy ecclesiology would have buoyed me against the deception in pragmatism. I wish that I had been asked hard questions on ecclesiology and polity. Why didn't someone ask me how to teach about the church to the church?

I would have agreed with the biblical theology of the local church that Nate outlined in the first chapter. I understood the primacy of the church in God's mission but I'd not slowed down to consider how that worked its way out in the practical dynamics of how the church was structured, organized, or led. In God's kindness and mercy, I began to learn about healthy ecclesiology while pastoring the church I planted. I made plenty of mistakes, many that I might not have made had I been trained and mentored in a healthy

New Testament church. I simply presumed upon ecclesiology and polity.

Sending churches can do their best work to prepare a church planter *before* he launches the new church. Sending churches mustn't presume that the planter and his team have put deep roots into the soil of healthy ecclesiology and polity. The sending church provides the foundation for a planter to learn, observe, test, and shape gospel ministry and biblical church life. Through mentoring relationships, the planter digs into the Word and substantial works on ecclesiology to frame his understanding.[1] He works with a safety net attached to the sending church. There, the pastors/elders train, instruct, refine, model, and give opportunities for the

---

[1] Consider the following books as a good starting point for reading, studying, and discussion: John S. Hammett, *Biblical Foundations for Baptist Churches: A Contemporary Ecclesiology* (2nd ed.; Grand Rapids: Kregel Academics, 2019); Mark Dever, *Nine Marks of a Healthy Church* (4th ed.; Wheaton, IL: Crossway, 2021); Mark Dever, ed., *Polity: Biblical Arguments on How to Conduct Church Life* (Washington, DC: Center for Church Reform, 2001); Jonathan Leeman, *Church Membership: How the World Knows Who Represents Jesus* (9Marks Building Healthy Churches; Wheaton, IL: Crossway, 2012); Mark Dever and Jamie Dunlop, *The Compelling Community: Where God's Power Makes a Church Attractive* (Wheaton, IL: Crossway, 2015); R. Stanton Norman, *More than Just a Name: Preserving Our Baptist Identity* (Nashville: B&H Publishers, 2001); Conrad Mbewe, *Foundations for the Flock: Truths About the Church for All the Saints* (Hannibal, MO: Granted Ministries Press, 2011); Nate Akin, *Convictional, Confessional, Cheerful Baptists* (Greenville, SC: Courier Publishing, 2024); Phil A. Newton and Rich C. Shadden, *Mending the Nets: Rethinking Church Leadership* (Greenville, SC: Courier Publishing, 2024); Phil A. Newton and Matt Schmucker, *Elders in the Life of the Church: Rediscovering the Biblical Model for Church Leadership* (Grand Rapids: Kregel Ministry, 2014); Matt Rogers, *A Workman Approved: Developing Future Pastors in the Local Church and Seminary* (Nashville: Rainer Publishing, 2018).

planter to test his gifts. If he flops in preaching, teaching, or leading, the safety net allows for him to be further trained, honed, and retooled to prepare him to lead a church plant. The sending church should never take it as a foregone conclusion that the planter is ready because of a predetermined timeframe. Instead, the sending church should approve the planter to lead a new work only when they've observed his character and gifts, listened to him teach and preach, and agreed on his understanding of ecclesiology. If he has failed to demonstrate character, competence, or sufficient commitment to biblical ecclesiology, then the church needs to pause. Good preparation doesn't mean perfection, but it does develop the planter's readiness to serve with no safety net.

In summary, what is the sending church doing?

- *The sending church anchors the planter with a clear, replicable definition of the church.* After sufficient involvement with the sending church, the planter should know what a local church is and how it should be organized.[2]

- *The sending church prepares and nurtures the church planter.* Preparation involves biblical, theological, and practical instruction. Helping the planter to establish healthy devotional patterns, personally and for family, will prepare him for being sent.

---

[2] See eight workable definitions from past and present churchmen for the church in Phil A. Newton, *40 Questions About Pastoral Ministry* (Benjamin L. Merkle, series editor; Grand Rapids: Kregel Academic, 2021), 235. My personal definition is: The church is God's people redeemed by Jesus Christ and baptized into His body by the Holy Spirit to glorify God through Christ-centered worship, service, and witness.

- *The sending church models healthy congregational dynamics.* The planter has the opportunity not just to study ecclesiology and polity but to see it lived out. The formative study of the church gives him the tools he needs to lead toward congregational health. The experience of a healthy sending church gives the planter a visual template for leading his congregation. He needs both formative and experiential elements.

- *The sending church provides patterns for effective plural elder shepherding.* The first elder plurality that I experienced was when the church I planted voted in three lay elders to serve with me. That was five years after we began. We made some early mistakes that we could have avoided if we had observed patterns of effective eldering earlier.

- *The sending church feels the ties with the church plant.* The sending church releases the planter and maybe a substantial core team to begin the work. They may rally together at the constituting and covenanting service. They continue through prayer and varied levels of support. That's why a church plant is typically called a daughter church. You maintain ties to your daughter even when she's on her own.

So, where do we begin? If your church plans to train and send out a church planter, what do you teach and model for him concerning the local church? What *must* he understand before you invest in sending him out? As we've already established, we want the planter and team to see the role of the church in the grand story of Scripture. But we want more than that. We also want them to move from merely speaking about the church in abstract terms to having a concrete sense of what they are describing. In this chapter, we'll consider the process through two questions: (1) What is a church? (2) Why must we narrow our view of the church?

What Is a Church?

We know the church isn't merely a building. The church is an assembly,[3] but not just any kind of assembly. It's an assembly of believers in Jesus Christ who have covenanted together as redeemed people who are united to Jesus Christ through His saving work. But some might object. What about a Christian campus organization or a Christian fraternity or a Christian service organization? Are they also a church? Quite simply, *no*. Despite meeting together in Jesus' name, the church is narrower. Its structure and purpose in the eternal plan of God are administered and secured through Jesus Christ. The church is far broader in that it exists throughout history and into eternity in the bonds of redemption through Christ and union by the Holy Spirit (Rev. 5:9–10; 1 Pet.1:2). No other Christian organization can make those claims.

---

[3] J. L. Dagg, *Manual of Theology: A Treatise on Church Order* (Harrison-burg, VA: Gano Books, 1990 from 1858, The Southern Baptist Publication Society), stated, "A Christian church is an assembly of believers in Christ, organized into a body, according to the Holy Scriptures, for the worship and service of God." He reiterates that the Greek term *ekklēsia*, translated as church, "denotes *an assembly.*... This word never denotes *the house* in which worshippers assemble," 74–75; italics original.

During the 4ᵗʰ century, the Nicene Council identified four marks of a church: one, holy, catholic, and apostolic. *One* refers to the church's union with God through Christ the Son, which countered ancient Arianism's denial of Jesus' deity. Jesus declared, "I will build my church," indicating that its existence is in union with Jesus (Matt. 16:18). *Holy* points to the church's source of holiness in the justifying work of Christ, noted by the repeated use of "saints" or "holy ones" to refer to the blood-bought church (e.g., Rom. 1:7; 1 Cor. 1:2). This counters the ancient Novatians who taught a rigid, legalistic Christianity, and Donatists who taught that the church's holiness was conveyed through the priests.[4] *Catholic* means universal, identifying the church through the ages. Jonathan Leeman explains that the church's *catholicity* is rooted in the gospel: "We are saying that our local gatherings, by gospel nature and design, belong to a global or universal gathering."[5] Finally, *apostolic* establishes the church built on the foundation of the gospel, indicating, "to be apostolic means that we hold to the same teaching proclaimed by the apostles revealed in Scripture."[6]

---

[4] "Novatian Schmism," R. C. Kroeger and C. C. Kroeger; and V. L. Walter, "Donatism," in Walter A. Elwell, ed., *Evangelical Dictionary of Theology* (2ⁿᵈ ed.; Grand Rapids: Baker Academic, 2001), 352–53, 846.

[5] Jonathan Leeman, "What is Catholicity and What Does it Require?" in Jonathan Leeman, ed., *Church Matters: Catholicity—Churches Partnering Together* (A Journal for Pastors; Washington, DC: 9Marks, 2023), 17. This entire journal focuses on catholicity and is highly recommended for a church planter to study.

[6] See Newton, *40 Questions About Pastoral Ministry*, 236–37; Hammett, *Biblical Foundations*, 57–69; Mark Dever, "Church," in Daniel L. Akin,

During the Reformation, many Christians wondered about the marks of a true church. John Calvin explained that true churches were marked by the gospel being purely preached and the sacraments rightly administered.[7] Martin Bucer in Strasbourg agreed, but he added excommunication as a third mark. As Paul Avis notes, "Love and discipline must be added to word and sacrament to form the true church."[8] John Knox lined up with Bucer, while English Puritans William Perkins and Thomas Cartwright saw discipline as necessary for the church's well-being but not for its existence.[9] Baptist theologian John Hammett summarizes the arguments from history by explaining that a true church must have the gospel in its preaching and its administration of the sacraments: "If it loses the gospel message, a group of people is no longer a true church."[10] Three prongs of the church hold it together. While all Christians should agree with these essentials, sending churches and planters must not waver from them as they partner to plant a new church.

ed., *A Theology for the Church* (Nashville: B&H Academic, 2007), 775–78.

[7] John Calvin, *Institutes of the Christian Religion* (2 vols.; John T. McNeil, ed.; Ford Lewis Battles, trans.; Philadelphia: The Westminster Press, 1960), 4.1.9.

[8] Paul D. L. Avis, *The Church in the Theology of the Reformers* (Eugene, OR: Wipf & Stock, 2002), 45.

[9] Ibid., 46, 50–51.

[10] Hammett, *Biblical Foundations*, 2nd ed., 69–73.

The Church Begins in Jesus

When Peter answered the question "Who do you say that I am?" Jesus first used *ekklēsia* to refer to the gathering of the redeemed: "Simon Peter replied, 'You are the Christ, the Son of the living God.' Jesus answered him, 'Blessed are you, Simon Bar-Jonah! For flesh and blood has not revealed this to you, but my Father who is in heaven. And I tell you, you are Peter, and on this rock, I will build my church, and the gates of hell shall not prevail against it'" (Matt. 16:16–18).

Jesus the Messiah builds the church through His vicarious suffering. Here's what Matthew adds after Jesus' declaration above: "*From that time* Jesus began to show his disciples that he must go to Jerusalem and suffer many things from the elders and chief priests and scribes and be killed, and on the third day be raised" (Matt. 16:21–23; italics added). That's not haphazard editing. "From that time" reiterates the gospel as central to everything the church is, will be, and does. Paul expresses this truth in Ephesians 2:19–21, "So then you are no longer strangers and aliens, but you are fellow citizens with the saints and members of the household of God, built on the foundation of the apostles and prophets, Christ Jesus himself being the cornerstone, in whom the whole structure, being joined together, grows into a holy temple in the Lord." Built upon the apostolic preaching of the gospel, the church is bound up in Jesus Himself.[11] John Stott noted that the apostles expected the church to believe and obey what they commanded. He wrote, "In practical terms this means that

---

[11] F. F. Bruce, *NICNT: The Epistles to the Colossians, to Philemon, and to the Ephesians* (Grand Rapids: Eerdmans, 1984), 304-05.

the church is built on the New Testament Scriptures."[12] Consequently, the church is Jesus' "own new society. . . . He lives in them, individually and as a community."[13] What are the implications for the church planter and sending church?

- The church belongs to Jesus, not to the pastor (Matt. 16:18). Any church planter will face emotional challenges during planting. The sending church can reiterate this truth, even years into the plant.

- The church centers its affections and practices in Jesus, which means the pastor must regularly evaluate his preaching and the church's ministry to be certain they do not veer from Christ (1 Cor. 2:2; 3:10–17). The sending church must evaluate the planter's preaching before sending him out. Ongoing contact with the planter will give opportunities to revisit this question.

- The church finds its reason for existence in obeying and worshiping Jesus (Matt. 28:16–20). The sending church's model of obedience and worship will provide a template.

- The church's pastors must seek to proclaim and teach Christ to "present everyone mature in Christ" (Col. 1:28–29). Probably nothing sticks in the mind of a planter more witnessing this truth lived out in the sending church.

---

[12] John R. W. Stott, *BST: The Message of Ephesians* (John R. W. Stott, NT ed.; Downers Grove, IL: IVP, 1979), 107.

[13] Ibid., 109.

- The church will eventually gather as one people in Jesus' presence (Rev. 21:1–14). Both the planter and sending church need to be nurtured on this promise.

The Church Is Connected to All the Redeemed

The image of the church is one body universally (Eph. 4:4) and one body locally in assemblies gathered throughout the world (Eph. 4:13–16). Herein lie two of the church planter's greatest challenges: (1) helping the new congregation to understand its connection to the larger body of Christ, and (2) teaching and modeling what it means for a local congregation to live in unity. While we may disagree on certain matters in the broader church, our affinity for the New Testament gospel binds us together.

First, the new church's broader connection keeps it anchored to the historical church. Jonathan Leeman explains that local congregations have imperatives related to the broader (even global) community of gospel-believing, gospel-proclaiming churches. He writes, "Specifically, the imperative of catholicity is *the covenantal and missional demand placed on individual churches to recognize and partner with other gospel-preaching churches around the world as occasion allows and in a manner appropriate to the Bible's institutional mandates for churches.*"[14] We're not ecclesiastical Lone Rangers, planting a church as though we're the only ones who preach Christ and who do ministry properly.[15] Attentiveness

---

[14] Leeman, "What is Catholicity?" 18; italics original.

[15] The work of the Southern Baptist Convention can make such partnership possible. While not the only model of local church collaboration, the SBC

during planting may eclipse a vision for the broader church. So the planter must battle against this tendency by praying publicly for other gospel-preaching churches, partnering in gospel-centered events, uniting in gospel outreach in the community, and beyond.[16]

Second, the new church must give attention to what unites its own members. Congregational unity doesn't just happen. Paul exhorts, "Walk in a manner worthy of the calling to which you have been called, with all humility and gentleness, with patience, bearing with one another in love, eager to maintain the unity of the Spirit in the bond of peace" (Eph. 4:1–3). Regenerate people must give attention to the character and practices necessary for unity. We've been called by the Spirit through the gospel to belong to Christ and, as Paul told the Galatians, to have Christ formed in us (Gal. 4:19). With relationships in the body, we must learn to walk with ("all") humility, gentleness, patience, love, and eagerness to know the Spirit's bonding power in peace. Without these qualities, the church may have great programs, lively services, strong polity, and admirable ministries, but it will

---

and its entities like the International Mission Board, the North American Mission Board, state conventions, six healthy seminaries, and innumerable local associations provide a context whereby churches can work together in shared endeavors. This is one of the reasons the Pillar Network strives to live in vibrant partnership with the SBC.

[16] To clarify, as Baptists, we will not likely plant a church with a non-credobaptism church; but we can support and encourage works if they preach the gospel. We can pray for them and financially contribute, as well as recommend others to attend. This is also true for partnership within the Southern Baptist Convention. We do not have to agree with every ecclesiological particularity of these churches to pray and partner where we can.

not have unity—the very thing that Jesus died, rose, ascended, and prayed for the church to have (John 17:20–26).

The Church Is the Focus of Eternal Attention

Out of all the institutions and organizations in the world, the church continues into eternity. Church planters will serve their congregations by giving them an eye for eternity, learning to live in the hope that's in Christ (Titus 2:13–14). The preaching, the prayers, the counseling, the worship leadership, and the pastoral care must all have the aroma of heaven.[17] Just read the book of Revelation and notice the Lamb's focus on the church for all eternity. If eternity's so important to Jesus with His Bride, the Church, then shouldn't we salt our pastoral labors with the hope ahead?

As one who has pastored for over four decades, if you asked me what I wish I had done more of in my ministry, it would be this: saturate the life of the church with a sense of expectancy of being in Jesus' presence. Build in them the hope we have in Christ through preaching, teaching, praying, and modeling. Jesus saved the church with a view to eternity. Let's get untangled from the turf wars in ecclesiastical circles and make sure we have such a view of the church.

The true church is one, holy, catholic, and apostolic. It will hold unwaveringly to the proclamation of the gospel and proper administration of the ordinances given by Christ to distinguish the church from the world. The three prongs to understand— its beginning in Christ, its connection to

---

[17] See Matt McCullough, *Heaven: Meditations on the World to Come for Life in the Meantime* (Wheaton, IL: Crossway, 2025).

all the redeemed, and its eternal attention—anchor local congregations and prevent ecclesiological drift. These convictions both narrow and broaden the church.

Why Must We Narrow Our View of the Church?

By "narrow," I don't mean a sectarian spirit that shuts others out who may not cross every T and dot every I. The gospel softens and warms us when we believe that it is the power of God for salvation to all who believe (Rom. 1:16–17). When I was a college student, I preached at a weekend youth conference in a church that had a strong sectarian spirit. They had narrowed the church to how a person dressed, whether or not the men had facial hair, and one permissible eschatological view. They had severely limited their relationship with anyone outside the church. One had to jump through all sorts of hoops to be in conformity to the pastor's view of the church and the Christian life. As a result, the church seemed far more about what they were against than what they were for. Instead of liberating, their approach to Christianity and the church brought on new levels of bondage. We should never let the world shape our view of the church. Instead, the New Testament frames the church for our congregations. We should narrow our teaching according to the Scriptures.

This necessary kind of narrowing pushes back on unbiblical pragmatic and utilitarian views of the church and upholds the beauty of the New Testament's picture.[18] The

---

[18] *Pragmatism* focuses on man-centered methods and goals rather than upon biblically formed ecclesiology. The full-fledged pragmatic view of the church may scarcely appear as the body of Christ, but instead, a machine

sending church has the opportunity to model this appropriately narrow view of the church, so that the church planter and his team might begin with the richness of the local
church.

As a seminary student, I remember being astounded
when I read Paul Minear's *Images of the Church in the New
Testament.* He identified 96 terms for the church. While we
might debate a few of his conclusions, most help us to see the
magnificence of the blood-bought church.[19] Consider a few
to reiterate with the church planter.

Christ's Body

We value every appendage, muscle, tissue, ligament, and mol-
ecule in our bodies. No wonder Paul explains the church as
a body (Rom. 12; 1 Cor. 12; Eph. 4; Col. 1). In both nature
and function,[20] the church is a body to cherish, enjoy, pro-

---

geared for producing people, money, buildings, and massive programs. Its
view of outward metrics of success may not equate to a holy, joyful, bibli-
cally-saturated, cross-bearing, fruit-of-the-Spirit producing flock of God.
Leading pragmatic church views (the Church Growth Movement of the
20th century and its 21st century descendants) may have good intentions,
but along the way the glory of Christ gets left behind. *Utilitarianism* leads
to reductionism in the church, stripping the church of its beauty and glory
as the body of Christ. In such cases, the church takes a backseat to the
pastor's drive for making a name for himself. The church ends up being all
about the pastor and little about the flock of God humbly and sacrificially
shepherded by the pastor.

[19] Paul S. Minear, *Images of the Church in the New Testament* (Philadelphia:
The Westminster Press, 1975).

[20] Wayne Grudem, *Systematic Theology: An Introduction to Biblical Doctrine*
(Grand Rapids: Zondervan, 1994), 858–59, distinguishes them in 1 Cor-

tect, preserve, nourish, and utilize. *Body* terminology vividly expresses the church's unity as each member serves the others *and* depends on the others. "For just as the body is one and has many members, and all the members of the body, though many, are one body, so it is with Christ. For in one Spirit we were all baptized into one body—Jews or Greeks, slaves or free—and all were made to drink of one Spirit. For the body does not consist of one member but many" (1 Cor. 12:12–14). My first introduction to this concept of the church as a body came through reading Ray Steadman's *Body Life*.[21] I had such an institutionalized view of the church that ecclesiological paralysis had stifled my leadership. I failed to see the organic nature of the congregation growing, maturing, forgiving, encouraging, and serving together as a living, Holy Spirit–indwelt body. Sending churches provide a framework of the church as the body of Christ for the planter to model in his leadership.

Christ's Temple

The Old Testament emphasizes the temple's centrality to Israel's existence and worship. In the New Testament, Jesus shows up and replaces the temple. Quite famously, He says to the Jewish religious leaders, "Destroy this temple, and in three days I will raise it up" (John 2:19). After His resurrection, His church then becomes the temple. That's why Peter can say that "[we are] living stones . . . being built up as a

---

inthians 12 and Ephesians 4.

[21] Ray Steadman, *Body Life: The Church Comes Alive* (Raleigh, NC: Regal Books, 1979). A more recent 1995 update of the book is available.

spiritual house, to be a holy priesthood, to offer spiritual sacrifices acceptable to God through Jesus Christ" (1 Pet. 2:4–5). In union with Jesus, the church becomes the temple that He indwells by the Spirit. Paul agrees, when he says the church, "being joined together, grows into a holy temple in the Lord. In him you also are being built together into a dwelling place for God by the Spirit" (Eph. 2:21–22). The images of the temple, the priesthood, and a dwelling place for God come together to fulfill the Old Testament temple in Jesus Christ. We do not wait for the temple to be rebuilt. It has already been built through Christ and His church. Both Christ and the church are called a temple, which proves the temple is no longer the focal point of God's people (John. 2:19; 1 Pet. 2:5). Instead, we see Christ at work in His church that He inhabits through the Holy Spirit dwelling in the corporate gathering of local churches, filling them even as the Shekinah filled the ancient temple and tabernacle.

Christ's Bride

The picture of the church as the bride of Christ in Ephesians 5:22–31 and Revelation 21–22 shows the intimacy of Jesus with the church. The church is first called "the Bride, the wife of the Lamb," and then the metaphors shift to show the Bride as the bejeweled "holy city Jerusalem coming down out of heaven from God, having the glory of God" (Rev. 21:9–11).

How do these pictures affect the church planter? He's not just pastoring a church to bide his time doing religious things. He's caring for the Bride of Christ until the consummation of the ages. So he must nurture the bride in preparation for eternity. I remember in a devotion time meditating on Revelation 19:6–8. It struck me that pastoral ministry is all about preparing the bride for the marriage to the Lamb. "'Hallelujah! For the Lord our God the Almighty reigns. Let us rejoice and exult and give him the glory, for the marriage of the Lamb has come, and his bride has made herself ready; it was granted her to clothe herself with fine linen, bright and pure'—for the fine linen is the righteous deeds of the saints." Pastors, through preaching, leading, shepherding, and modeling the gospel, prepare the bride for the wedding day. In the same way, the sending pastor and church model this kind of eternal preparation in the local church.

Christ's Flock

Borrowing language from Ezekiel 34, the New Testament writers use the term *flock* to describe the church. It expresses a gathering of redeemed people who need to be led and cared for by the shepherds. After years of neglect by Israel's national and spiritual leaders, the Lord rebukes the corrupt shepherds and then promises He will raise up faithful shepherds for His flock. "Woe to the shepherds who destroy and scatter the sheep of my pasture!" declares the Lord. Therefore thus says the Lord, the God of Israel, concerning the shepherds who care for my people:

> You have scattered my flock and have driven them away, and you have not attended to them. Behold, I will attend to you for your evil deeds, declares

the Lord. Then I will gather the remnant of my flock out of all the countries where I have driven them, and I will bring them back to their fold, and they shall be fruitful and multiply. I will set shepherds over them who will care for them, and they shall fear no more, nor be dismayed, neither shall any be missing, declares the Lord (Jer. 23:1–4).

Pastors are a direct answer to Jeremiah's prophecy. They faithfully feed the flock with the Word and the gospel. Jesus' pointed instruction to Peter after the resurrection gives pastors in every age clarity on their work: "Feed my lambs. . . . Tend my sheep. . . . Feed my sheep" (John 21:15–17). Paul exhorted the Ephesian elders, "Be on guard for yourselves and for all the flock of which the Holy Spirit has appointed you as overseers, to shepherd the church of God, which he purchased with his own blood" (Acts 20:28; CSB). Peter exhorts the same, "Shepherd the flock of God that is among you, exercising oversight . . . being examples to the flock" (1 Pet. 5:1–4).[22]

We must see how these images shape and direct the sending church's actions.

The sending church's ecclesiology will likely be mirrored in the church plant, especially as it matures. This reality strengthens the sending church's responsibility to model the one, holy, catholic, and apostolic pattern of the historic

---

[22] Other prominent images of the church in the NT include the church as Christ's household, people, family, priesthood, holy nation, chosen race, servants, friends, and sons. See Minear's *Images* list, 268–69.

church. It also encourages attentiveness to the New Testament pictures of the church, so that the richness of what Jesus is doing might be evident in the sending and daughter churches. I'll note three final applications to consider:

1. A church with an unhealthy ecclesiology should focus on developing the marks of a healthy church before attempting to train church planters.[23] I'm not suggesting the sending church must arrive at a superlative state of health (whatever that may be), but they should be well on their way in modeling what a church is before they attempt to build that vision in the planter. Is the sending church on a good path toward healthy ecclesiology? Then move ahead as a sending church. The planter will learn as the church works through some of the ongoing issues of maturing the church.

2. The future church planter needs to be immersed in the sending church's life. He shouldn't treat the sending church as a lecture hall, but as a busy kitchen where he can prepare and serve up spiritual vitality, in which he can be a prep chef involved in the process while learning from the head chef.

3. As the planter teaches his core team about the church, he should invite members of the church, along with elders, to listen to his discussion on healthy church life. They can be a sounding board

---

[23] See Dever, *Nine Marks of a Healthy Church*, 4th ed.

for him as he trains his core team, perhaps even giving testimony of the church's struggles to get to where they are now as a Christ-mirroring church.

Without a thoroughly biblical sense of what the church is, then none of what we suggest in the rest of the book will matter. The temptation looms in our world, our church culture, and our own hearts to run to pragmatic how-to solutions. We must do the hard work of building a robust, clear foundation on which our practices can be built.

What does healthy ecclesiology have to do with a sending church and church planting? That will be our consideration in the next chapter.

CHAPTER 3

WHAT DOES THE CHURCH DO?

Phil A. Newton

Developing a robust ecclesiology does far more than just satisfy theological curiosity. It sets the stage to apply the doctrine of the church to the whole of ministry. If we do not understand the nature of the church—its existence as the body of Christ, its connection to the Old Testament temple, its relationship to the catholic body, its dependence upon apostolic authority in preaching and teaching, and its mission—then one can easily slip into patterns that miss the mark of a New Testament church.

Many churches drift into pragmatism and unhealthy practices simply because they've never plunged deep roots into the fertile soil of sound ecclesiology. They slip into pragmatism because they're seeking to do what they *think* pleases

God without reference to biblical authority. This may lead to manipulative practices that call into question a pastor's reliance on the power of the Spirit. Pragmatic churches are left to their own methods and means to achieve what they perceive the church should do. Finally, pragmatism develops *unhealthy practices* that tend to promote a man or a ministry method or an institution rather than the glory of God. If that sounds too strong, then look at the landscape of American church life.[1] An unthinking acceptance of pragmatism left us with the Church Growth Movement of the 1970s and 80s.[2] The Church Growth Movement normalized "movement practices" for ministry which ultimately obscured what the Bible said about the church and gospel-centered ministry.[3]

---

[1] Consider David F. Wells' searing analysis of the modern church in *No Place for Truth: or Whatever Happened to Evangelical Theology?* (Grand Rapids: Eerdmans, 1994) and *The Courage to Be Protestant: Truth-lovers, Marketers, and Emergents in the Postmodern World* (Grand Rapids: Eerdmans, 2008).

[2] For my analysis of the Church Growth Movement's pragmatic emphasis, see "The Pastor and Church Growth: How to Deal with the Modern Problem of Pragmatism," in John H. Armstrong, ed., *Reforming Pastoral Ministry: Challenges for Ministry in Postmodern Times* (Wheaton, IL: Crossway, 2001), 263–80.

[3] Movement practices, adopting Donald McGavran's *Understanding Church Growth* (3rd ed.; Grand Rapids: Eerdmans, 1990) axioms and principles, have proliferated in some global contexts. I'm for multiplication. But it must be approached biblically. David Well's books referred to in footnote 1, offer a strong critique in this area. As correctives, see the following works that treat aspects of pragmatism, movement methodology, and anemic evangelism, missions, and ecclesiology. David F. Wells, *Above All Earthly Pow'rs: Christ in a Postmodern World* (Grand Rapids: Eerdmans, 2005); Jared C. Wilson, *The Gospel-Driven Church: Uniting Church-Growth Dreams with the Metrics of Grace* (Grand Rapids: Zondervan, 2019); Tom Wells, *A*

Churches sometimes splinter when they trade gospel-centrality for quasi-evangelical extremes.[4] Far too many churches conduct performances instead of gathering for humble, joy-filled worship. They operate like a well-oiled religious machine but never explain how and why disciples of Jesus can faithfully make disciples. They crave the applause and appeal of the world instead of denying themselves, taking up their cross daily, and following Jesus.

A healthy sending church may not eliminate a planting pastor's weaknesses, but it can limit ecclesiological aberrations from taking root in the new church by investing in the planting pastor's spiritual maturity, theological integrity, and ecclesiological foundation. Deep friendship, accountability, and mentoring leave little room for falling into unhealthy patterns. The sending church doesn't just train a potential planting pastor, it attempts to put the entire future congre-

---

Vision for Missions (Edinburgh: The Banner of Truth Trust, 1985); J. Mack Stiles, *Marks of the Messenger: Knowing, Living and Speaking the Gospel* (Downers Grove, IL: IVP, 2010); Will Metzger, *Tell the Truth: The Whole Gospel to the Whole Person by Whole People* (Downers Grove, IL: IVP, 1984); Mark Dever, *The Gospel & Personal Evangelism* (IX Marks; Wheaton, IL: Crossway, 2007); Kevin DeYoung and Greg Gilbert, *What is the Mission of the Church? Making Sense of Social Justice, Shalom, and the Great Commission* (Wheaton, IL: Crossway, 2011); and for an extreme example of where movements go, see the examination of Doug Coleman, *A Theological Analysis of the Insider Movement Paradigm from Four Perspectives: Theology of Religions, Revelation, Soteriology and Ecclesiology* (Evangelical Missiological Society Dissertation Series, Pasadena, CA: WCIU Press, 2011).

[4] See an examination of a few extreme views in "Church Matters," *A New Christian Authoritarianism? Christian Nationalism, Theology, and Magisterial Protestantism*, 9Marks, vol. 1.

gation on the right path for decades of fruitful ministry.[5] The sending church must build into the planter and core team what the church does and how it functions.

What Does the Church Do?

Lest we think the church exists by filling calendars with activities, we need to pause to develop clear paths for leading local congregations. Early in ministry, I remember gauging the church's health by the calendar of activities. That soon came crashing down on me, as I pursued busyness and getting people together for nice religious activities instead of directing them toward what the church is called to do. Obviously, I can't specifically identify what *your church* needs to do, but I can give you four categories that will evaluate whether your church is on track in its ministry.

Follows Jesus

That's what Jesus told His early disciples: "Follow me" (John 1:43). The local church exists as a body of regenerate people following Jesus. Even the term *disciple* means someone who is a learner, someone taught by the one he follows. That implies devotion, attentiveness, and single-mindedness—in this case, toward the Lord Jesus Christ. We know we're beginning

---

[5] This is not to imply that the work rests solely on the sending church. Once again, partnership with denominational entities can help. I praise God for Southern Baptist seminaries who strive to partner with the church to train pastors. In addition, many within the International Mission Board, the North American Mission Board, and State Conventions are striving to create robust training systems that churches can use to prepare men for the work.

to follow Jesus when we start to resemble Him in the way we think, talk, live, and treat others. After describing what the Christ-like life looks like, Paul captures this aim in Ephesians 5:1–2. "Therefore be imitators of God, as beloved children. And walk in love, as Christ loved us and gave himself up for us, a fragrant offering and sacrifice to God." Imitating or mimicking the Lord God, as children mimic their parents, is made manifest by walking in love the way Jesus walked. Do we keep this preeminent in our preaching, leading, and planning for the church?

A sending church should model what it means to follow Jesus. The mentoring pastor must provide for those he trains an example of living as a disciple of Jesus Christ. One of my early mentors died while I was a young church planter in my mid-30s. His walk with Christ in public and private left an indelible mark on my life. I wanted to follow Jesus as he did. That relationship spilled over into how I sought to model following Jesus before my congregation.

Worships Jesus

God seeks true worshipers who will worship in spirit and truth (John 4:23–24). Don Carson captures what this means for our worship gatherings.

> There are not two separable characteristics of the worship that must be offered: it must be "in spirit and truth," i.e. essentially God-centered, made possible by the gift of the Holy Spirit, and in personal knowledge of and conformity to God's

47

Word-made-flesh, the one who is God's "truth,"
the faithful exposition and fulfillment of God and
his saving purposes.[6]

Does our worship reflect this trinitarian consciousness and
express God's worthiness and glory? Do we approach worship "in spirit" from the depths of our union with Christ by
the Spirit and "in truth" with authenticity of the revelation
of God in His Word? Sending churches must model biblically rich, experientially real, and joyfully evident worship as
they prepare to send out planters and teams.

My wife and I are members of a five-year-old church
plant in Memphis. The impact of the churches and pastors
who mentored our pastors can be seen in our corporate worship. They include worship elements modeled by their sending congregations—a biblical call to worship, a moment of
silence, a prayer of praise, a confession of sin, a corporate
Scripture reading, a pastoral prayer, expositional preaching,
and weekly Lord's Supper. These practices cultivate a weekly
rhythm. So does the joyful, passionate singing that they've
seen modeled by these churches. Our young church is en-
riched because several congregations invested in our pastors'
ministries and prepared them well.

---

[6] D. A. Carson, *The Gospel According to John* (Grand Rapids: Eerdmans,
1991), 225.

Serves Jesus

The best way to think of serving is by doing a study of the New Testament "one another" passages.[7] Around 30 different "one another" commands orient the church in how we should serve one another. We must pray for, encourage, build up, and be hospitable to each other. We must stir each other up to love and good deeds. We must be kind to and love one another. We can easily slide by these commands as optional or insignificant, but they are the very essence of Christian service, certainly inside the church but also inevitably spilling over to those outside the fellowship of the saints.

We might think a church planter just needs the X's and O's of theology and ministry. But he needs to see life in the body of Christ. His core team needs to have experienced a healthy body life. They need to know what they'll be missing in life together when they plant a new church, which will motivate them to replicate a healthy body life in their new church.

Makes Disciples

Jesus left the church marching orders in the Great Commission. We're told to go and make disciples of all nations, baptizing them in the name of the Triune God and teaching them to obey everything He commanded (Matt. 28:18–20). If we're going to be a New Testament church, then we must intentionally seek to disciple others—both locally and be-

---

[7] See Phil A. Newton and Rich C. Shadden, *Mending the Nets: Rethinking Church Leadership* (Greenville, SC: Courier Publishing, 2024), 60–61 for a list of the thirty or so "one another" commands.

yond our community. That's the pattern in the emerging church (Acts 1:8). Being involved in global missions is never about *whether we should,* but rather how has God particularly equipped our church to *engage the nations with the gospel.* The sending church must instill a mission trajectory for the church planter, so that from the start of his pastoral labors, he leads the church in mission.[8]

The church must act according to the desires of her Lord. Yet to act, the church must grasp the way Christ designed her to live.

How Does the Church Function?

Think about the day-to-day picture of the church's life. Every church is made up of gathered people who have covenanted together in Christ for the sake of the gospel. They are preparing each other for eternity, to serve one another with brotherly love, and to impact their sphere of influence with good news. It might seem strange to some, but biblical church polity actually shapes how the church functions in daily life. As the church orders its life, structure, decision-making, and leadership according to New Testament design, they're better prepared to faithfully serve Christ and share the gospel.[9] No

---

[8] See Andy Johnson, *Missions: How the Local Church Goes Global* (9Marks Building Healthy Churches; Wheaton, IL: Crossway, 2017) for a helpful guide on how to develop a mission conscious and engaged church.

[9] While the present chapter only hints at a few ideas in church polity, other resources fill the gaps. See *Church Matters:* "Polity: What It Is and Why It Matters," 9Marks, vol. VI; Newton and Shadden, *Mending the Nets*; Mark E. Dever, ed., *Polity: Biblical Arguments on How to Conduct Church Life* (Washington, DC: Center for Church Reform, 2001).

doubt, you may think of more categories than I'm proposing, but these four characterize the overall life of the church that the sending church instills in their church planter and his team.

United People Acting Congregationally

Fascinatingly, even though it would have been much easier in the early church for a few leaders to make all the decisions and command the church, New Testament churches are ruled congregationally. That doesn't mean that every member voted on everything that happened in the church's life. But many major decisions regarding the church's gifts, resources, and involvement, the leaders decided together. For example, we find the congregation acting together to set apart the Seven who would free the apostles for their pastoral labors (Acts 6:1–7).[10] When gospel work broke out in Antioch through the ministry of unnamed Christians, the church responded: "The report of this came to the ears of the church in Jerusalem, and they sent Barnabas to Antioch" (Acts 11:22). The church was so attuned to mission endeavors that they sent one of their finest members. This hints at the mission-oriented practice of congregationalism in the sending church.

We see congregational action as well when the Antioch church set apart and sent out Barnabas and Saul for extensive

---

[10] See Benjamin L. Merkle's forthcoming work, *Authority in the Church* (Nashville: B&H Academic, 2026), where he argues against calling the Seven *proto-deacons*. He agrees they have some bearing on how much of the church has understood the office of deacons but points out the lack of biblical identification of them as deacons. His insights on deacons serving the elders sheds much light on the NT office of deacons laboring alongside elders.

gospel mission work (Acts 13–14). Under the leadership of apostles and elders, the church found pleasure in receiving Paul and Barnabas' report on Gentile conversion. They consequently sent Silas and Barsabbas to join them in reporting the decisions from the Jerusalem Council (Acts 15). Paul instructed the Corinthian church to act decisively in their assembly to remove a member who flaunted their covenant by gross immorality (1 Cor. 5).

Throughout the New Testament, we see the gathered body act on issues related to pastoral care, mission and discipleship, doctrinal unity, and congregational purity. *Structurally*, they identify with Christ; *outwardly*, they witness and expand kingdom work; *inwardly*, they guard the church's purity.[11] That's how the church unites to act congregationally.

---

[11] Jonathan Leeman, *Don't Fire Your Church Members: The Case for Congregationalism* (Nashville: B&H Academic, 2016), 51–52, provides an extensive look at elder-led congregationalism. He summarizes the office of church members in the priest-king office that Adam lost when he sinned in the Garden, but through Christ has been regained for the redeemed in Christ. "Christians occupy this office, furthermore, in all three ways outlined with Adam. There is a *structural aspect* of imaging, identifying with, or representing Christ. There is an *outward activity* of witness, expanding, or cultivating Christ's kingdom. And there is the *inward activity* of guarding, protecting, or consecrating that kingdom life. Christians *identify with Christ* through baptism into the membership of a church and the Lord's Supper. They *witness or cultivate* the kingdom life through evangelism, pursuing good deeds, and working as unto Christ in everything. And they *guard or protect* the kingdom life by seeking holiness in their own lives and in the lives of their fellow saints" (italics added).

Submissive People Led by Plural Eldership

There's a difference between healthy congregationalism and what we might call absolute or total or strict congregationalism. In absolute congregationalism, the church cedes no power to formal leadership or else it controls the token leaders. It laboriously makes all decisions in the corporate gathering. This practice is unwieldy and not corroborated by Scripture.[12]

Healthy congregationalism also prevents one man from ruling the church. I remember speaking in a church years ago where the pastor ruled. His voice was followed . . . *period*. Everyone walked on eggshells around him. One of my close friends served on his staff and felt totally stifled by the man's heavy hand. That's not biblical! Ironically, he would have called his church "congregational." But Paul's and Peter's exhortations to elders counter any such authoritarianism (1 Tim. 3:2–4; 2 Tim. 2:24–25; 1 Pet. 5:1–3).

Instead, New Testament churches identify a plurality of qualified elders who teach, lead, and care for the flock. These men are responsible and accountable for faithfulness to the congregation (1 Tim. 3:1–7; Titus 1:5–9; 1 Pet. 5:1–4). Certainly, a congregation has the voice to approve

---

[12] I use the adjectives "absolute" and "healthy" to distinguish those who think the church is a pure democracy in which every member is a priest individually, and consequently has no consideration for submission to spiritual leaders as the New Testament teaches, rather than the corporate priesthood of all believers found in healthy churches that functional congregationally with plural elder leadership. See my chapter in "Congregationalism Is Not Democracy," in *Church Matters—Polity: What It Is and Why It Matters*, 9Marks; vol. VI:45–48.

a given elder after he's been appropriately examined by the existing elders. But just because elders are accountable to the congregation doesn't mean that they exist to do the bidding of the congregation.

Elders do not receive their orders from the congregation which installs them. Instead, the elders or pastors/overseers are undershepherds of the Great Shepherd.[13] They're ultimately accountable to the Lord to maintain right doctrine, regularly preach and teach God's Word, model for the church toward spiritual maturity, and guard the flock against those who disrupt its unity and purity. Simply put, elders lead the church as they exemplify what it looks like to follow Jesus.[14] A healthy church submits to its leaders as they exercise the ministry of the Word.

The elders exercise authority of counsel rather than authority of command, as Jonathan Leeman has helpfully

---

[13] See Benjamin L. Merkle, *40 Questions About Elders and Deacons* (Grand Rapids: Kregel Academic & Professional, 2008) about the synonymous use of pastor/elder/overseer, the office of deacons, and the functioning of elders within the congregation.

[14] For more details on plural elder leadership in a congregational framework, see Phil A. Newton and Matt Schmucker, *Elders in the Life of the Church: Rediscovering the Biblical Model for Church Leadership* (Grand Rapids: Kregel Ministry, 2014; Newton and Shadden, *Mending the Nets*; Phil A. Newton, *40 Questions About Pastoral Ministry* (Benjamin L. Merkle, series editor; Grand Rapids: Kregel Academic, 2021); Juan Sanchez, *The Leadership Formula: Develop the Next Generation of Leaders in the Church* (Nashville: B&H Publishing, 2020); Jeramie Rinne, *Church Elders: How to Shepherd God's People Like Jesus* (9Marks Building Healthy Churches; Wheaton, IL: Crossway, 2014).

explained.[15] A sending church should model healthy plural elder leadership and include the church planter in their meetings and congregational care.[16] It should also model what it looks like to have healthy respect for its elders. This modeling happens in members' meetings and throughout the life of the church. As this happens, the church planter will long to see this model formed in his own congregation.

Devoted People Shaped by Ministry of the Word

Through the preaching, teaching, and discipling ministry of the pastors and teachers, the church journeys toward unity, maturity, and the fullness of Christ (Eph. 4:13). Elders lead with a trajectory that is oriented toward spiritual maturity (Col. 1:28). In other words, they don't lead with pastoral cleverness or ingenuity. They know that spiritual maturity is the result of the teaching of the Word. So pastors commit themselves to the exposition of the Holy Scripture; they show the power of the gospel to justify, sanctify, and glorify those gathered. The sending pastor provides a pattern for the planter to emulate.

Perhaps there's no more important function of the church than its devotion to Christ through the ministry of the Word. Through this process, the Holy Spirit hones, shapes,

---

[15] Jonathan Leeman, *Authority: How Godly Rule Protects the Vulnerable, Strengthens Communities, and Promises Human Flourishing* (9Marks; Wheaton, IL: Crossway, 2023), 149–165.

[16] See Nathan Knight, *Planting by Pastoring: A Vision for Starting a Healthy Church* (9Marks; Wheaton, IL: Crossway, 2023), for his helpful perspective on the elder/pastor practices in planting.

refines, revitalizes, renews, and fills God's people so that they might serve, witness, and display the glory of Christ. Pastors preach the Word with humble dependence on the Spirit to apply the Word with power. Over time, the congregation develops ears to hear the Word and hearts to receive it with obedience. This leads to fruitful member-to-member discussion. Together, pastors and the congregation grow in the joy of digging together into Holy Scripture, seeing the whole counsel of God as a Christ-centered story that manifests the seamless plan of God for His people. When church planters are sent out by churches modeling this kind of devotion, they will long to see the same reproduced in their churches. This will affect the way they pray, study, prepare, and preach, longing to know the Spirit's power for effectiveness.

Sending People Focused on Kingdom Work

A sending church cultivates its members to think beyond their tight circle of friends to see the need to engage in kingdom work. They know that the Scriptures teach that Jesus died for people from every tribe, language, people, and nation (Rev. 5:9). They want to identify where those unreached by the gospel live. With joy, they track the outward movement of the gospel from the 120 gathered in the Upper Room to Judea, Samaria, and the remotest parts of the earth (Acts 1:8). They love hearing from missionaries and church planters; they love welcoming internationals into their fellowship.

A sending church cultivates a praying people who know the names of the missionaries they're engaged in supporting, encouraging, and visiting. A sending church models prayer for the nations in its corporate gatherings. A sending church arranges its budget to include the nations and church planting efforts around the world. A sending church seeks to train up workers to be sent into the harvest.[17] A sending church willingly goes through the diligent and sometimes-painful process of training up people they love—only to send them out to plant or do mission work for the sake of Christ's kingdom. The level of love, sacrifice, tears, and hard work cannot be minimized when a church follows Antioch's example in Acts 13 to send out a core team to plant a new church. They prepare for months and years and then, by God's grace, they commission and send those they love. The ecclesiological foundation they laid puts the church plant years ahead in its development because these missionaries understand what they're about as a people of God. Instead of learning lessons the hard way, they've learned them the right way—through a faithful congregation led by pastors who have modeled for them what it looks like to be a healthy local church. That kind of foundation prepares the church planter and his core team to replicate what they've been living in for months and even years.

Here are some final recommendations to establish healthy ecclesiological foundations for new churches.

---

[17] For more details on how to train workers to send into kingdom work, see Phil A. Newton, *The Mentoring Church: How Pastors and Congregations Cultivate Leaders* (Grand Rapids: Kregel Ministry, 2017) and Matt Rogers, *A Workman Approved: Developing Future Pastors in the Local Church* (Nashville: Rainer Publishing, 2018). See also Jamie Dunlop, *Budgeting for a Healthy Church: Aligning Finances with Biblical Priorities* (9Marks; Grand Rapids: Zondervan, 2019), for a comprehensive book on how to budget towards mission engagement.

1. Ask the planting pastor to write detailed position papers on ecclesiological and pastoral issues: preaching, ministry, missions, evangelism, and polity, to name a few. Discuss, critique, and sharpen what the planter has written.

2. Ask the planter to interview three pastors outside the sending church. He should talk about their walk with Christ, healthy family practices, pastoral ministry, and any counsel he may have.

3. Spend some time with the church planting team. Ask them what they've learned most as a member of your church. Field questions from the planting team so that sending church members might discuss with them.

PART 2

PREPARING A CHURCH PLANT

CHAPTER 4

WHEN IS A CHURCH READY TO PLANT A NEW CHURCH?

Brandon Langley

In 2016, we planted a church with the dream of becoming a church planting church in the New Orleans Metro area. That dream didn't become a reality until 2025. On that glorious Sunday, we commissioned two elders and twenty-seven members to plant a church in a neighborhood twenty minutes away. It took nine years for us to be "ready" to plant a church.

It's not that we didn't want to plant sooner. We weren't stagnant during those nine years. We were preaching, praying, discipling, and supporting church planting both locally and globally. But we were not yet ready to send out our own church planting team.

Why weren't we ready? There is a sense in which no one is ever truly ready to have their first child. Parenting is on-the-job training. You can read all the books and seek all the advice, but stepping into parenthood is still a leap into the joyful and sleepless unknown. Church planting is similar. At some point, the church must take the plunge into the scary and uncertain world of sacrificially sending their first planting team.

In Part 1, we suggested that church planting must be built on the foundation of robust ecclesiology. Now that we've rooted planting in the biblical storyline and in the biblical definition of a church, we are ready to turn our attention to the work of a sending church in preparing to multiply.

Readiness and Urgency

Some might suggest that our patient plodding toward "readiness" was inconsistent with the urgency of the mission. People are dying every day without Jesus. Shouldn't we pick up the pace and plant more churches whether we're ready or not? In his book *Church Planting Movements*, David Garrison argues for church planting that is "rapid and multiplicative."[1] Garrison writes, "'How rapid is rapid?' You may ask. Perhaps the best answer is 'faster than you think possible.' Though the rate varies from place to place, church planting movements always outstrip the population growth rate as they race toward reaching the entire people group."[2] Unfor-

---

[1] David Garrison, *Church Planting Movements: How God is Redeeming a Lost World*, 6th ed. (Midlothian, VA: WIGTake Resources LLC, 2004).

[2] Ibid., 21-22. Later Garrison writes, "Some missionaries insist on taking

tunately, Garrison's position leaves the nature and practice of the New Testament church in the dust.

Instead, I insist that we take the time to lay a good foundation. This doesn't stand in contradiction to the urgency of the missionary task or to Scripture's teaching. Paul commands all of us to *take care* how we build the temple of God's people on the foundation of Christ (1 Cor. 3:11–18).

To be clear, we didn't wait nine years to send a church planting team because we believed we needed the money, the building, or the programs to create a modern American expression of church life. We weren't saving up to put on the best show in town so that we could draw in the spiritual seekers with our contemporary worship and sleek branding. A church is a community of baptized believers who are devoted to the apostles' teaching and the fellowship, to the breaking of bread and the prayers (Acts 2:42). So what do you really need to plant a church? Why should you wait, and when should you pull the trigger? Isn't readiness subjective? The church should assess at least five categories of readiness to discern when to plant—and when it's time to do it again.

Congregationally Ready

When Paul and Barnabas returned from their first missionary journey, they went back to their sending church in Antioch. Luke recounts this special moment: "When they arrived and gathered the church together, they declared all that God had done with them" (Acts 14:27). The entire

---

the time to 'lay a good foundation' with a small group, rather than sowing the gospel widely and expecting a church planting movement," 244.

church gathered because the whole church had prayed, fasted, and commissioned these men. Their mission was congregationally celebrated in part because it had been a result of congregational action.

Church planting cannot be the sole decision of the pastors. Nor can it be driven only by the aspiring planter. Healthy sending requires congregational affirmation and participation. The New Testament presents a church polity in which the congregation authoritatively determines its leadership, membership, and stewardship.[3] Planting a church affects all these areas and it will be felt throughout the church body.

Church planting is hard. When done well, it hurts. Members may be asked to sacrifice resources, send their closest friends, and adjust to a new ministry dynamic. Others may be asked to leave behind the comfort of the community they love to join the planting team. I write this just three weeks after sending our first church planting team. It feels like we are recovering from an arm amputation—as it should. Those we sent were family. We miss their spiritual giftings, their beautiful voices on Sunday mornings, and the sweet fellowship we enjoyed for many years. There is a good and glorious hurt that comes with gospel goodbyes.

That's why your congregation must be convinced—by Scripture—that church planting is one of the most faith-

---

[3] For a comprehensive argument for congregational church government see Jonathan Leeman, *Don't Fire Your Church Members: A Case for Congregationalism* (Brentwood, TN: B&H Academic, 2016). For a more concise resource on congregationalism consider Jonathan Leeman, *Understanding the Congregation's Authority* (Nashville, TN: B&H Books, 2016).

ful and fruitful ways to advance the kingdom of God. Your church is ready to plant when its members are willing to vote "yes" to the discomfort of sending for the glory of God. If your church planting plan couldn't pass a majority congregational vote, it's not time to plant. Everyone needs to be on board. Pressing forward without congregational support risks dividing the church through a split rather than multiplying through a plant. This doesn't mean that you need unanimous agreement, but if significant disunity remains, it will be prudent to keep teaching, casting vision, and praying.

I love the story of Ken Rucker who pastors New Branch Community Church in Buford, Georgia and serves as a board member with The Pillar Network. Ken's church facility was at capacity. They had a sizable percentage of members driving from an adjacent community. Ken and his elders sensed that God was leading their church to send a plant, but they weren't sure who would lead the work. Of all the elders, Ken lived closest to where the new plant would be established. Though he was the founding pastor of the church he loved and had served for many years, he pushed through his hesitation and submitted his name for consideration. Because Ken served as the lead pastor on staff, the church plant proposal would include a major staffing change for the sending church—one that required 90% approval in a congregational vote according to their bylaws. They made the proposal, took the vote, and—to the surprise of the elders—the vote failed with an 86% approval. Perhaps you could argue that those who voted "no" were missing God's will or that those criteria were too high, but Ken and the elders trusted the providence of God through the expressed will of the congregational vote and the agreed-upon process of their bylaws. To Ken's surprise, he and his wife felt relief wash over them. They went back to the drawing board, developed a new proposal with a different elder who would serve as the planter, and the vote passed the 90% threshold. They were now congregationally ready to plant a church.[4]

Spiritually Ready

"The horse is made ready for the day of battle, but the victory belongs to the LORD" (Prov. 21:31). Readiness isn't just about logistics. You can have the horse ready and still not be prepared for battle. Church planting is a victory that belongs to the Lord.

In Acts 13:2, the Holy Spirit said, "Set apart for me Barnabas and Saul for the work to which I have called them." And again, in verse 4, "Being sent out by the Holy Spirit…" Sending is the Spirit's work. So how can you know when the Spirit is moving in this way? Should we expect an audible voice in a worship service? A prophetic declaration?

The Bible teaches that the Spirit leads us into truth (John 16:13), unifies us (Eph. 4:3), sanctifies us (2 Cor. 3:18), and empowers our witness (Acts 1:8). One way the Spirit leads is by stirring godly desire (Rom. 8:5; Gal. 5:16). The first qualification for the office of overseer is aspiration (1 Tim. 3:1). In other words, you cannot conclude that God is leading you to be a pastor unless God also gives you some

---

[4] For more information on New Branch Community Church, check out their website: https://www.newbranch.com/.

desire to be a pastor. The same principle applies to church planting.

Has the Spirit created a burden for a particular community? Is there unity among the elders and the body? Are people stirred with the aspiration to join a planting team? Our desires are not sovereign and they are not always holy, but if God is leading a church toward church planting, he will also be leading the desires of some to participate.[5] Since "the king's heart is a stream of water in the hand of the LORD and he turns it wherever he will" (Prov. 21:1), we can preach and pray and trust that God will stir the hearts of those he calls to church planting.

We need Spirit-given desire, but we also need Spirit-empowered discernment. We know God is always working to fulfill the Great Commission and we know the need is great, but where do we start? There is always too much work to be done and too much need for any one church to meet. Should your church send missionaries to the unreached and unengaged in the 10/40 Window? Should you focus on planting in the inner city, the rural town with little gospel witness, or

---

[5] The doctrine of God's providence carried out through the work of God's Spirit in his people should lead us to believe that the Spirit will shape the desires of God's people for church planting in his perfect timing. In his monumental book on God's providence, John Piper writes, "Jesus does not just propose that there be a people gathered from all nations. He promises it and performs it. 'I will build my church, and the gates of hell shall not prevail against it' (Matt.16:18). He can do this without failing because he is at work in his people 'to will and to work for his good pleasure' (Phil. 2:13). He is '[equipping them] with everything good that [they] may do his will, working in [them] that which is pleasing in his sight' (Heb. 13:21)." John Piper, *Providence* (Wheaton, IL: Crossway, 2020), 663.

the community just 30 minutes away where many of your church members live? Are there particular cities or neighborhoods more strategic than others? The Great Commission is an overwhelming endeavor on a human level and it's impossible to choose what to do and how to do it based purely on logical deduction.

Paul intended to go into Asia, but he was "forbidden by the Spirit" (Acts 16:6). So he pivoted and developed a new plan to go to Bithynia. But the Spirit of Jesus did not allow him (Acts 16:7). Instead, he received a vision of a man from Macedonia calling to him (Acts 16:9). God's guidance is rarely as dramatic as a vision in the night, but the New Testament consistently models a sensitivity to the Spirit that is cultivated through prayer, fasting, listening, and immersion in the Word. Andrew Murray writes,

> Our whole relation to God is ruled in this, that his will is to be done in us and by us as it is in Heaven. He promised to make known His will to us by His Spirit, the Guide into all truth. And our position is to be that of waiting for His counsel as the only guide of our thoughts and actions. In our church worship, in our prayer meetings, in our conventions, in all our gatherings as managers, or directors, or committees, or helpers in any part of the work for God, our first object ought ever to be to ascertain the mind of God.[6]

---

[6] Andrew Murray, *Waiting on God* (Chicago, IL: Moody Press, 2013), 78.

Consider this simple test of spiritual readiness: Are you praying? Have you led your church to pray and fast? In Acts 4:31, after they prayed, "the place in which they were gathered was shaken, and they were all filled with the Holy Spirit." The prayer gathering should be the engine of a church's mission together. If you don't have a regular gathering for intentional prayer built into the rhythm of church life, start here. Lead the church to pray big, intentional, missional prayers—the kind of open-handed prayers that both frighten you and excite you. Prayer precedes spiritual guidance. In the same way, spiritual guidance precedes church planting.

Situationally Ready

We don't know exactly how the Spirit shut the door on Paul's plans to travel to Asia and Bithynia. It could have been a spiritual impression upon Paul's mind and heart or it could have been situational as with other cases in the New Testament. Paul was often forced out of a city by circumstances of divine providence, not because he had any kind of spiritual inclination to pick up and move. God is sovereign over your church's situation, and it's possible that the details of your circumstances might provoke genuine promptings either to act or to wait.

Has God grown your congregation but limited your gathering space? Are you overflowing your facility? God is not surprised by that reality. Perhaps He has done this so that your church might overflow into a new church plant. Has God drawn people from other communities so that they are driving long distances to gather with your church? If so, could it be that God is forming the beginnings of a new core team who can invite their neighbors to hear the gospel? We have seen God working in this way through our situation. We were outgrowing our facility, and I presented the options to our church over a year ago. We could plant a church, build a bigger building which would put our church into debt, move to two services and fracture the community life of our church family, or just stop evangelizing altogether and turn visitors away at the door. The last option is clearly not a biblical option. Thankfully, our church expressed a clear and unified desire to pursue planting a church. I am certainly not arguing that church planting should only be pursued when you're out of options, but circumstances can motivate readiness.

When we began to look at the details of our situation, it drove us into a more concentrated season of prayer. Over time, we saw the plan unfold. We had a sizable portion of our membership driving from the same community 20 minutes away. Through a lot of ups, downs, twists, and turns, a dwindling Baptist church in that area actually voted to close their doors and donate their facility to us for the purpose of planting a new church. God orchestrated our situation, and we walked through the doors God was opening.

The situation doesn't have to be perfect. Ours certainly wasn't smooth sailing. There will be difficulties to overcome. After all, you're fighting a spiritual war (Eph. 6:10–12). But you must fight to view your circumstances through the lens of God's providence. Take an honest look at where your church is spiritually and situationally. Ask for wise counselors from both inside your church and outside your church to assess and provide wisdom as to what would be prudent.

Your situation, however difficult or inconvenient, is full of opportunity that is orchestrated by the hand of God. Spurgeon mused, "Blessed is the man who sees God in the trifles! It is there that it is hardest to see him; but he who believes that God is there, may go from the little providence up to the God of providence."[7]

Financially Ready

Your church is not situationally ready if it is not also financially ready. Good stewardship is a command. Our whole life and ministry could be interpreted through the paradigm offered in 1 Peter 4:10–11:

> As each has received a gift, use it to serve one another, as good stewards of God's varied grace: whoever speaks, as one who speaks oracles of God; whoever serves, as one who serves by the strength that God supplies—in order that in everything God may be glorified through Jesus Christ. To him belong glory and dominion forever and ever. Amen.

God gives us grace and we steward that grace in such a way that he receives the glory.

That is the Christian life and that is the mission of the Christian church. He gives us our salvation, our spiritual

---

[7] Charles H. Spurgeon, *Providence*, sermon 135, preached February 8, 1857, The Spurgeon Library, https://www.spurgeon.org/resource-library/sermons/providence/#flipbook/.

giftings, and our resources. We steward them to spread his glory to every nation and generation.

There are two ways that we can fail at our stewardship responsibility. We can waste God's resources, or we can hoard them. The balance we want to strike is wise stewardship.

In the example of the prodigal son, he wasted all his money on himself. Jesus explains, "He squandered his property in reckless living. And when he had spent everything, a severe famine arose in that country, and he began to be in need" (Luke 15:13–14). Churches can recklessly spend money on themselves in ways that hamstring their ability to send or support future church plants. If the church's overhead is high, you may not yet be ready to plant a church. Church planting doesn't have to be expensive—you don't need a fancy building and state-of-the-art sound equipment. But if you send a sizable team of members who are faithful to give, and your church cannot survive the loss of their generosity, then some significant changes need to be made before sending. That doesn't mean you will never be ready, but it may mean you need to lead the church into a season of financial trimming and biblical teaching. Being financially ready isn't just about the numbers in the bank. It's also about the stewardship philosophy of a church that prioritizes missional sending.

Wasting God's resources is one side of poor stewardship, but in a world obsessed with safety and certainty, hoarding money may be the bigger temptation. In Jesus' parable of the talents, three servants are given five talents. The servants who invested the talents and multiplied what the Master gave them are called good and faithful. The servant who buried his talent to keep it safe is called slothful and wicked (Matt. 25:14–30). When we read the parable of the talents, we tend to think about the individual. But the message applies to congregations as well. We aren't called to bury what God has given us, nor should we build larger and larger barns to hoard what we have (Luke 12:15–21). Our aim, therefore, is stewardship that is generous, but not foolish.

Consider your church's operational budget. Is it lean? Are you poised like a battleship ready to deploy, or a luxury cruise liner keeping the customers comfortable?[8] What would it look like for you to budget any margin for future church planting so that you could more freely and open-handedly send faithful and generous members without financially tanking your current ministry? Could you consistently budget a sizable percentage each year to go into a "missional savings" account? From that account you could bless church plants with a startup grant, and when it's time to send you could freely send that percentage of your membership without destroying ongoing ministry in your community. Planting requires sacrifice, but it also requires stewardship. Church planting starts with a healthy spending philosophy that prepares the church for sending well.[9]

---

[8] J. D. Greear, *Gaining by Losing: Why the Future Belongs to Churches That Send* (Grand Rapids, MI: Zondervan, 2015), 25.

[9] For a helpful book on church budgeting consider Jamie Dunlop, *Budgeting for a Healthy Church: Aligning Finances with Biblical Priorities for Ministry* (Wheaton, IL: Crossway, 2019).

Pastorally Ready

Finances are important but not the most important. After all, you can technically have people join together as a biblical church and meet in a home or public space with no money at all. You do, however, need a church planter, and raising up a church planter can be harder than raising funds. You need a man who is not only elder-qualified, but who desires the work. In other words, you need a miracle of God's grace.

When the apostle Paul addresses the Ephesian elders in Acts 20, he credits God with the miracle of making them pastors. He says, "The Holy Spirit has made you overseers" (Acts 20:28). Likewise, God is the one who ultimately raises up qualified men who are ready and willing to plant a church. Being pastorally ready means to a man that a group of people are willing to follow man into the work of church planting.

While God ultimately raises up a pastor, He often uses other Christians in the process. After all, pastors teach faithful men who will be able to teach others also (2 Tim. 2:2). Often, when a church gets planted out of a church led by a plurality of elders, the planter is one of the already-qualified men. So, if you have multiple elders, look around the table and ask whether God would send one of you.

If the church planter is not currently sitting around the elder table, then hopefully he is in an established pipeline of ministry preparation. God raises up church planters through the shepherding ministry of the church, pastoral residencies, internships, and mentoring relationships. Church multiplication cannot happen without pastor multiplication, and this takes time and intentionality. Those who advocate for a rapidly multiplying church planting movement often appeal to Paul's travel itinerary, but they often don't consider the years of Paul's preparation. Elliot Clark writes:

> Paul wasn't commissioned by the church officially until he had spent fourteen years proving himself through evangelism, teaching, and faithful ministry (Gal. 2:1). If we consider also his lifetime of training in the Hebrew Scriptures even before his Damascus road experience, then our calculation of Paul's ministry preparedness increases significantly. . . . This is essential. Local churches must regain their responsibility to prove, affirm, and send qualified missionaries.[10]

If you don't have a church planting missionary whom the church would affirm as biblically qualified (1 Tim. 3:1–7; Titus 1:5–9; 1 Pet. 5:1–4), then you're not yet ready to send a church planting team. If you have a man who aspires to plant, yet no one is willing to follow him, then you're not yet ready. One could even argue that you actually need more than one elder-qualified man since Paul was never sent out to do the work without a sufficiently qualified and gifted co-laborer.

This is where church-to-church partnerships make church planting more plausible for many churches. If a church is congregationally, spiritually, situationally, and fi-

---

[10] Elliot Clark, *Mission Affirmed: Recovering the Missionary Motivation of Paul* (Wheaton, IL: Crossway, 2022), 95.

nancially ready to plant but in need of a pastor to lead the work, the Lord may provide the right man through partnership with other like-minded or denominationally connected churches in your region. A group of doctrinally aligned and missionally driven pastors meeting together regularly can be helpful. One church may be ready in some of the above categories while another church may be ready in complementary ways. Together, they can send a church-planting team. It's my hope that the church plant we just sent will one day partner with us to plant another church, and in this way both our churches will multiply sooner than we would have in isolation. Associationalism can become the key for more churches to be ready to plant more churches more often.

Church planting is always an act of faith. But assessing congregational, spiritual, situational, financial, and pastoral readiness gives us a framework for discernment.

Ask the right questions.

Pray for the Spirit's leading.

Trust God's providence.

And when the time comes—take the plunge to plant in faith.

Then do it again and again until we see Jesus face to face.

CHAPTER 5

HOW DO I FIND A PLANTING PASTOR?

Dave Kiehn

The call to plant churches is not a modern trend—it is the ancient and ongoing mission of Christ's church. From the moment Jesus declared, "I will build my church" (Matt. 16:18), the gospel has gone forth when faithful men preach Christ and form local assemblies in every corner of the world. Today, the need remains urgent. Towns, cities, and neighborhoods remain without a faithful gospel witness. We know we should plant churches. So where do we find the right men?

At my local church, we've seen firsthand the joys and challenges of raising up church planters. It's not a quick process, and it's never one-size-fits-all. But by God's grace, there are biblical patterns and practical steps we can take to identify, equip, and send faithful shepherds. This chapter seeks to encourage and to guide pastors, elders, and church leaders who are praying and planning to multiply their gospel influence.

The church planting process begins not with strategy, but with supplication. It continues with faithful example, discerning evaluation, strategic partnerships, and sacrificial sending. In the following sections, we'll explore what it means to look up, look down, look in, look out, and look forward as we seek to obey Christ's call to make disciples and plant churches.

Look Up:
Begin with Prayer and Dependence on God

At the foundation of any work of the Lord is prayer. Before we strategize, network, or train, we must *first look up* to the God who raises up shepherds after His own heart. Church planting, at its core, is not a human enterprise. It's a divine calling. The laborers must be sent by the Lord of the harvest (Matt. 9:37–38). Therefore, the search for a faithful church planter does not begin in a classroom or with a committee—it begins in the prayer closet.

The instinct of the church should be to pray first and wait for the Lord's leading rather than act first and pray later. We see this lesson modeled throughout the Scriptures. Before Jesus began His public ministry, He spent forty days in the wilderness fasting and praying. Before He chose the twelve apostles, He spent the entire night in prayer to God (Luke 6:12). If the Son of God did not proceed without prayer, how can we presume to take the work of church planting into our own hands without first seeking the Father?

As a local church, we must approach church planting with humility. We don't presume to know who should plant churches. We don't assume we can read a man's heart or predict his endurance. Only God can do that. So we ask persistently, fervently, and specifically. We ask God to raise up men from within our congregation, from within our city, and from other faithful churches and seminaries. We plead with the Lord to stir hearts, to clarify callings, and to affirm gifts that will build up His Church.

John Piper has often said that "prayer is the open admission that without Christ we can do nothing."[1] That's not just true of personal holiness—it's true of missions, of multiplication, and of church planting. If the power does not come from above, the effort will bear no lasting fruit. We may build an organization. We may gather a crowd. But we will not plant a church in the biblical sense of the word unless God is in it from beginning to end.

In our contemporary landscape, we face the allure of pragmatism found in so many books, strategies, bootcamps, and blueprints for church planting. We think that if we can just find the right man, with the right gifting, and place him in the right context, success will follow. But spiritual fruit does not grow from strategic formulas. It grows when the Spirit of God works through humble, faithful people. And prayer is the first fruit of humility.

The early church understood this. In Acts 13, when the church in Antioch was about to send out Paul and Barnabas,

---

[1] John Piper, *Desiring God: Meditations of a Christian Hedonist* (Rev. ed.; Sisters, OR: Multnomah, 2003), 81.

79

what did they do? Luke tells us, "While they were worshiping the Lord and fasting, the Holy Spirit said, 'Set apart for me Barnabas and Saul for the work to which I have called them.' Then after fasting and praying they laid their hands on them and sent them off" (Acts 13:2–3). Before anyone was sent, the church fasted and prayed. It wasn't just a moment of prayer tacked on to a business meeting—it was a season of earnest intercession, waiting on the Spirit of God to speak.

Prayer was not a prelude to ministry—it was the heart of ministry. Likewise, in Acts 6, when the apostles were confronted with the growing administrative needs of the church, they refused to neglect "prayer and the ministry of the Word" (Acts 6:4). As Garrett Kell has emphasized, "Plead with God to raise up pastors for you to invest in. Pray that he'd raise up pastors to serve alongside you, pastors to send out from you, and pastors to one day replace you."[2] A praying church is a discerning church, and a discerning church is a fruitful church.

This is why, at the church I serve, we've tried to make prayer a foundational part of our ministry, especially when it comes to identifying and equipping future leaders. We pray in our elder meetings for God to raise up men. We ask our members to pray specifically for the next church planter. We include petitions in our corporate gatherings that God would send laborers into the harvest. We do not simply announce opportunities for leadership—we pray for God to

---

[2] Garrett Kell, "Pastors, Train Future Pastors," in *9Marks*, June 30, 2020; accessed online: 26 June 2025; https://www.9marks.org/article/pastor-train-future-pastors/.

burden the right men with a calling and to give us eyes to see them when they rise up. Prayer heightens the attentiveness of the church's leaders to see what God is doing in their midst.

Prayer also prepares *us*. It humbles our ambitions, slows our rush to action, and helps us to walk by faith rather than sight. It reminds us that success in church planting is more than numbers, brand names, or popularity—it's about faithfulness. When we pray, we are not just asking God to move—we are preparing our hearts to obey when He does.

It's important to recognize that sometimes the Lord's answer to our prayers takes time. We may pray for years before a suitable man emerges. That's okay. Prayer aligns our hearts with His will, not to pressure God into acting according to our timeline. In His perfect time, He will raise up the right laborer for the right field.

So, before you do anything else—before you form a committee, before you draft a budget, before you start scouting neighborhoods—*look up*. Look up to the God who sees what we cannot see. Look up to the God who knows the hearts of men. Look up to the One who is building His church, and the gates of hell shall not prevail against it.

Look up, and pray.

Look Down:
Model Faithfulness as the Lead Pastor

If prayer is the foundation of finding a church planter, then pastoral example is the blueprint. The men you train or evaluate will take their cues from you. As Paul said to the Corinthians, "Be imitators of me, as I am of Christ" (1 Cor. 11:1). That's not an arrogant statement—it's a pastoral one. We must *look down*—not in pride, but in responsibility—recognizing that faithful shepherding must be modeled before it can be multiplied.

Christ calls church leaders to be faithful rather than charismatic, obedient rather than innovative. Future planters are watching how we live, how we shepherd, and how we suffer. They are learning from our preaching, but also from our patience, our gentleness, and our perseverance in difficulty. We cannot expect to raise up faithful church planters if we ourselves fail to model what faithfulness looks like over the long haul.

Faithful pastoring is not a spotlight ministry; it's a shepherding ministry. It's not about building a platform—it's about building up people. As Alistair Begg puts it, "The pulpit is intended not as a showcase for a preacher's performance but as the place from which a pastor gives Christ-exalting, biblical instruction."[3] That includes the sheep in your flock and the potential shepherds-in-training sitting among them.

The sobering truth about pastoral ministry is that we are always teaching—even when we're not consciously doing so. How you treat the least visible members of the church, how you respond to criticism, how you handle conflict, how you prioritize your time—these are all shaping the next generation of leaders. They're watching. They're learning. They're forming their own picture of what pastoring should be.

---

[3] Alistair Begg, "The Pulpit: Its Powers and Pitfalls," *Truth for Life*, Parkside Church, Cleveland, OH, 20 September 1999; accessed 28 June 2025: https://www.truthforlife.org/resources/sermon/the-pulpit-its-power-pitfalls/.

I remember one brother who came to our church with great zeal for church planting. He was passionate, articulate, and had a heart for reaching the lost. But he lacked a clear picture of faithful, long-haul pastoring. Over time, simply being around our elder team—watching how we navigated church discipline, how we prayed for struggling members, how we counseled in grief and joy, how we opened our homes, how we labored week after week in expositional preaching—transformed him. He didn't just learn what to do—he learned *how to be a pastor.* That came not through a class, but through a model.

If you want to find a faithful church planter, you must first be a faithful pastor. Your preaching must be expositional, doctrinally rich, and Christ-centered. Your pastoral care must be personal and consistent. Your leadership must be marked by humility, patience, and the fruit of the Spirit. Your life must be above reproach, in doctrine and in devotion. As John Owen wisely exhorts, "A minister may fill his pews . . . but what that minister is on his knees in secret before God Almighty, that he is and no more."[4] That truth holds in both planting and pastoring. If the man behind the pulpit is marked by holiness in his personal life and integrity in his relationships, the fruit of his ministry will reflect it. If his life doesn't have it, the fruit will be seen in the congregation.

We must remember that the soil of ministry is often stubborn. It's easy to get caught up in short-term metrics—

---

[4] Costi Hinn, "Private Lives Define Public Leaders — For the Gospel," *For the Gospel* (blog), February 1, 2025; accessed 28 June 2025: https://www.forthegospel.org/read/private-lives-define-public-leaders?rq=john%20owen%2C%20. Citation from Owen not identified.

attendance numbers, program success, platform recognition. But faithfulness in the pastorate is often seen in the mundane, behind-the-scenes ministry. It's sitting with a grieving widow. It's preparing another meal for a struggling family. It's preaching the Word on a Sunday when you feel tired and discouraged. These moments matter because these moments train the next planter to trust in God, not in himself.

At our church, the most powerful leadership development tool is our elder team. Men grow by watching other men love the church. That's why we invite potential leaders into our lives, not just into our meetings. We want them to see how we speak to our wives, how we discipline our children, how we pray in private, how we rest. It's not just about theology—it's about trajectory.

And here's the key—your quiet faithfulness is never wasted. It may never be recognized by a platform or podcast, but it is forming the next generation of church leaders. As Paul exhorted Timothy, "Keep a close watch on yourself and on the teaching. Persist in this, for by so doing you will save both yourself and your hearers" (1 Tim. 4:16). Your example—how you live out that verse day after day—may be the very thing God uses to inspire a man to plant a church in faith and fidelity.

So, pastor, look down. Examine your life and doctrine. Model what you want to multiply. Be the kind of shepherd you want to send out. And trust that as you plant the seeds of faithfulness in your daily ministry, God will raise up faithful men to carry that model forward into the harvest.

Look In:
Identify and Invest in Men Within the Church

If we've looked up in dependent prayer and looked down through faithful modeling, then we are ready to *look in*—to examine the flock God has already entrusted to our care. The men we need to plant churches may already be sitting in our pews, serving behind the scenes, quietly loving people, and living lives of humble faithfulness. Our task is to identify them, test them, invest in them, and help them discern whether the Lord may be calling them to shepherd His people.

The best church planters are not always the most dynamic personalities or the ones who stand out in a crowd. Often, they are the men who have already demonstrated a heart for people, a love for the Word, and a pattern of service in the life of the church—men who are already doing the work of pastoring in seed form. These are the ones to pay attention to.

At the church I serve, we are constantly looking for faithful men to invest in. Not just the loud ones or the charismatic ones—but steady, Scripture-loving, people-serving brothers who may not yet realize that God has gifted them to teach and shepherd. We strive to make our approach to leadership development intentional rather than haphazard. We believe it must be intentional and relational. We've structured a leadership pipeline that begins with discipleship and gradually moves toward theological training, character evaluation, and hands-on ministry involvement. Zach Eswine wisely emphasizes the importance of faithfulness in obscurity: "The pastoral vocation is not about greatness. It's about faithfulness in the small, mostly overlooked things."[5] That truth has been proven time and again. Many of the best future pastors and planters aren't asking for a microphone—they're asking how they can help a struggling brother, lead their family in the Word, or serve the saints more effectively. These are the men to look for. And often, they're hidden in plain sight.

Your role as a pastor is to spot the embers and fan them into flame. You must look with spiritual eyes—not just for ability, but for humility. Not just for gifting, but for godliness. When Paul gives qualifications for elders in 1 Timothy 3 and Titus 1, he spends far more time on character than charisma. That's intentional. God's leaders must be holy before they are helpful.

We must assess both *gifting* and *godliness*. The man may be able to explain Scripture, but does he love people? Can he handle criticism without losing his temper? Is he patient with the weak? Does he confess sin and receive correction well? Is he the same man at home that he is at church? Does he take joy in serving others when no one sees? The late John MacArthur long emphasized this principle in his teaching: "The character of a pastor is not optional—it's essential."[6] A man may preach a fine sermon, but if he is proud, self-willed,

---

[5] Zack Eswine, *The Imperfect Pastor: Discovering Joy in Our Limitations Through a Daily Apprenticeship with Jesus* (Wheaton, IL: Crossway, 2015), 272.

[6] John MacArthur, "The Character of the Pastor," *Grace to You*, Grace Community Church, Sun Valley, CA, January 27, 2019; accessed 28 June 2025: https://www.gty.org/sermons/81-35/the-character-of-the-pastor.

or harsh, he undermines the gospel he preaches. Paul told Titus to appoint elders in every town, but only those who were "above reproach." That must be our standard as well—not perfection, but clear, consistent godliness.

Once you identify a man with both character and some measure of gifting, begin to invest. Bring him close. Invite him into your life. Let him watch you counsel, prepare sermons, visit the sick, resolve conflict, and teach. Give him opportunities to lead small group discussions, teach a Bible study, lead a prayer meeting, or preach a short message—*under supervision.* These are not tryouts; they are training grounds.

One of the most helpful things you can do is *normalize slow growth.* Encourage these men not to rush into ministry but to let the Lord shape them over time. It's easy for young men to be impatient—to want the pulpit without the preparation. But remind them that the Lord often calls before He sends, and there's usually a season of hidden, humble formation in between.

Walk with them through life. Don't just give them tasks—give them your time. Let them see your weaknesses and how you run to Christ. Let them see the tears, the prayers, the disappointments, and the joys. Help them understand that ministry is more than just about preaching well—it's about *living well.* Show them that to be a shepherd is to bleed for the flock.

Look in. Take the time to observe, invest, and equip the men God has placed in your church. You may be surprised. The man you're praying for may already be there, faithfully stacking chairs, teaching children, and quietly leading his family. Don't overlook him. Bring him close. Pray over him. Train him. Walk with him. And trust the Lord to reveal and refine his calling.

God raises up leaders from among His people, often in the most ordinary ways. Our job is not to manufacture pastors, but to *recognize* the ones the Spirit is already forming, and to equip them to do the work of ministry for the glory of Christ and the good of His church.

Look Out:
Seek Partnerships with Like-Minded
Churches and Seminaries

Sometimes, even after praying fervently, modeling faithfully, and searching carefully within our own congregation, we find that we do not yet have the man God is calling to plant a new church. Or perhaps we have a brother who is close—he has the heart and some of the gifting—but he is not ready to be sent out alone. In these moments, we must *look out*—beyond our walls, beyond our immediate sphere, to the broader body of Christ. The church is a family, a network of believers working together to advance the gospel. We are not meant to do this work in isolation.

The Apostle Paul did not plant churches alone. He worked in gospel partnership. He relied on trusted brothers like Timothy, Titus, Barnabas, and Silas to carry the mission forward. The New Testament church was a collaborative effort, a partnership of churches and leaders united in the gospel task. We must emulate this same spirit of cooperation and open-handedness. The mission is too big for any one church or leader. This is one reason why the Pillar Network strives to joyfully partner with the Southern Baptist Convention of churches. Through church-to-church partnerships and collaboration with national and state entities we are able to align with others to both find potential pastors and send healthy churches.

Richard Baxter's words still ring true, "A church must not be a name or a form, but a company of living saints; built together, spiritually united to his Son, that believers may grow up into him in all things."[7] In our contemporary culture, churches often become focused on their own identity, their own style, or their own vision to the exclusion of gospel partnership. But true kingdom expansion happens when gospel-centered, Bible-preaching churches unite. We must cultivate relationships with like-minded churches that share our commitment to Scripture and faithful ministry. These partnerships can become rich sources for identifying gifted men but who may need additional seasoning, mentorship, or opportunities to hone their character and pastoral competence.

Our church has been blessed by ongoing relationships with seminaries as well as connections with faithful churches within our Southern Baptist Convention and beyond. These partnerships provide multiple avenues for training and testing potential planters.[8]

---

[7] Richard Baxter, *The Reformed Pastor* (Edinburgh: Banner of Truth Trust, 1981 from 1656 ed.), 15–16.

[8] We praise God for the health of six SBC seminaries—Southern Baptist Theological Seminary, Southeastern Baptist Theological Seminary, Midwestern Baptist Theological Seminary, New Orleans Baptist Theological Seminary, Southwest Baptist Theological Seminary, and Gateway Semi-

One such avenue is a pastoral residency or internship. Seminary education equips men with vital theological knowledge, but there is no substitute for hands-on experience in the local church. A residency or internship places a man in the thick of ministry—preaching, counseling, hospital visits, elder meetings, discipleship—under the oversight of seasoned pastors. This on-the-job training is invaluable. It transforms theoretical knowledge into practical wisdom and spiritual maturity.

We also participate in theological intensives and conferences where men can deepen their doctrinal understanding while connecting with mentors and peers who are on similar journeys. These gatherings foster community and accountability and help young pastors grow in confidence and competence.

Although a seminary degree is helpful, it does not give an automatic stamp of readiness to plant a church. Many good men graduate seminary with sound doctrine and theological skill but lack the seasoning that comes from long, faithful service in the local church. Pastor and professor Jared Wilson captures this idea when he says seminaries have their lane, and it's an important one, but the local church is the divine arena for making disciples.[9]

---

nary—that provide excellent partnerships with churches. In addition, many State Conventions and the North American Mission Board have training resources that local churches can, and should, consider using.

[9] See Jared C. Wilson, *Gospel-Driven Ministry: An Introduction to the Calling and Work of a Pastor* (Wheaton, IL: Crossway, 2021), to see how Wilson unpacks this ministry perspective.

The local church is the crucible where theory meets reality. It's where a man learns to shepherd imperfect people, to navigate conflict with grace, and to carry the burdens of a flock that is often ungrateful and weary. This seasoning takes time. It takes humility. And it requires a church willing to invest in a man's growth over the long haul.

When we look out to other churches and seminaries, our goal is to find godly men who *can be trained*—men who have the potential, the desire, and the basic character but who still need mentoring and experience. We want to be a church that other churches and seminaries trust with their future leaders.

This means being willing to invest in men we may never ultimately retain. Some men will come to us for a season, grow under our teaching and care, and then move on to plant churches elsewhere. We do this not because it benefits us, but because it benefits the kingdom. We want to be a sending church, a training ground, a hub of gospel multiplication.

Partnerships also guard against isolationism and narrow-mindedness. They remind us that the gospel is bigger than our local context, that the body of Christ spans regions and nations. When we open our eyes and hands to the broader church, we join a movement far greater than ourselves.

In practical terms, this means:

- Maintaining active relationships with trusted seminaries and their faculty.

- Hosting pastoral residents and interns who have been vetted by their sending churches.

- Engaging in regional and national church-planting networks.

- Regularly consulting with other pastors about potential planters.

Encouraging men in our congregation to consider seminary or cross-church mentorship if they show gifting but need further equipping.

In all this, prayer remains central. We pray for wisdom to discern true calling and readiness. We pray for humility to partner well with others. And we pray for God to open doors for these men to be trained, tested, and sent with the Lord's blessing.

So, *look out*—not just to find men but to *train* them well. Be a church that others trust to shape their future leaders. Be willing to invest in those you may never retain, for the sake of churches you may never see. Because the mission is not about keeping good men—it's about sending them. And that sending is a sacred trust.

Look Forward:
Prepare to Send with Sacrifice and Joy

After you have looked up in prayer, looked down by modeling faithfulness, looked in to identify and train men within your church, and looked out to broader partnerships, the final step is to *look forward*—to prepare your church to send a faithful church planter with both sacrifice and joy. This is a critical moment in the life of any congregation, and it demands both sober reflection and spiritual celebration.

Sending a church planter is a deeply spiritual act—a holy commissioning, a sacred sending out of brothers and sisters who are beloved members of your church family. These are not just employees or volunteers; these are men you have prayed over, discipled, walked alongside, and loved. You are releasing them into a mission field that will test them in every way imaginable. It is the church's highest privilege and heaviest responsibility to send such men forth with the right heart and posture.

Charles Spurgeon once famously said, "If sinners be damned, let them leap to hell over our dead bodies."[10] While his language is stark, the passion behind it captures the urgency and cost of gospel ministry. We must feel this same urgency in raising up and sending out faithful men to proclaim Christ. The eternal weight to the work, the souls of men and women at stake must move us. The church planter you send is not just planting a building or launching a program—he is stewarding the gospel to a people in need of salvation.

Because of this urgency, we must teach our churches to see sending not as an exceptional event but as a normal part of gospel life. Too often, churches view it as a loss, a blow, or a disruption when a member or leader leaves to plant a church. But sending brings forth rejoicing, not because we're glad they are gone, but because we are glad they are going—for the sake of the gospel, for the sake of people who need Jesus, for the sake of the kingdom's expansion.

---

[10] Charles Haddon Spurgeon, "The Wailing of Risca," December 9, 1860 in *The Metropolitan Tabernacle Pulpit Sermons* (London: Passmore & Alabaster, 1861), 7:13.

We must preach and teach about the biblical pattern of sending. The Apostle Paul's example is instructive: he did not hoard gifted men in one place; he sent them out with a team, a blessing, and a network of ongoing support. The sending church is a sending family, praying and providing and rejoicing from afar.

Financially, the sending church must be sacrificial in their giving. Many planters start with little more than a vision and a small core group. The sending church has responsibility to provide seed support—whether through direct funding, helping raise support, or connecting the planter with other churches. Sacrificial giving demonstrates the church's commitment and love.

Emotionally, the sending church must be prepared for the pain of separation. The planter and his family will leave familiar friends, routines, and support systems. Congregations must grieve well and encourage well, staying connected through prayer and visits. The pastor and elders should provide ongoing counsel to both the planter and the sending church to maintain healthy relationships.

Practically, the sending church must provide ongoing training, encouragement, and accountability. Planters need mentors, networks, and resources to persevere. Church planting is often exhausting, isolating, and discouraging. It takes perseverance and faithfulness over the long haul. If we prepare our planters to suffer well, through teaching about endurance and sanctification—and if we prepare our churches to support well, through prayer, encouragement, and practical help—then we will send with strength.

We should also prepare to walk with our planters through the hard seasons. Inevitably, church planting will bring opposition—from without or within. There will be spiritual warfare, discouragement, and times when the fruit seems small or absent. The sending church must be a source of steadfast prayer and encouragement during these valleys. It is a mark of true gospel partnership that we rejoice in the mountaintop moments and weep in the valleys.

And finally, *look forward with hope*. Perhaps the church your planter establishes will one day send others. This is the Great Commission in motion: one church planting another, which plants another, until Christ returns. This multiplication is God's ordained method for the expansion of His kingdom.

Think of the ripple effect. The faithful planting of one church leads to a cluster of gospel communities in a region, which in turn births more churches. The kingdom spreads. The name of Jesus is exalted. The gospel goes forth with power.

Sending a church planter is a spiritual investment in that future. It is an act of faith, trusting that God who began this good work will bring it to completion (Phil. 1:6). It is also an act of worship, offering up our best sons for the sake of the Savior's mission.

So, pastor, church leaders, and members, prepare your hearts and prepare your church to send with both sacrifice and joy. Walk in step with your planter through prayer and provision. Teach your people to rejoice in the sending, knowing that though you are releasing a beloved brother, you are also releasing the gospel to go forth in power.

CHAPTER 6

WHERE SHOULD WE PLANT A CHURCH?

Matt Rogers

Not long ago the word "vision" was all the rage in pastoral ministry and church planting conversations. The word "visionary" was a five-star adjective used to define successful pastors. Breakout sessions of national conferences championed steps pastors could take to grow their visionary capacity.[1] "Without vison the people perish" (Prov. 29:18), and death would surely be the fate of leaders who failed to tap into their full visionary potential.

Or so we were told.

---

[1] I became a Christian in the early 2000s and was on a church staff shortly thereafter. One of the first books I remember reading about Christian leadership fits this visionary genre perfectly: Andy Stanley's *Visioneering: Your Guide for Discovering and Maintaining Personal Vision* (Colorado Springs: Multnomah, 2005).

Over time it became clear that vision was shorthand for man-centered pragmatism. Get an idea. Develop a path to bring that idea to life. Rally the troops. Take the hill. Whatever the cost.

This vision premise applies to the work of church planting. After all, starting a new church is inherently a work of vision. There *is not* a church and then there *is* a church. What could be more visionary than that?

And yet, I'd rather be diligent than visionary. The work of church planting requires diligence more than vision. In contrast to the theoretical concept of vision, diligence implies that faithful pastors follow God's vision for His church. Rather than inventing their own guidelines and guardrails, faithful pastors search diligently in God's Word to find the whys and hows and whats of church planting.

The wisest man who ever lived invites us to "consider the ant" (Prov. 6:6–8). Diligence should be a defining attribute of pastors and sending churches seeking to multiply. Many pastors aspire to lead a church that plants and revitalizes other churches. Those pastors might stumble into a church planting opportunity, but happenstance is no substitute for a nuanced and well-defined plan to proactively pursue the task of multiplication. The proverbial ant, in contrast, "prepares its provisions in the summer; it gathers its food during harvest (Prov. 6:8). Later, the writer suggests that "there is profit in all hard work, but endless talk leads only to poverty" (Prov. 14:23) and "the plans of the diligent certainly lead to profit, but anyone who is reckless certainly becomes poor" (Prov. 21:5).

Among the critical decisions a diligent sending church must make is where they will plant a new church. In Chapter 4, Brandon provided guidance on the various factors of "readiness" that should be considered by a sending church. As he rightly said, a church will never be fully ready the way a parent is never totally prepared to have a child. At some point, you must jump. But the question then becomes— Where do we jump? This matter cannot be left to the winds of chance. Pastors need a plan. In this chapter, I will outline four ways a sending church can apply diligence to the question of where to plant. Along the way, I'll attempt to show strengths and weaknesses of each approach and conclude by suggesting the best method is probably some combination of the four.

Method #1
The Place of Greatest Need

This method is sensible since we want to start new churches in the places where 1) there are the fewest number of churches, or 2) there is an overwhelming number of people. So we go where the people are. It's common for sending churches to look over their city or their region and notice places with a lack of gospel churches. Were we to put a dot of light on a map for every healthy local church, there would be places that are dark. It might be a section of the city or a sociological subset of the population that are overwhelmingly under-served. If you have limited resources, some suggest that we must prioritize the places of greatest need.

The inherent challenge of this method is clear—there is so much need that it's virtually impossible to rank where the need is greatest. This is especially true if the sending church considers the entire world as a potential place for church planting. There are needs everywhere. While some countries may be considered "reached" by sociological research, you'd be hard-pressed to find many places in the world that could not use more healthy churches.[2] The overwhelming need is also true when we limit consideration to the U.S., especially in major, urban areas. All major cities need more churches.

To narrow the options, diligent sending churches could consider places of need in their immediate community. This focus limits the options and presents sending churches with greater knowledge of what's most needed. For example, if the sending church attempts to target an unreached nation around the world, they are at a disadvantage unless they know a faithful pastor, church, or missionary in that location who can help them understand where to plant a church. But elders likely know their own city and region. They know the dynamics that impact planting in that location and the plac-

---

[2] There's much discussion about the missiological strategy implications of defining various people groups as "reached." Often the term "unreached" is used to denote places with less than 2% believers. The thought is that places with more than 2% are then able to take the responsibility for evangelizing their people and no longer need to rely on outsiders to send missionaries or church planting teams. Yet, there are all sorts of challenges. First, we all know that simply because people profess faith does not mean they are genuinely converted or growing in faith so these numbers could be inflated. Next, these numbers often do not take into account whether there are healthy churches to which these 2% of Christians are connected. Finally, it does not follow that even those places with greater than 2% genuine believers could not still benefit from other churches sending missionaries or church planting teams. See https://joshuaproject.net/resources/articles/has_everyone_heard.

es where a healthy church is most needed. They know over-looked areas or demographics of the city that are not being reached and can diligently attempt to plant there.

Method #2
The Place the Pastors Have Previously Identified

All churches should begin by praying for the Spirit to guide how and when they should multiply. Of course, individual pastors should make church planting a matter of person-al prayer. They should ask God to help them see what He would have them lead the church to do. We must press be-yond merely the lead pastor or the mission pastor praying about this matter. Pastors should commit to praying about multiplication as a group. They should organize their elder meeting such that they are not merely praying about the past or present needs of the church body, but also praying for future guidance in the work of multiplication. As op-portunities for multiplication come along, the diligent pas-tors should commit to seek the Lord's help and direction through prayer, rather than praying after they've already made up their minds about what they want to do. We know that the Apostle's path in the book of Acts was often de-toured based on such supernatural guidance, clarity, or im-pediments (Acts 16:6–10).

I'm aware of the significant conversations regarding the extent to which modern missionaries and evangelists should seek to replicate the Pauline example.[3] My point here isn't to

---

[3] For instance, see the classic missiological treatment of Paul's missionary methods in Roland Allen, *Missionary Methods: St. Paul's or Ours?* (Grand

argue for a one-to-one correspondence between the Apostle's work and ours, but simply to acknowledge that God provides guidance to his people in unique ways, often through prayer. This seems especially true in matters of prudence, such as where a sending church should plant a new church. We don't want to rely on our human instincts alone about a place that seems ideal to us and miss an opportunity God might have us prioritize that, at least on the surface, doesn't make as much sense.

Members of the church should diligently pray also. Pastors don't have to have fully developed plans for how and when we are going to multiply in order to ask the church to pray that God would send leaders and make the way possible for multiplication. A steady prayer of a healthy church should be for God's help to multiply. It may even be helpful to set an exploratory vision before the church, such as, "The pastors sense that God might be leading us to start a Hispanic church in the city. We don't have the answers right now of exactly how we are going to do that, but we would love for you to join us in praying that God would make a way." There is power in the church knowing that we are expecting God to send our members and pastors out on mission. Multiplying churches are continually led by the unique outworking of God's providence through answered prayer.

Churches desiring to multiply can ensure that a sending assumption permeates their preaching so that people are re-

---

Rapids: Eerdmans, 1962) and a different Pauline argument that interacts with Allen, Eckhard J. Schnabel, *Paul the Missionary: Realities, Strategies, Methods* (Downers Grove, IL: IVP Academic 2008).

minded of the need to pray. Existing preachers can and should use their preaching to convey their own work in sharing the gospel so that people see the connection between evangelism and the need for more and more churches. Preaching should also highlight the regular means of multiplication within a church, such as the start of a new small group, so that people are accustomed to hearing about new endeavors. A multiplying church can periodically have outside preachers who have been faithful to lead churches to multiply share about the work and testify to God's power, plan, and provision in their own church plants.

Sending churches should not rush the process. There's real beauty in waiting to see how God answers prayer. It may start with the conviction among a few pastors of a planting need and then, weeks or months later, God sends a new family to the church with a husband who is biblically qualified and desires to plant a church in that area. Or the church may sense an opportunity through prayer and then, a year later, a dying church in that area gives them a building in which they can plant a new church. Be willing to wait until the Spirit breathes His blessing, favor, and power on a planting initiative.

The potential downside of this method is clear. If we aren't careful it's easy for a sending church to wait to the point of passivity. Take a pastoral team of five. Must we wait until all five have the same level of clarity? Must we require unanimity among them? Should they all share the same sense of conviction on when and how and with whom? If we answer these questions affirmatively, then we could paralyze ourselves. Compound this reality if we extrapolate those questions to the whole church membership. It's unlikely that all, or even most, will align exactly on how the church should plant. Yes, by the time the church commissions and sends, congregational polity means that the church must bless, send, and pledge to support the plant. But it's less necessary that the church's members all align on the front end since pastoral leadership will allow for intentional shepherding toward what is best. Prayerfulness need not mean passivity.

Method #3
The Place Where People Already Live

This method is not applicable to international church planting or domestic planting in other cities. But when you are considering planting in your own city, you can start by looking at where your people already live.

Let's take the normal U.S. city and imagine that a healthy local church has key families who are driving 45 minutes across town to get to the church.[4] There may be factors that make the drive worth it. In many cases, however, people are commuting such a long distance because they can't find a healthy church in their immediate area. Pastors who know their flock can see these trends and may decide to sending a church planting team to start another healthy church.

This method is an ideal place to start for churches who aspire to be a sending church. Localized planting provides

---

[4] 45-minutes is an arbitrary number. In some cities, a commute of 15-minutes would be enough to justify another church plant. This is particularly true in large cities with high population density where people tend to live, learn, work, and play in a tight geographical circle.

something akin to training wheels. This method allows for the greatest level of intentionality because the elders are able to target a location and develop a plan without needing the input of others. The close proximity also allows the sending church to maintain a level of connection and care with the planting team that would be difficult if those sent are an ocean or even just a flight away. The local planting model allows for more experimentation since it's easier to finesse a timeline for planting when people aren't having to box up a house. This method also provides the unique ability to build a core team and instill healthy ecclesiological DNA when you ask faithful church members to continue to serve a church closer to their homes. Finally, the core team members are likely connected to relationships in these locales that make it easier for them to invite neighbors or coworkers to the new church.

Localized planting creates an easier path for an already-existing elder team to send one of its own to lead the new church. Once these churches get into the nitty-gritty of multiplication, the elders will have to make a number of decisions that lack a clear biblical prescription; therefore, a healthy elder team must trust and respect one another. As Dave mentioned in the previous chapter, perhaps the most important decision those pastors will make is who will lead the new work. It's far easier to send a pastor whom you already know, love, and trust. Existing relationships possess the trust needed between a sending church and a planting team.

All these benefits should not imply that this method is without challenges. Though training wheels help children grow in confidence to ride a bike, we all know the fear-filled, tear-inducing, panic-stricken moment when the training wheels come off. Likewise, sending churches and local plants face many challenges. It's easy to cast an aspirational vision for a plant across town, but people must actually go, which means distance themselves from relationships they hold dear. It means they must say goodbye to ministry programs such as a beloved youth group or children's ministry. If the plant will be led by one of the pastors of the sending church, the pastoral team and the church as a whole will grieve when he leaves. The sent pastor and his family will also grieve. They may still live close to the sending church and to many of those they'd given their lives to serve for years, but now they sense they are starting all over. Finally, because of the close proximity, there can be a sense of uncertainty among the planting team akin to dating. They might try it out for a time, find that the allure of the new isn't what they hoped, and return back to the sending church. Or they might press the plant to replicate the ministry structures and programs of the sending church too quickly without giving time for good, slow growth to take place. In contrast to the planter who moves to a new city with a few trusted friends, knowing these people have made sacrifices to join the planting team, the local planting pastor might not have the same level of confidence that his team will stick.

Method #4
The Place A Planting Pastor Is Invested in Going

A final method is to rely on the sense of direction given to a potential church planter. It is unwise for a sending church to force a location on a potential planter when that person has a conviction of another path.

If future church planter is a blank slate when it comes to his planting location, then he can humbly submit to the elders of the church and their existing vision for the church's planting endeavors. Wise elders are well ahead of this process and will have already thought through locations that would make sense to send a church plant.

In most cases, however, the potential church-planting pastor has some sense of the context where he would best serve. He might sense a fit in a rural village community with high poverty. He might be drawn to an unreached people in Southeast Asia. In my experience, there are two ways this can play out.

Sometimes, the prospective pastor needs to loosen his grip on an ideal place and bend his direction in line with where the elders sense God leading the church. For example, a brother who desires to be sent to Latin America may soon discover that his sending church has been praying about a Spanish-speaking church plant in a Hispanic community across town. Or you might have a brother who longs to plant a church in Europe but who may consider planting in an urban North American location where the church has been involved for some time. In both examples, the pastor's desires and the church's vision are similar but not exact. In these cases, it is wise for the prospective planter to consider adjusting his location bullseye to match the church's.

Other times, the church shifts to match the planter. Consider a rough parallel in football. Your starting quarterback is a run-n-gun, quick tempo, run-first, ask-questions-later type. But he gets hurt. His backup is the opposite—a drop-back passer who prefers to scan the field from the pocket and pick the defense apart with his precision. You'd be foolish to call the same plays for each quarterback. Instead, a coach plays to the strengths of the man on the field.

The same is true for a sending church seeking to pick a place to plant a church. Why force a potential planter into a location that's a bad fit? In our haste to plant a church (or be seen as a church-planting church), we can press someone to go somewhere that's not wise.[5] Consider some key factors. What is the planter's background? It may be tough to take a blue-collar man from a farming family and ask him to plant in inner-city Philadelphia. What do his wife and family think? Don't drag a planting family into a location kicking and screaming just because that's where the elders want to plant. Where has the planter been fruitful in the past? This doesn't mean the planter has to have lived in the location before but consider his work in cross-cultural ministry in the States before you buy plane tickets and send him to Tokyo.

The person is always more important than the place. Start with a biblically qualified pastor and discern together where that man is best positioned to do ministry. Get the right person, and in some ways it doesn't matter where you put that man. Every location in the world could use a healthy church, so develop and send that man to pastor

---

[5] I've seen this happen too often in connection with financial backing. A sending church or a church planting organization determines that they will fund planting work in certain locations and not others, so a planter zeros in on those highly funded areas and overlooks a spot that might be a better fit. He might claim to feel called to plant in an urban context because that's what's funded, when he'd be better suited to plant in the mountains of Appalachia.

God's people somewhere and you'll be serving the kingdom in meaningful ways.

Once you get a true pastor, diligence relates to the intersection of God's sovereignty, pastoral instincts, and humility. You can't mechanize the process of picking a place to plant. God's always going to be at work ahead of you, so it's vital that both the sending church and the church planter keep their spiritual antenna up for what God's doing around. You might plan to plant a church in Pittsburgh when a dying local church offers you their building if you'll send someone. You'd be foolish not to at least consider if the man you were planning to send to Pittsburgh should pivot.[6]

Then there are pastoral instincts, especially among the pastors of the sending church. We need discernment to know when we should press someone to consider a place they might not otherwise go and when it's better to adjust based on the gifts of the planter God has sent. You'll be well-served not to

---

[6] Most (not all) of the planters that I know have seen just this reality play out. They had a place in mind. Maybe it was just something they'd talked about with their spouse. Or it might have been a shared conversation with the sending church or its pastors. There was a dot on the map and they were moving toward it only for something to cause them to pivot. The same is true for many international workers that I know. They sensed God's leading to a certain people group, but visa issues or a health crisis changed their plans and they ended up elsewhere. This is all part of the process! I fear that we often communicate "God called me to this certain people group or this certain city," and in so doing we put pressure on ourselves to go to that dot on the map or else we feel like a failure. I want to be more open-handed. God called you to His work in the world through the local church and, over the course of your life, this may lead you to several different places or roles, and the fact that you detoured to another place does not necessarily mean you were unfaithful.

rush the process, but give time for conversation, reflection, prayer, and revision to take place as you all seek God's path forward for the plant.

Finally, both the sending church and the planter will need a healthy dose of humility. Where you plant a new church is a big decision. The sending church may have had years to pray and think about what they sense God doing. They know there will be cost incurred in sending and sending well. Their elders are likely considering the implications should they plant across town versus planting in another state. It's a significant decision for the planter, who is not only selecting where he will plant, but also where he will raise a family. These decisions often involve one's extended family as well. Once upon a time, the grandkids had lunch at their grandparents house each Sunday. Now they'll celebrate holidays via FaceTime. It takes great humility on the part of everyone in the room to work diligently to a place of shared direction and investment.

Such diligence is a long-term goal because planting a church is filled with twists and turns. But diligence is a far better pursuit than the mystical sense of "vision" that commonly shows up in these conversations. So keep diligently wrestling with these four methods over a long period of time with a group of trusted pastors. There's no "right" method for every situation. All of them can work. So diligently consider each and enjoy where God puts your church plant on the map.

PART 3

ESTABLISHING A CHURCH PLANT

CHAPTER 7

HOW DO YOU DEVELOP A HEALTHY LEADERSHIP TEAM FOR A PLANT?

Matt Rogers

Meet William, Jose, and Ben. They've been friends since college when they worked together to lead ministry on campus and in their church. It was then that they first started talking about planting a church together. These three young men were compelled by a vision to see healthy churches planted among all people and determined to give their lives to pursue this mission together.

What could go wrong?

In the case of William, Jose, and Ben, the challenges weren't doctrinal or ecclesiological. They were on the same page there, though they might disagree at times about implementation of their vision in the church. Their disagreements over substantive issues were minor. What ended up torpedoing the work was the difficulty of working together as a team.

The three had changed significantly. No longer were they the frothin' at the mouth youngins' of their college ministry years. Their roles had also changed. Ben was now the lead pastor, so he wasn't merely linked to William and Jose as friends. He was now their pastor and, since Jose was on staff, Ben was also his boss. In addition, their lives had gotten vastly more complex. All three were now married with kids and their wives did not have the same level of friendship that the men possessed. Finally, these three were wired differently. Their ministerial instincts were different—as were their spiritual gifts—so they started and ended at different places when making decisions or implementing projects in the church. It was a recipe for disaster.

Within three years of planting, Jose took a pastoral job in another state, William left the church to attend another in town, and Ben was all alone trying to rebuild his planting team, all the while dealing with the reality of broken relationships with the two other men he thought he'd be serving with forever.

It would be nice if this story were a fictitious example of a rare experience. But it's not. The scenario outlined above happens time after time, leaving hurt churches, distant relationships, and squandered resources. Although each situation is unique, those seeking to plant churches or send church planters would be wise to consider the topic of team dynamics. This is the first step toward implementing a planting vision.

In Part 2 of this book, we discussed how you know when your church is ready, who you may ask to lead the work, and where you should plant. Now we turn our attention to the delicate work of implementing this vision. Faithful and fruitful church planting requires intentional team formation and careful fostering of team health.

Biblical Foundations for Team

It wasn't too long ago that the normative model for church planting was a lone pastor and his family moving to a new area in the hopes of starting a church. This pattern followed closely the senior pastor, deacon board, and support staff hierarchy that was common in many churches.

In recent years, we have awakened to the biblical and practical necessity of multiple pastors leading singular churches. We ought to celebrate the fact that we live and minister at a time when most sending churches and church planters understand the need for multiple pastors.[1]

What's clear from Scripture is that teams of leaders were sent to share the gospel and establish churches in new regions and to pastor those newly established churches. For example, the Antioch church chose leaders—Barnabas and Saul—and set them apart to take the gospel to the Gentiles (Acts 13:1–3). After the decision of the Jerusalem counsel, Paul determined to go back to the various churches they'd

---

[1] For those wanting a refresher on the rationale for plurality consider Phil Newton and Matt Schmucker, *Elders in Congregational Life: Rediscovering the Biblical Model for Church Leadership* (Grand Rapids: Kregel, 2014); Mark Dever, *9 Marks of a Healthy Church* (Wheaton, IL: Crossway, 2021); Phil Newton, *40 Questions about Pastoral Ministry* (Grand Rapids: Kregel, 2021); Alexander Strauch, *Biblical Eldership: An Urgent Call to Restore Biblical Church Leadership* (Colorado Springs: Lewis and Roth Publishers: 2003); Phil A. Newton and Rich C. Shadden, *Mending the Nets: Rethinking Church Leadership* (Greenville, SC: Courier Publishing, 2024).

established to strengthen the work. Again, they did so in teams—with Barnabas and Mark going in one direction and Paul and Silas in another (Acts 15:36–41). Subsequently, as Paul continued his work into Europe he did not want to go alone, but chose a reputable disciple named Timothy to join him in the mission (Acts 16:1–5). Everywhere you look in the book of Acts the plural pronouns "we" or "they" are used to speak of those sharing the gospel and planting churches (see Acts 13:4, 13–14, 42; 14:7; 17:1; among others).

Additionally, the New Testament affirms that teams of pastors led churches. When Paul sent Titus to Crete, he urged him to appoint pastors in every town among each church (Titus 1:5). Paul's tearful goodbye to the Ephesian church was addressed to the elders there (Acts 20:17). When speaking to these elders, Paul addresses them as a group of overseers and pastors, not simply a singular leader (Acts 20:28). Similarly, Peter exhorts elders to faithfully shepherd God's flock until the Chief Shepherd, Jesus Christ, returns (1 Peter 5:1–5).

We also know from the biblical evidence that team dynamics were difficult, even among the first apostles and pastors. In the passage already cited, the division of Barnabas and Mark from Paul and Silas was not the result of missionary strategy, but a difference of opinion over whether Mark was trustworthy moving forward. Barnabas thought so, Paul disagreed, so they split (Acts 15:36–41). These men were doctrinally aligned, and no sin implied with either party. And yet, they held different assessments on who was qualified to partner in the mission. Of course, sinful attitudes sometimes slip into partnerships. Although they weren't pastoring together, Paul and Peter disagreed sharply over practices related to the Gentile mission, which led Paul publicly to confront his brother over his sin (Gal. 2:11–14). There were also theological differences among leaders, which led to the gathering in Jerusalem to determine how the disciples should respond to the spread of the church into Gentile territory (Acts 15). This cursory summary of the biblical evidence leads to two provisional conclusions: churches are led by teams of pastors, and team leadership is often fraught with complexity.[2]

All Out or All In

When facing team complexities, the sending church and the church planter often follow two common rationales. The first is to ignore the subject, at least in any formal way. We build teams after biblical norms and simply assume that the dynamics will take care of themselves. After all, isn't the Christian life all about dying to self and seeking unity amidst diversity? Surely pastors should be able do that with anyone the Lord sends as a teammate.

We're also tempted to avoid the subject for fear that addressing it reeks of pragmatism. We've been to conferences where personality profiles were sliced and diced and have

---

[2] Over the years I've often returned to Peter Scazzero's Emotionally Healthy series and found myself challenged and encouraged. His first chapter in *The Emotionally Healthy Church* (Grand Rapids: Zondervan, 2003) describes how the holistic health of a pastor and his team impacts the overall health of the church. This point is a bit adjacent to the main theme of this chapter, but it is worth considering how disunity is fostered due to a lack of emotional health in leaders and not necessarily the result of differences in personality or gifts.

come away feeling overwhelmed by all the labels and typologies applied to this subject.[3] It can feel like a gimmicky form of pseudo-psychology to apply secular principles of team dynamics to pastoral ministry. So leaders put their head in the sand and just try to work out the relationship friction as it comes without any clear plan.

This is a dangerous approach. To explain, consider the work of parenting. We all know there is evil in the world seeking to destroy our children. We can close our eyes and pretend that it's not happening. We can assume that the right combination of time and maturity will give them the skills they need to resist the allure of worldliness. No parent worth the title would be so passive. It's negligent to know something can do great harm and not to address the issue— whether you are a parent, a sending church, or a church planter.

In contrast, others go all in on the subject of team dynamics. When I started planting churches in the early 2000s, the vogue discussion was about tri-perspectival leadership

---

[3] Yes, I'm generally a hater when it comes to personality profiles and typologies, but I must admit that I've found benefit at seasons in my life in having some labels to think about how I'm wired. Gallup's *Strengths Finder* (Washington, DC: Gallup Press, 2007) was helpful in learning to articulate how I functioned and what I enjoyed as a leader. More recently, Jeremie Kubicek and Steve Cockram's *The 5 Voices: How to Communicate Effectively with Everyone You Lead* (Hoboken, NJ: Wiley, 2016) has proven useful. In each case, I've found the most value in using these tools for team discussions and not personal introspection. Their highest value comes in helping me understand and relate to others on my team, learning common language for how I might help them thrive and shaping how we might interact in the most fruitful ways.

using the three-fold paradigm of prophet, priest, and king.[4] The prophet served as the outspoken visionary and primary preacher. The priest excelled in mercy and compassion and gave care to the flock. The king worked to ensure that the structure and organization of the church was secure, so he must be gifted in administration. The ideal church planting team, so I was told, was made up of one kingly pastor, one priestly pastor, and one prophetic pastor.

In our day, this paradigm isn't as prominent. A new model has taken its place: APEST. Taken from Ephesians 4 and popularized by Alan Hirsch, APEST is an acronym for the 5 types of leaders that God gives to the church—Apostle, Prophet, Evangelist, Shepherd, and Teacher.[5] There's significant overlap with the tri-perspectival pattern here. The apostle is the pioneering leader who always wants to take new ground. The prophet is the one who declares truth, often in the face of the prevailing culture. The evangelist is gifted and motivated to share the gospel with the lost. The shepherd, like the priest, gives his time to caring for needs and showing mercy to the hurting. And the teacher is the one who provides biblical teaching and instruction to the church.

---

[4] This language seemed to be the go-to way those in the so-called *Young, Radical, Reformed* subset of evangelicalism talked about team dynamics in leadership.

[5] Hirsch is prolific in his writing and this language shows up in a number of his books but his book *5Q: Reactivating the Original Intelligence and Capacity of the Body of Christ* (Jacksonville, FL: 100 Movements, 2017) is built completely around the concept. Due to Hirsch's influence in prominent church planting groups like Exponential, APEST has become something of a household term for some subsets of evangelicalism.

Those arguing for the APEST paradigm suggest that the health of the church's mission hinges on having a pastor or key leader who fits each of these roles. This means that church planters should form teams on their one APEST type. According to APEST voices, planters are ideally apostolic, prophetic, or evangelistic, so they need to surround themselves with shepherds and teachers for the work to succeed.

While I disagree with the common APEST interpretation of Ephesians 4, my greatest fear is more than just a disagreement over biblical interpretation.[6] In both cases, whether in tri-perspectival leadership or APEST, there is a clear effort to bind the conscience of the pastor or sending church by suggesting that *this* is the biblical model for team formation. So if a team doesn't fit the APEST paradigm, then it's considered unbiblical and unlikely to succeed. It seems that such an argument goes beyond the Bible's intention and attempts to build an entire model of team formation around a single passage.

More compelling, it seems, is to suggest that the Bible commends teams of interdependent and complementary leaders, and that pastors and churches are free to use Spirit-given wisdom to determine the best structure for form-

---

[6] I see Paul speaking of four roles, not five—with the later term being a hyphenated shepherd-teacher and referring to the office of pastor. "Shepherd" denotes their function in the church—they tend to the flock—and teacher refers to their most prominent function in the church—they instruct the saints by teaching God's Word. God gave the Old Testament prophets and the New Testament apostles to lay the groundwork for the doctrine and mission of the church. Evangelists refers to those who go to establish new churches in new places, roughly akin to how we might use the term missionary.

ing and maintaining team health. Rather than mandating a certain typology, wise leaders assess the unique personality and gifts of various leaders to form complementary teams. This approach allows them to rely on biblical ethics and virtues—love of neighbor, humility and honor, biblical conflict resolution—as they strive to maintain team health.

Complementary Team Formation

The place to start is in the team formation. Sometimes, church leaders want to plant a church so badly that they'll put any willing and moderately capable leaders on the team without thinking through their personalities or gifts. Pastors are scrappy, so they often find co-pastors.[7] Some form a team from their sending church and leave that church to plant with two or three planting pastors. Others reach out to friends from their past and invite a man they already know and trust to plant with them. Still others find fellow pastors in the field—perhaps someone who is already pastoring in the city in which they are seeking to plant, or someone who is a faithful member of a church in the area but hasn't been invited to consider pastoral ministry in the past. Over time, the planter may be able to raise up men from the church

---

[7] It's worth noting here that it's not enough merely to desire to be a pastor, nor should you pursue the work simply because a friend invites you to consider helping him plant a church. Pastoral ministry is an honorable vocation for those biblically qualified for the work. This matter should not be taken lightly. Consider Bobby Jamieson's *The Path to Being a Pastor: A Guide for the Aspiring* (Wheaton, IL: Crossway, 2021) for a thorough treatment on what it means to aspire to the work of pastoring according to Scripture.

itself and disciple them onto the team. The issue for most is not how to find someone to pastor alongside them but how to ensure that the pairings are a good fit.

Most of us would never be so haphazard with even our volunteer roles in the church. We recognize that taking an introverted accountant and asking him to rock babies might not be best, either for the accountant or for the baby. Putting a tone-deaf, wannabe crooner on stage to lead congregational music might not be best. So why take any man who's pastorally qualified and gifted and put him on a team where he might not be free to use his gifts most effectively?

Because I'm convinced of the biblical necessity of the gathered assembly and the centrality of the preached Word, this is the place to begin with team formation. Put simply, the most effective method for church planting seems to build a team around a pastor with preaching gifts. Over time, it will be wise to share the pulpit, but the early years of planting need a consistent voice week-in and week-out. Both visitors and members alike need a pastor who gives himself to exhort, encourage, and lead the church through his preaching. Such men come in all shapes and sizes. Some are extroverted and passionate. Others, like me, are more comfortable in the shadows but love to help people see and understand God's Word. Good preachers can also harness their communication gifts to lead the church in other ways. Whether this happens in church meetings, small group Bible studies, or over coffee with prospective members, church plants thrive when there is a clear and steady voice leading the way.

Then—much like a sports team built around a certain player—I would attempt to form teams on the basis of the complementary gifts needed to support the man identified to preach.

The concept is not original to me, but when I speak about gifts I tend to use the terminology of green light, yellow light, and red light. "Green light" gifts are things a leader does naturally, almost unconsciously. "Yellow light" gifts work like an internal switch. The leader can do these things, but it takes intentionality. In fact, doing them well and for a long period of time drains that person's battery. Finally, "red light" gifts are those things that you just can't do well, even with great thought or training. I've already suggested that church plants should start by identifying a person with green light gifts in preaching and leading.

From there, the next move is often to think about that leader's red light gifts. There are no omnicompetent leaders so there's no shame in acknowledging this. The shame comes from not supplementing these weaknesses with others who can help. The areas to consider are both hard-wiring, personality, and gifts. You want to matchmake a team of people who are complementary.

In an ideal world, you'd have two people whose red light and green light gifts were almost completely opposite. For example, you might pair an introverted, contemplative preacher with an outgoing evangelist. Or a charismatic preacher who's the life of the party with a solid administrator who is loyal and comfortable with hidden grunt work. Because these leaders would also have yellow light gifts that they could use if they had to, it's easier for them to switch on these yellow light gifts for the first few years of the church's life and then appoint more leaders as God begins to build His church.

Neighbor Love

Once a team has formed, the real work has only just begun. Church planters are often new to pastoral ministry. They're using leadership gifts they've not fully developed so the early years of team relationships will be critical. Again, parenting provides a practical comparison. You labor in the grade-school years to teach your son or daughter to relate to other humans, especially their siblings. If these relational skills are not cultivated at a young age, the long-term implications can be disastrous. The same holds for a team of leaders in the church. We have to be intentional in the early years so that the team matures in a healthy way.

If you form a team of complementary leaders, then they will inevitably frustrate one another. Much like the premise that opposites attract in marriage, interdependent pastoral teams are appealing but the dynamics of these differences can lead to conflict.

The sending church has a critical role to play here. Ideally, it will be conscientious on the front end to appoint men as pastors who have a track record of neighbor love. They build healthy relationships and aren't known to be explosive or divisive. We then hold these men to account when the pressure builds. All pastors know the challenge of a married couple who comes to you for counsel far too late. There's little you can do to help at this point. Team dynamics work similarly—if the sending church loses sight of these relationships and simply waits until the church planting leaders reach out for help, many times the difficulty will already be nearing a breaking point. The sending church should establish a regular time to sync up with the team of new leaders, both as individuals and as a team, and to ask good questions about the nature of their shared relationships. Sending churches might include these questions: What do you appreciate about this brother? What irritates you? In what ways do you wish you were like him? In what ways do you wish he was like you? What will it take for you to work well with this brother? What does he need to know about you to work well with you?

Humility and Honor

Anyone who's read the Gospels knows the tight connection Jesus draws between leadership and humility (Matt. 20:26–28). We intuitively know that pride and young men seem to walk hand-in-hand. We would hope that due diligence has taken place beforehand to ensure that a man appointed to pastor is growing in humility, but we'd be naïve to assume that his pride would not become more visible when he steps into the work of planting a church. The intensity of the effort combined with the inherent challenges of pastoral ministry means that residual pride is going to surface and will need to be confronted.

There's both a proactive and reactive way for a planting pastor to confront pride and to grow in humility. Reactively, we need sending churches that will call out pride when they see it. This requires proximity. Someone must be in the leaders' lives enough to see how they handle it when they don't get their way, how they respond when someone else gets the spotlight, or what they do when someone challenges or criticizes them. This type of proximity will likely mean that the sending church pastor and the planters connect regularly. A proactive pastor can ask good, simple questions like: 1) Where do you feel frustrated right now? 2) What obstacles are you facing? 3) Where is conflict evident in the plant and how are you handling this pressure? Ideally, over time, these kinds of conversations happen among the church plant's pastors, but for a season, there will likely need to be some outside voices who speak up and challenge leaders when pride is evident.

Proactively, the best way to grow in humility is to give yourself to showing honor. Writing to the church in Rome, Paul writes, "Take the lead in honoring one another" (Rom. 12:10). Of course, honoring another person could inflame their pride, but that's beyond any team member's control. What's important is that we aim to do a good job of positioning others on the team for wins and lending strength to help them do their job and do it well. The more we each give ourselves to making someone else thrive, the more our attention is taken off ourselves, and the more team chemistry is solidified. A sending church can come alongside church planting pastors to help them see ways they can create wins for others. Sending churches can help young leaders who are often hyper-consumed with their own cares to look out for the interests of others (Phil. 2:1–4).

A final way honor is demonstrated is through what we say. There's a fine line here—we don't want to be leaders who merely blow smoke and tell everyone that they are doing a great job, even when they aren't. But our words do matter. The way we speak to people—and the way we speak about people when they aren't around—says much about our heart's disposition. Sending churches can help planting pastors learn to speak to each other about concerns and not about each other. They can press pastors to see the good that others bring to the team and celebrate the wins others receive, even if those wins come at a cost to them personally.

Conflict Resolution

Church planting pastors will not do this perfectly, so we'd be wise to intentionally coach them to develop healthy practices related to conflict and conflict resolution. Simply put, pastors who cannot square back up after hard conversations, dropped balls, or embarrassing miscommunication will not persevere. Those who are easily offended or who respond in passive-aggressive pity-parties will find the work excruciatingly difficult. Not only will pastors have to do this with one another, but they will also have these types of interactions with church members. One of the more difficult things to get used to, especially in leading a church, is the reality that someone is always upset about something, and many times they are also upset with you. If we place all our hope on a conflict-free horizon, we will find ourselves swiftly discouraged when the horizon remains just out of reach. Rather, we must learn to cope with the white noise of conflict in God-honoring ways.

In my experience, this is an area where the old paradigm of model, assist, watch, and leave (MAWL) is incredibly helpful. Even before sending planting pastors, I want them to watch me navigate conflict. Since conflict is always happening, it's pretty easy to bring future pastors into a difficult situation and allow them to watch how I use my words to bring clarity, how I speak with a measure of grace and truth, what I do when the temperature continues to rise, and all of the other soft skills needed to handle conflict well. Then, once sent, I can assist the brothers in navigating conflict. They still manage the church's challenges but I'm available to help from outside. Rather than waiting for them to bring up places of conflict, I can simply ask, "So tell me about some conflict you are facing and how you are handling it." Since the conflict is now theirs as an autonomous congregation, it's also much easier for them to appreciate the counsel or help that is provided. Over time, the sending church will be able to step back and watch them work through a hard situation. Rather than walking with them every step of the way, it can engage after the fact and ask them about what they learned or what they might do differently. Over time, the new, fully formed elder team will be able to work through the conflict on their own.

These factors are not a surefire way to avoid team implosions. But they are a strong apologetic for the value of an intentional, ongoing relationship with a sending church. Giving proper attention to this undervalued area of church formation will spare leaders from relational pain down the road and serve to strengthen the foundation of the churches we do plant so that they survive and thrive.

CHAPTER 8

WHERE DO THE PEOPLE COME FROM?

Matt Rogers

When someone says they want to start a family, you know they intend to have a son or a daughter, or maybe one of each. Or they might mean that they are pursuing adoption, but even in this case, you know where the kids are coming from.

Not so for a new church. When someone says they want to start a new church, there's a natural question: Where will the people come from? Who will join in the effort? You might have a biblically qualified pastor and his family, but that family alone isn't a church—at least not yet.

As I attempted to show in the last chapter, you might have a well-constructed team of interdependent pastors and leaders. But again, that team isn't necessarily a church—at least not yet. A new church will need a group of Christians who invest their lives in being members of this new church. In this chapter, I want to show you where you might find people for the new church and share some upsides and challenges of each type of person.[1]

A Word on Terminology

Church planting resources refer to the group of people who want to plant a church with many different terms. Some call them a "launch team."[2] This term emphasizes the role these people play in helping to launch Sunday services for the church plant. If we aren't careful, this term could denote a performative model of the church that drifts toward pragmatism and consumerism. Others simply call these people "members," seeking to highlight the fact that there is nothing extraordinary about this group—they are just members like everyone else who will join the church. I understand the impulse here, yet there's something important to be said about the first members, especially those who go out with a church plant before the potential church has even covenanted together. At this point, these people are not technically members of the new church.

---

[1] A number of years ago I wrote a version of these models along with Ed Stetzer. That eBook on core group formation can be found here: https://www.newchurches.com/e-book/building-your-core-team/.

[2] Such language was popularized by books like Nelson Searcy's *Launch: Starting a New Church from Scratch* (Grand Rapids: Baker Books, 2017). The term "launch" is also common for denominations or networks as a tag on their church planting arm. I'm not suggesting that all those who use launch terminology are pragmatists. The term may simply be a metaphor connecting the start of a church to a space shuttle hurtling into space. But words have meaning. And when we talk about starting churches as "launching" something, it's often a short step to a performative model of church that caters to consumerism. Define clearly the terms used to describe teams.

As the first and foundational members, these individuals have a unique role to play in the healthy development of the church. I prefer the term "core group" or "planting team." Both terms highlight the fact that this is a group and not just one or two people. It also emphasizes the foundational nature of this group. They are "core" to the work that God is doing in planting a new congregation. Most often, I use "planting team" to refer to the church-planting pastor and other pastoral or staff leaders and "core group" to refer to lay Christians who are committed to developing the new church.

Motives

Before we look at where the core group comes from, let's consider why someone might want to join it in the first place. When we started a new church in 2009, a trusted mentor advised me: "In the early days of church planting, it's as important who doesn't join your church as it is those who do." I didn't want to listen at the time. After all, if there's anything a new church desperately needs, it's people. Surely anyone who was willing and able to join with us would be an asset. But my mentor's words proved true. I soon learned that the wrong people could do much harm, especially when those people attempt to join a core group.

First, some just love the planting pastor and his family and want to follow them in whatever they are doing. This motive seems commendable yet love for a person is not enough to handle the demands of starting a new church. Others want to join a core group because they like the city or the place in the city where the new church will be located.

Some might feel enamored with the idea of moving from their quaint suburb to a major urban hub to plant a church. Or they might long to escape a certain climate or lifestyle. In my experience, a love for the place may compel a person or family to relocate, but it won't keep them there. Others may join a core team for convenience. Perhaps they live closer to the church plant. This may be workable for some, but if you build a core group solely based on convenience, then you're unlikely to get the level of maturity and servant-heartedness you need.

Other reasons people join a core group are more destructive. Some people simply like change, so they get bored with one church and move on to the next. Or they might not have many relationships and they see the church plant as something new, different, and interesting. People who are quick to leave one church for the next will likely not stay long. Once the new wears off, they'll be on to something different. Others get frustrated with their church and see the church plant as a place to "get church right." This impulse may be sound people should flee unhealthy churches and root themselves in a healthy congregation. But preferences (ecclesiological or methodological) too often lead well-meaning people to bounce from one church to the next. Those who don't know the difference between biblical conviction and personal preference make for bad core team members because, given enough time, they will get frustrated with something at the plant. Finally, some people are divisive and see a church plant as an easy target. They may have tried to torpedo their former church by being a busybody. They might desire levels of church leadership that are beyond their maturity. It may be hard to wreck an established church, but a wolf brings real harm to a young church plant.[3]

On the other hand, there are good reasons for people to join a core group. Ideally, the team is filled with those who are committed to the mission of God and the work of the local church. Regardless of where the team comes from, you must spend time with them to develop a foundation for shared ecclesiology.[4] Some may want to join because they see a way to use their gifts in a unique way through the church plant. For example, a larger church might have many people capable of caring for children, whereas the new church has

---

[3] This is an argument for waiting to covenant together for a season after the core team begins to solidify. Sometimes it takes time for wolves to show their true colors and the last thing a church plant wants is to have to practice church discipline early in the life of the plant. It may be wise to take a season where the core team does a Bible study together while still meeting with the sending church or another partner church where they are members and wait a few months before constituting membership in the church plant.

[4] See chapters 1–3 of this book for the ecclesiological foundations you'd want to make sure were in place among core group members. This chapter focuses primarily on where you find the people for the team and not what you do with them once you have them. The *New Churches* podcast has a series on development factors that a planter should focus on as he builds his church-planting team. This podcast, along with the *Building Healthy Church Series* from 9Marks, provide some helpful foundations you want to build into your team: https://www.newchurches.com/podcasts/new-churches-podcast/team-essentials-theology-mission-and-teaching-in-church-planting-teams/. I've found that teaching through a book dripping with ecclesiology, like Ephesians, can be a good idea for team formation. If the core group comes primarily from the sending church, then the planter can work through Ephesians for months leading up to the plant. If the core group is scattered, then it could be wise to take time to work through these ecclesiological foundations as a Bible study before the church launches.

none. Or an existing church with a facility might not need the same type of volunteers that a church doing set-up and tear-down in an elementary school does. Other reasons that we've already discussed can be good or bad. For example, loving the new planting pastor and his family, or wanting to move to the new location.

With these healthy motives in mind, let's consider some places you might look for core team members.

Place #1
New Believers Who Already Live Nearby

Some will cast a vision for this model using the phrase "plant from the harvest." By this, they mean that it's better to start churches by reaching the lost than simply moving Christians from an existing church to a new church plant. This approach encourages planters to move into a new location, form natural connections with non-believers, and seek to share the gospel with them. As those people come to faith, you then seek to train them to understand the role of the local church and use their gifts to serve on the core group. These individuals already live in the place you are seeking to plant, so there's no need for them to relocate. They are already embedded in homes, jobs, and schools. They have established relationships in which they can share the gospel and connect people to the church. Finally, those who have recently become Christians are often passionate about the work of evangelism, so your core group would be full of those who are zealous to talk to others about Jesus.[5]

---

[5] A book like *Church Plantology* by Peyton Jones (Grand Rapids: Zonder-

This approach isn't without its drawbacks. First, it's slow. It might take years to get stabilized.[6] Let's say a planting pastor from South Carolina is sent to Los Angeles to plant a church. This is something my Baptist State Convention in South Carolina has prioritized in recent years. Praise God for faithful leaders who've been willing to move across the country to plant churches and train pastors. This work is meaningful and important. And it's slow—especially if you only seek to develop a core group from non-Christians. This certainly doesn't mean you don't move across the country to share the gospel, but it does mean that you may want to think about other ways to build a planting team than solely from among the lost.

Another drawback is that this model seeks to develop a church with those who are all relatively new to the faith. While it is true that anyone who has been reconciled to

---

van, 2021) makes a compelling case for the priority of evangelism in church planting. While there are challenges to this approach, which I itemize in this chapter, I do think it's a needed challenge to many in the "healthy church" camp to consider how we can do a better job of anchoring our church-planting activity in a genuine love for the lost and urgency that many would come to faith. Karson Merkel's chapter in this book attempts to highlight that very theme.

[6] This isn't to suggest that something is slow therefore it's not worth doing. Healthy churches take time to develop and so does the fruit of evangelism. But those taking this route will likely need a funding model to sustain the slow growth and, in many cases, those who start with few, or no Christians find that they grow discouraged in the work before they see conversion happen. Also, to depend on converts for a core team seems to undervalue the role of the gathered church in evangelism itself. One of the best ways for Christians to be involved in the work of evangelism in a new city is for them to have a healthy church to invite the lost to attend.

God through Christ can and should share the gospel (2 Cor. 5:17–21), it's another thing to ask a group of novice believers to take on the various demands of church leadership. Not only that, but young Christians are often ill-prepared to disciple others (Titus 2:1–8). Finally, the Parable of the Sower suggests that many of those who seem to come to faith will not endure, so to build a core group using this model alone will likely result in a group with many who do not persevere (Matt. 13:1–9, 18–23; also called Parable of the Soils). In my estimation, planting from the harvest is a marvelous goal. Evangelistic intentionality must be a part of every church plant, but all core groups are going to need some mature Christians. So where might they come from?

Place #2
Friends of the Planting Pastor

A good place to look for core group members are long-time friends of the planting pastor or his family. These might be college roommates who once served together in campus ministry. It could be people the planter or his wife have led to faith or discipled through the years. Maybe it's people who have seen the fruit of the planter's ministry and want to support that good work. It could be family members who want to lend strength to plant and support the planters.

With new people, the planter will have to earn trust, but long-standing friends and family already have that trust. With this approach, the planting pastor knows his team well and will be better able to put them into roles that fit. Furthermore, long-standing relationships are less likely to be flaky. If a family member moves to help you plant a church, there's a good chance that person will not bail at the first sign of difficulty. Finally, close friends and family can help with many practical needs. I've seen rich benefits when a planter has his in-laws move with them to start a new church if for no other reason than to have someone to help with babysitting for the pastor and his wife to get a date night from time to time.

There are challenges to this option, however. Relationships with close friends and family can be complicated, and when those relationships get sideways, it can be tough to recover. Ask anyone who's tried, and they will tell you that it can be hard to pastor your parents or siblings. And just because two people were best buddies in college doesn't mean their relationship will remain healthy in the changing roles necessary to start a church.[7] When conflict flares within the church, it's one thing for a church member to get mad and leave, but it's another thing altogether if that person is a family member or close friend.

Another dynamic to keep in mind is that these relationships can create an insider culture that's hard for new people to break in. Imagine you plant a church with thirty people on a core team who all have connections that extend back for years. They have their own insider jokes. Their own hangout rhythms. Their kids already know each other. Now

---

[7] In my 20 years of experience, I've found far more brothers who dreamed about planting a church together in their 20s who have a tough go of it when they try to plant together, than I have seen this model work. The changes brought about by time and age, coupled with the changing relationships necessitated in a church plant, often make it tough for old buddies to make ideal church planting partners.

add a new family to the mix. The core team might not even be aware of how awkward this can seem to outsiders.

Finally, if you take long-standing relationships from various walks of life and backgrounds, it could be the case that you form a core team of people who differ on key doctrinal or ecclesiological matters. Simply because someone loves the planter isn't enough, if that person isn't primarily sold on the mission and vision of the church they are seeking to plant together.

Place #3
Anyone Who Wants to Come from the Sending Church

To address the last challenge in the preceding model, some suggest that you should build a core team from your sending church. If you do this, you've got a group of people already committed to certain ecclesiological convictions. By virtue of shared membership, the planting pastor can easily connect with these people and even meet with them as a small group for a time before they're sent. Building a core team from the sending church allows that church to have real buy-in to the plant. Not only do they know the planter and his family, but they also know many people who went with them to start the church. This diverse circle of relationships makes it more likely that the sending church maintains vibrant partnership as the plant moves forward. I'm differentiating this place to look for core group members from the model that will follow because some sending churches choose to make an all-call to any members who want to go.

While such an all-call is fairly easy, it's not without risk. Doing so could set the church planter up with a difficult core group if the people who say they want to go are young in the faith, socially awkward, or difficult to work with. The planter could certainly tell some of these people "no" but that requires him to have hard conversations that might otherwise be avoidable. An all-call might also lead to too many people on the core team. This could hurt the sending church, especially if that church isn't large, by taking away too many key leaders. But more importantly, a core group that's too large can stunt the evangelistic urgency of the plant from the start. Some pejoratively call this "plopping" rather than "planting." If you just plop a bunch of Christians in a new place, you have the same risk of creating an insider culture, not striving to reach the lost, and juggling myriad demands that come from having a small church right from the start. Many prefer to limit the all-call and choose to look elsewhere.

Place #4
A Select Group of Christians from the Sending Church

Some decide to hand-select a group of Christians from the sending church. The sending church pastors and/or the church planter determine this group based on who they think would support, enrich, and encourage the work of the plant. This requires a high trust relationship between the planter and the sending church. There's nothing worse for a sending church than for a planter to pick his team without discussing this with other pastors. But in a trusted eldership, the brothers can work together to discern who would be a good fit.

I've seen churches that keep a list of different types of people: 1) those who seem to be a home run, 2) those who might be good to ask, and 3) those whom the sending church would rather not go for various reasons. From there, the pastors can make personalized asks to these individuals, which communicates to those being asked that they are valued and sought after.[8] It allows the pastors to form a core team of people with different gifts, backgrounds, and maturity levels. Finally, this allows the sending church to have some say in how large the core team gets, which protects against some of the fears of "plopping" too large of a group.

Selecting core team members in this way does open the door for hurt feelings. Those who are not asked to go or who are asked to remain behind may feel slighted. Personally selecting core team members can undermine the work of God's Spirit because if we're not careful, we can communicate that it is the pastor and not the Spirit calling someone to go. Or we could pit ourselves against the Spirit in the person's conscience by asking them to stay when they feel pressed to go, or vice versa. People could feel they are letting us down if

---

[8] Here it is imperative that the planter honors the sending church. For example, the sending church pastors may know of an issue with a prospective team member or need that person for an upcoming ministry objective. The planter may not know all the reasons why the sending church thinks that some would be a good fit and others not. What's important is that the prospective planter honors these requests and communicates clearly with the sending church. This is especially true if members of the sending church approach the planter and ask about joining the core team rather than the planter going to them with an invitation. If this happens, it's vital that the planting pastor comes to the sending church pastor(s) and says, "Hey, such and such approached me and said they'd really like to join our church planting core group. They were not one of the people we discussed for me to pursue so I just wanted to let you know that they'd asked me and see if you are good with me inviting them to join us?" This level of openness builds trust and helps to avoid tension down the road.

they sense that God is leading in a different direction. Finally, as already noted, for this path to work there must be high trust between the sending church and the planting pastor. You can easily sabotage future partnership if you aren't forthright in the core group building process.

Place #5
Interested Christians from Partner Churches

A final option is to seek out partner churches in the area and ask them to send people. It's easier to imagine this model if we think about a church in the Southeast planting a church in Chicago. It's unlikely that the sending church will have 20 people willing to move to plant, though that's possible in some cases.[9] Most churches are going to have to depend on partnerships in the new city to find healthy Christians to join the team.

There are two options. First, a church might already cooperate with a network like Pillar that provides these known relationships.[10] If so, the sending church should reach out to

---

[9] This is most likely the case when you have a large and young church. Large churches can more easily absorb the loss of a big group leaving at any one time. And the younger the church is, the more likely their members are at the front end of careers or families where it's easier to pick up and start over again in a new place.

[10] Partnership at this level is one of the key reasons to align with a group like The Pillar Network (www.thepillarnetwork.com). By virtue of the shared ecclesiological convictions of Pillar churches, a sending church can assume certain things about another Pillar church and thereby entertain the idea of grafting members from that church into their church-planting work, knowing that these members are likely to come to the work with certain foundations already in place.

other Pillar churches in that area, tell them of the intention to plant a church, and strategize together about who might be a good fit to partner with the plant. It's unlikely that a church would have many people desiring to go since they may not know the planter or the sending church. But it's possible that these area churches, simply by making an all-call invitation, would produce a handful of viable options. Partnership with local associations or state conventions within the SBC could be another way to find people from local churches willing to invest in a new work.

If the church isn't in a network like Pillar, then partnerships can be more difficult since the sending church would need to vet the health of the partner church to discern if their sending members would be a good fit. These churches have to depend on the web of relationships they have for someone to point them to like-minded churches who may be able to send people. However, it's a tough sell for a sending church pastor to cold call a prospective partner church and ask them to give people to a plant. It will be far better if there are trusted relationships already in place.

The challenges to working with partner churches are obvious. Even the best church-to-church partnerships involve differences that may make alignment challenging. Since these team members don't already know the planter, it will take time for relationships to form. And, perhaps the most difficult, if these team members live in another city it will be tough to do much together as a team prior to the planter moving to the city, whereas a core team built from the same sending church can have months of in-person meetings ahead of time.

Each of these options for core team formation presents some strengths and challenges. The nature of the sending church and the planting pastor will influence the number from each group. It's important that the planting pastor keep in mind the challenges, particularly if the team is weighted toward people from one of these groups. In my mind, the best place to find people for the core team is the sending church since you can hand-select a few people. From there, invite others from the sending church to consider going, while giving the caveat that the planting pastor may need to refine the group based on who is interested. Then invite the planting pastor to think about friends or family who might be interested and selectively invite them. These groupings should form the basic building blocks of a core team. Later, the church plant can add members from partner churches and, ideally, some people God saves to the team. This well-rounded team can become the core group through whom God does His work of building His church.

CHAPTER 9

HOW DO I HELP THE SENDING CHURCH LOVE CHURCH PLANTING?

Clint Darst

Church planting is a labor of sacrificial love. It requires significant time, energy, resources, and people. Once you've decided to lead your church to pursue church planting, you must make it a priority to motivate your church—the one doing the sending—to make the individual and corporate sacrifices necessary to start the new work. In his famous sermon, "The Expulsive Power of a New Affection,"[1] Thomas Chalmers argues that moral transformation comes not primarily from restraining worldly desires, but by replacing them with great-

---

[1] Crossway published this sermon in their *Short Classics* series: Thomas Chalmers, *The Expulsive Power of a New Affection* (Crossway Short Classics; Wheaton, IL: Crossway, 2020).

er affections birthed out of the gospel of grace and unto the glory of God.

Borrowing from Chalmers, I believe the best motivation for our congregations to make the investment necessary to plant another church is expulsive love for God, His gospel, His church, and those far from God. This love motivates our churches to joyfully sacrifice for the advancement of the gospel through church planting. In this chapter, my desire is to help you motivate your sending church with this expulsive power for the task of church planting so they will be fully invested in the work. I will seek to do this by briefly considering Christ's compassion for the crowds and His command to pray for laborers to be sent out, as recorded in the familiar text of Matthew 9:35–38. I will then suggest six applications to help connect your congregants' affections to individual and corporate investment in church planting.

Christ's Compassion
Should Fuel Our Efforts

First, pastors must cultivate the right compassion in our congregations. Fallen human compassion has a limited shelf-life. We cannot merely seek to use compelling stories and statistics about the lost in a particular community and expect our congregations' affections to stay white-hot for missions generally or church planting specifically. Stories and statistics can be helpful additions to conversations about church planting, but if we win our churches to church planting primarily with stats and stories, then we risk our congregations' compassion becoming desensitized or overwhelmed. The numbers and stories may tug on heart strings at first, but over time they blend and blur. This may lead some members to feel like the process sounds too much like a startup business proposal from someone trying to solicit financial backing. Instead of being burdened that human beings made in the image of God are headed to an eternal hell, they might just wonder what you are trying to convince them to do. Other, perhaps more tender members might despair over how many churches are needed, considering the vast lostness and suffering in the world. They might feel like your effort is too small and become discouraged. Or they might hear "successful" church plant stories and turn them into unrealistic expectations if this new work doesn't lead to the same results. Therefore, we must fuel these efforts with a tank of compassion that never runs out.

The Lord Jesus in His earthly ministry went to all kinds of people in all kinds of places on His mission to seek and save the lost. We get a glimpse into the very heart of God[2] in Matthew 9:35–38. Jesus gazed upon the crowds with pity and pain because so many were harassed and helpless like sheep without a shepherd. This grace and mercy led Him to leave heaven and dwell among fallen humanity to declare the gospel, to display good deeds, and to perform miraculous works that confirmed His Messianic identity and mission.

---

[2] This point is true for domestic church planting and international missions' sending. Sometimes pastors can be so zealous that their church 'loves the nations' that they leave this conceptual or theoretical. We don't want people to merely love the idea of missions but to attach themselves to God's heart for the lost and find motivation in the nature and character of God and his work through Christ. See John Piper, *Let the Nations Be Glad! The Supremacy of God in Missions* (30th anniv. ed.; Grand Rapids: Baker Academic, 2022) for a thorough and insightful treatment of this theme.

This compassionate love ultimately led Him to climb Calvary's cross and die to bring lost sheep into His eternal shepherding care. This compassion, this *splanchnizomai*, this pain of pity in the basement of the Savior's bosom, ignited and propelled the disciples into Christ's mission.[3]

Christ's compassion for suffering sinners must permeate our preaching and teaching, personal discipling and counseling, and illustrations and applications. This is what must fuel our church planting efforts. If we do this well, our people will not only begin hearing about the lost or the need for church planting when we have a church plant to put in front of them. They will already sense Christ's love and, in a sense, will already be asking, "So what are we going to do?" When we do this, the Spirit works in the hearts of our people and transforms them from one degree of glory to another, conforming us to the image of Christ. Let us not merely appeal to human compassion to be mustered from within, but regularly take them to the One who invites suffering sinners, "Come to me, all who labor and are heavy laden, and I will give you rest. Take my yoke upon you, and learn from me, for I am gentle and lowly in heart, and you will find rest for your souls" (Matt. 11:28–29).

---

[3] In ancient Greek culture, the bowels, rather than the heart, were the seat of one's emotional life. The noun form of the verb could refer to one's literal entrails or feelings of love, affection, and pity. For a fuller discussion of this verb and its semantic range and relationships see Frederick W. Danker, Walter Bauer, and William Arndt. *A Greek-English Lexicon of the New Testament and Other Early Christian Literature* (Chicago: University of Chicago Press, 2000), 938; Johannes P. Louw and Eugene Albert Nida, *Greek-English Lexicon of the New Testament: Based on Semantic Domains* (2nd ed.; New York: United Bible Societies), 25.49.

One way we can bring Christ's compassion to light is by reminding our members of their own testimonies. Remind them of the pain and vanity of their life without Christ. Remind them of how often their idols overpromised and underdelivered. Remind them of the weight of their guilt and shame. And then remind them how the Good Shepherd rescued them by laying down His life for them and taking it up again on the third day. Remind them how He guides them into green pastures with his flock so that they are no longer alone and abandoned to their idols. Stir up their gratitude for the Christ who saved them and the church that He placed them in. Remind them that someone, at some point, planted every church that exists. Help them trace their story of salvation through the work of the church. And then teach them to look at the needs of the crowds again through Christ's compassionate eyes.

Connect your stories and stats to the love of God in the cross of Christ. Let the church feel the pain that Christ's heart revealed. Show them crowds full of sinful sufferers who are harassed and helpless like sheep without the Good Shepherd. Remind them that those crowds are full of sinners whose sorrows are multiplying because they are running after other gods (Ps. 16:4). Those crowds might be full of political, cultural, and social figures, full of friends or foes. But no matter who makes up those crowds, they are full of individuals who either have the soul-satisfying Savior as their faithful Shepherd or they have soul-sucking idols dragging them unto an eternal hell. Our churches need to live with open eyes and broken hearts because, having been united to the Savior, they now look through the eyes of Christ and love with the very heart of Christ. They need to remember God's saving compassion for them and for those who do not yet know Him. And if they feel the compassionate love of Christ for the lost and dying world, then this expulsive power will cause them to act. Church planting will be one of many manifestations of their actions. Therefore, we must not only fuel them with Christ's compassion. We must show them how Christ's command shapes our ministry.

Christ's Command to Pray
Should Shape Our Efforts

I think it is fair to assume that the disciples saw our compassionate Lord's grimacing face as He looked upon the crowds and were in turn moved with a new compassion they had never experienced before. Then Jesus turned to them and stated the great cause of his pity, "The harvest is plentiful, but the laborers are few" (Matt. 9:37). The great problem is a lack of laborers for an abundant harvest. There are so many people and so few preachers. Therefore, He calls them to action: "Pray earnestly to the Lord of the harvest to send out laborers into his harvest" (Matt. 9:38). Notice, the first command isn't to go preach, but to pray. Before sending out the disciples to do the work, He made sure their dependence was upon the Lord of the harvest rather than on their own strength, might, or even *their own* compassion. He had them looking at the crowds through His eyes so that they might feel His compassion for those crowds. He had them living with open eyes and broken hearts. Then He grounded their dependence in the One who is sovereign over the harvest.

Our Triune God cares far more about the harvest than we do, and the good news is that He is sovereign over it. He is the Lord of the harvest. He knows when to sow, when to water, and when to reap. He has and will give the tools to His servants and send them into the part of the harvest field that He desires them to labor in. He will grant instruction on who is to sow and who is to water and who is to harvest. Or, to use the metaphor of the Psalmist, He is the Lord and unless He builds the house those who build it labor in vain (Ps. 127:1). But those who have open eyes, broken hearts, and calloused knees from praying to the Lord of the harvest can be confident that Christ will answer the prayers He commanded us to pray. None of our labor is in vain (1 Cor. 15:58). He will supply laborers to reap worshippers from every tribe, tongue, and nation. The Lord of the harvest will raise up more laborers until the harvest is complete. His compassion compels Him to, and his sovereign power guarantees He will not fail. One of the things I love about the book you are reading is how often this point has been made. In virtually every chapter, the authors have pointed us to prayer because the work of sending and starting new churches is ultimately a work of God.

Matthew 10 opens with Jesus calling the disciples to Himself. He gives them authority and then directs them to go and be the answers to their own prayers (Matt. 10:1–5). The Lord gives us the grace to see what He sees and feel what He feels. He commands us to plead with Him to do something about the needs of the world, and then He sends us out with beautiful feet. When we are on our knees in prayer, our hearts are humbled and emboldened for His mission; our hearts gain the wisdom needed to steward the good gifts that He has given us for His purposes; He unites our heart to His mission to seek and save the lost; He grows all His disciples unto maturity in Christ; He reminds us that this world is not our home; and He reminds us that living for eternity is far more valuable, wise, and rewarding than living for this life.

When our eyes are looking where He is looking, and our hearts are feeling what He is feeling, then our prayers will be about what He sees and feels. Our feet will be willing to walk into whatever self-sacrificial good works He has called us to because we long to see His gospel advance. It is in the compassion of Christ that we find that expulsive power of a new affection that Chalmers spoke of. Those new affections include a passion for seeing the gospel advance causing self-sacrificial desires to drive out old self-serving desires. This results in new affections that want to see harassed and help-less sheep with no shepherd come to know the Good Shepherd through faithful laborers. This new affection driven by Christ's compassion and committed to Christ's command to pray leads us to the Apostle Paul's logic: "How then will they call on him in whom they have not believed? And how are they to believe in him of whom they have never heard? And how are they to hear without someone preaching? And how are they to preach unless they are sent? As it is written, 'How beautiful are the feet of those who preach the good news!'" (Rom. 10:14–15). If the congregation is motivated by the compassion of Christ and committed to pray to the Lord of the harvest to send out laborers, then they will be ready to love and invest in the future church plant.

The faithful pastor's responsibility is to equip the saints for this work.[4] The pastor begins with prayer and then he must help lead the church to discern: Whose feet will be beautiful by going? Whose feet will be beautiful by sending? Whose feet will be beautiful by giving? If we really believe that churches plant churches, then how will all of this come together in such a way that when the new church is sent out, it is not just by pastors, but by the whole church (or group of churches) who have a deep affection and investment in this new work? When our congregations are living with open eyes, broken hearts, and calloused knees, then we must help them walk with beautiful feet. We do this by connecting the compassion and command of Christ to practical love and investment in the church plant. With the biblical motivations for church planting in place, we can now turn to six practical suggestions to help cultivate that corporate and individual involvement in a future plant.

Make Church Planting a Normal Emphasis in Your Corporate Gatherings

First, to cultivate congregational love and investment into the future church plant, you should strategically emphasize church planting in your corporate gatherings. You can do this in your pastoral prayers by regularly asking for the Lord to send laborers to particular cities or communities because of specific needs there. You can do this at members' meetings by asking the congregation to pray for the young men the pas-

---

[4] Walter L. Liefeld, *1 & 2 Timothy, Titus*, (NIV Application Commentary; Grand Rapids: Zondervan Academic, 1999), 160.

tors are investing in with the hopes of sending them out. You can regularly connect Christ's compassion and commands to applications in your sermons. Give the stats, give the stories, and then call the members to pray that our compassionate King would send gospel laborers to meet these needs among specific communities. Finally, consider prioritizing a residency where your congregation can watch a laborer grow and develop over time and then be sent out.[5] As a part of the residency, consider giving the resident opportunities to sit in on elders' meetings, conduct pastoral prayers, teach discipleship classes, and preach at your regular services. This will allow the resident to develop as a shepherd. It will also allow the congregation to benefit from his ministry, see his progress in the faith, and to know the individual well enough to affirm his character and giftings so that they feel comfortable commissioning him for this new work (1 Tim. 4:15).

---

[5] Our church prefers at least two years with a resident whom we intend to send out to start or strengthen a church. We have found that it is best to have at least a year of exposure to how our ecclesiology and philosophy of ministry is lived out prior to another year (or more) of helping get the new work started. We provide a stipend and housing for our residents and allow them to raise support or work as needed. For more details on pastoral residencies and varied training approaches, see Matt Rogers, *A Workman Approved: Developing Future Pastors in the Local Church and Seminary* (Nashville: Rainer Publishing, 2018); Phil A. Newton, *The Mentoring Church: How Pastors and Congregations Cultivate Leaders* (Grand Rapids: Kregel Ministry, 2017); Colin Marshall, *Passing the Baton: A Handbook for Ministry Apprenticeship* (Kingsford, Australia: Matthias Media, 2007).

Create Clear Pathways for Individual Involvement

Second, think strategically about how to create clear pathways for individual members to get involved. At the beginning of our residency, we have our potential planters join a community group[6] and participate as faithful members in our church. Then, after they become interwoven in the fabric of the life and ministry of our church, we have them start a new community group and encourage people that have interest in going with the church plant to consider visiting or joining that community group.[7] This helps facilitate a season where members can explore interest and discern if they want to join the work while building a relationship with and a trust in the potential planter.[8] These steps connect nicely with the encouragement Matt gave in his chapter about where you can look for a planting team. Our church, as a sending church, wants to send some of our members to join our church plants and we want to make it as easy as possible to discern whether or not they should go.

---

[6] Our Community Groups meet weekly in the Spring and Fall Semesters to discuss and apply the sermon text, pray, and fellowship together.

[7] This is especially helpful if planting locally, since people can easily join with a team in the part of the city where they already live.

[8] This does not guarantee they will be a part of the core team per se. The elders walk with the pastoral resident through building a core team that will be commissioned based on the needs of the team and the spiritual health of the individuals interested. This is a delicate process that requires pastoral oversight and involvement. See Chapter 8 in this book, Matt Rogers, "Where Do the People Come From?" as he shows how to navigate this core team process.

We also set up the Church Planting Resident to have regular interest meetings throughout their residency. We encourage interested members to attend. Additionally, we encourage members to attend even if they have no plan to go out with the plant but would like to know how to pray for and partner with the plant as members of the sending church.

Create Pathways for Ongoing Connection

Third, be intentional about how you will facilitate ongoing connection between the sending church and the plant. Members who join your church after the plant has been sent out will need an opportunity to learn about and develop affection for this work. Regular corporate prayer and ministry updates will be helpful. In addition, if the church plant is in proximity, you might form a rotation of volunteers from your church to help by serving in kids ministry or on hospitality teams, especially in the early days when the core team is thinly stretched. You can also consider swapping pulpits, celebrating anniversaries, and partnering in community outreach and missions. In addition to financial support, you could take their elders to conferences and events with the elders of your sending church. If you have an annual pastor's retreat, consider inviting the plant's elders to join and have their own planning retreat with you.[9] Lastly, consider

---

[9] We paid for their accommodations, sent them our planning retreat agenda and schedule ahead of time so that they could adapt and use it for their annual planning if they wanted to. At the retreat we invited them to join in on devotions, meals, and fellowship time with us and have their own planning sessions when we had ours.

adding information and links on your website that point people to this work. Mention it in your membership classes and feature information and updates wherever you feature ministry partners.

Celebrate Kingdom Wins

Fourth, with the compassion of Christ fueling this work, make sure to take every opportunity to celebrate kingdom wins—not only you as the pastor, but the entire church. One of the things that I find most encouraging about the early church is the refrain of "success" as the Word of God advances in various places. It is the Word of God that "increased," "multiplied," and "continued. . . to prevail mightily" (Acts 6:7; 12:24; 19:20; cf. Col. 1:5–6). For your church to continue to invest in and love the plants that are sent out, she must have a kingdom mindset that gets excited not only about your own personal growth (though that is wonderfully exciting), but about the Word's growth through every faithful church and ministry. Instead of celebrating record attendance on Easter Sunday, celebrate total attendance at your church and the church plant. When someone comes to faith and is baptized at the new plant, celebrate that with the sending church. Help the congregation celebrate kingdom growth so that their hearts are increasingly knitted to the church plant and to all faithful churches that are advancing the gospel of grace. Here again, denominational partnerships provide a meaningful context for such celebration.

Gently Shepherd through Sending Fatigue

Fifth, you should anticipate "sending fatigue."[10] This is even more likely if the Lord gives you grace to plant locally, especially more than once. Our church has sent out three plants locally in the last four years. We sent out many key leaders who each had a tremendous impact on our faith family. We express the tension when another beloved member commits to leave by saying, "We are sad to see you leave but excited to see you go." This cost will hit some people (pastors included) harder than others. Do not be surprised or frustrated by this. If your church is healthy and people are growing in grace together, then sending and leaving *should* be hard. People have taken relational risks, dropped vulnerability walls, and served alongside some of the brothers and sisters that are leaving. It may have taken them years to get to know and love these members and now they are leaving. They may have walked through difficult seasons together, so it is hard to part.

You may have invested deeply in the lives of some of these members and assumed they were "lifers." As they leave, you not only have to lead others through sadness and disappointment, but you must deal with your own. With these emotions comes the simultaneous encouragement that people are willing to go, and that God is using the local church He has called you to be a part of to expand His kingdom.[11]

---

[10] I first heard this phrase in a conversation with Tony Merida, pastor of Imago Dei Church in Raleigh, NC.

[11] This process can be very difficult on pastors if there are members you have specifically discipled who you assumed would not want to go. I encourage you to make sure to process these complex emotions of simulta-

It can be a very complex emotional experience. Be faithful and gentle with the sheep who have a hard time sending out beloved members (even if it's the sheep looking at you in the mirror). Care for them and encourage them. Remind them that the harvest is plentiful, but the laborers are few. Remind them that you've all been praying that the Lord of the harvest would do this very thing and you all can trust that He is gentle and lowly and will give you rest for your souls, even in this work.

Anticipate that Great Day when Sending Ends

Lastly, make sure you regularly offer hope by pointing to the great day when we will all be gathered around our Good Shepherd. It is hard to send out people you have poured into for decades. It is hard to lose some of your biggest givers and best leaders to two church plants within the same 12-month period. It is hard to lose much of the diversity the Lord has graciously given your church. It is hard. But the Lord of the harvest loves the nations. He has compassion for crowds, and He has compassion for you. He called you to pray and send or pray and go. But He also promises that one day sending will end. Can you imagine how joyful it will be when

---

neous excitement and disappointment with another pastor on your elder team or even from another church committed to sending. There is a strange temptation to feel underappreciated when the very thing you've been praying for happens. You want people to want to go, but not *those* people. It is helpful to have a brother pastor who knows you well to shepherd you through this time. He can help you discern between indwelling sin that needs to be repented of, and sacrificial sadness that needs to be commended, celebrated, and encouraged.

your church members get to meet those who came to faith, perhaps generations later, through their love and investment that went into church planting? The sending fatigue will be eclipsed with unending joy.

A few years ago, a sister whom God had done an incredible work in had to relocate and join another faithful church. Nearly a year later, she sent an email that captured the expulsive power of eternal hope that our people need to joyfully invest in church planting:

> Several months ago, I was thinking about you all and was overcome with tears of sadness that I don't get to be with KCC each week anymore. But then God graciously brought this beautiful thought to mind. This is only a temporary separation that I am experiencing, and one day, I will get to worship with you all again for eternity. There will be no more physical distance and there will be no end to our praising God together. My tears of sadness were then overcome with tears of joy for the goodness of our great God and His marvelous promises. I am truly undeserving of His lavish grace and I cannot wait for Heaven![12]

The compassionate love of Christ compels us to pray to the Lord of the harvest to send out laborers. It causes us to live with open eyes, broken hearts, calloused knees, and beautiful feet. And laborers with beautiful feet can't help but desire

---

[12] Quoted with permission of the writer.

to plant churches where the Good Shepherd will care for those who were once harassed and helpless. Therefore, let us do all that we can to equip the saints for this ministry by creating corporate and individual pathways for them to love, invest, celebrate, and stay connected to future church plants. And though we will likely have to shepherd the sheep through some sending fatigue along the way, within the good providence of our compassionate King, we know that heaven is going to be full of people that were helped to get there through the efforts of ordinary Christians and churches.

CHAPTER 10

WHAT IS THE ROLE OF WOMEN IN CHURCH PLANTING?

Sarah Rogers

As I drove a group of tired high school seniors and college students home from a missions conference, we debriefed in the car. Everyone felt excited about God's work in the world and wrestled with ways that they could be part of it. Some of the older students already had their sights set on applying for the Journeyman program[1] or serving with a church plant. The younger students were excited to keep exploring how the Lord might position them to use their lives for His glory among the nations. Amidst all the excitement, one young woman spoke up, "All of the speakers were set on working

---

[1] See https://www.imb.org/students/go-2-years-journeyman/ for more information on this introduction to international missions service.

for God's glory around the world, but the men seemed to be the ones doing real ministry while the women seemed only to talk about being wives and mothers. I'm struggling to see my place in the work as a single woman, and I'm wondering if marriage and children would prevent me from serving in the church or missions at all."

I was struck by the tension she felt and expressed. I am a married woman with five children who recognizes and takes seriously the high calling of marriage and motherhood that the Lord has given me. At the same time, I was losing sleep and drawing from stores of energy long unused to serve college students on this trip. Not only was I serving on this trip, but I love the local church and labored alongside my husband in the church planting process, teaching and counseling women, and serving on mission from my neighborhood to the nations. I was serving in the church and giving my life for God's mission, the very things this girl in my car was wondering if she'd ever be able to do. Clearly, there were some misconceptions we needed to address.

Churches need the gifts, support, and partnership of women in the planting process, and women need the order and care of their local church.[2] In Part 3, we've described how you go about building a team and cultivating buy-in from the church. Now we want to show how that team and

---

[2] There are several helpful books written on the topic of the role of women in ministry. Among them, I've found these most helpful: Ligon Duncan and Susan Hunt, *Women's Ministry in the Local Church* (Wheaton, IL: Crossway, 2006); Gloria Furman, *The Pastor's Wife: Strengthened by Grace for a Life of Love* (Wheaton, IL: Crossway, 2015); Jani Ortlund, *Help! I'm Married to a Pastor* (Wheaton, IL: Crossway, 2021).

the sending church are served and supported by faithful women. In this chapter, I'll aim to show the women reading this book how they can aid in planting work and to help the pastors along the way by giving them ideas about how to deploy women so that they thrive.

Use Your Gifts

To begin with, women are gifted by God to serve His church. Sidelining half of the church's members simply due to their gender would squander innumerable gifts that God intends to use to bless His people through His church. Since I hold complementarian convictions, I whole-heartedly believe that there are God-ordained roles for men and women in the church, and I want to honor the divine intention of structuring the world and the church such that men and women have distinct, yet complementary gifts.[3] However, I fear that our attempts to discuss these differences sometimes highlight the various roles that women are prohibited from holding in the church (such as serving as pastors), rather than also emphasizing the myriad of ways women can build up the church as they use their gifts.

---

[3] This isn't the place for a thorough discussion of complementarianism so I commend to you the following books for a defense of this position: Kevin DeYoung, *Men and Women in the Church: A Short, Biblical, Practical Introduction* (Wheaton, IL: Crossway, 2021); Jonathan Leeman, ed., *Complementarianism: A Moment of Reckoning* (9Marks Journal; Washington, DC: 9Marks, 2019); Jonathan Leeman, ed., *Complementarianism and the Local Church* (9Marks Journal; Washington, DC, 2017); Keri Fulmar, *How Can Women Thrive in the Church?* (9Marks; Wheaton, IL: Crossway, 2021).

Almost every Sunday at my church, I meet someone who is visiting for the first time. After asking a few questions to get to know them, one of the first things I tell them is where they can find the bathrooms. We're in an older building and the bathrooms can be difficult to locate, so I welcome church visitors as I would welcome someone into my home, making sure they know where to find what they need. As I learn about them, I'm already thinking of who they would relate well to because of similar backgrounds, current circumstances, or other data points that my questions reveal.

Of course, it's not merely women who can show hospitality in this way, but many women know how to welcome others in and help them find their place. Not surprisingly, one-third of women working outside the home are in education and the health service industry,[4] while another one-third are stay-at-home moms.[5] A majority of women daily focus on serving vulnerable populations. Utilizing and developing these skills day in and day out positions women to be valuable gifts to the church as they leverage those skills in the body of Christ. Not only that, but having women serve the church in these ways bolsters the work of the pastors who may be giving attention to some aspect of the liturgy or to their sermon, while unintentionally overlooking the guest

---

[4] Stephanie Ferguson Melhorn, "Data Deep Dive: Women in the Workforce," *U.S. Chamber of Commerce*, https://www.uschamber.com/workforce/data-deep-dive-a-decline-of-women-in-the-workforce.

[5] "Employment Characteristics of Families—2024," *Bureau of Labor Statistics*, https://www.bls.gov/news.release/pdf/famee.pdf.

who just needs to find the bathroom so he or she can listen to that sermon.

These are not just skills that are developed as a result of family or work dynamics. Christians know that the Spirit gifts every believer supernaturally so that we exercise gifts for the building up of the body (1 Cor. 14:12). All believers, men and women, should seek out the ways the Spirit has gifted them and use those gifts to build, serve, and disciple other believers in their local church. These gifts are going to accord with all of Scripture's teachings, meaning that women will not be gifted to pastor a church because that gift is reserved for qualified men. But in all the ways that the Spirit gifts women to build up the church in accordance with Scripture, they should be encouraged, expected, and given opportunity to exercise those gifts. Men, especially pastors, have a role to play here. Much like the young girl in my car coming home from the missions' conference, some women in our churches feel overlooked and undervalued. It's incumbent upon pastors to come alongside these ladies, help them to see how and where they can serve, and provide encouragement as they do (Eph. 4:11–16).

How can women know what gifts the Spirit has given them? Spiritual gift inventories have fallen out of use in some of our church circles, often for good reasons. A better way to discover your gifts is to ask the Spirit to help you as you read about the gifts in the New Testament, assess what areas stir you up when you think about serving, and then to look for areas of need in your church. Another way to discover your gifts is to ask other people. Sometimes other people see us better than we see ourselves. Ask those you trust to tell you where they see fruit in your work. As you give yourself to service in the church, the Spirit will use other believers to encourage you in areas of gifting or redirect you when you serve in an area outside of your gifting.

When Matt and I moved to Greenville, South Carolina to plant a church in 2009, another woman led our children's ministry. When she needed to step down two years in, I agreed to lead until we found a replacement. I do not have gifts of administration, as I quickly discovered while leading this ministry. I did my best to complete the necessary background checks, volunteer trainings, and Planning Center check-ins to help parents feel safe, children feel welcome, and volunteers feel equipped. But these were not my strengths. So the ministry suffered. While I was thankful to serve and bridge a need in the church, I was equally thankful to pass off those responsibilities to someone whose giftings and desires matched this area of service. On the other hand, I had an increasing desire to teach the Bible and was convinced that many generations would be impacted if women grew in their knowledge and love for the Scriptures. Working with our pastors, I hosted a Bible study in my home and received encouragement on my faithfulness to the text, helpful illustrations that simplified the concepts, and contagious passion for women to read and understand Scripture for themselves. My pastors also read and listened to my teaching. They gave encouragement and feedback to hone my use of this gift. The Spirit, the Word, and the Church should call out, affirm, and champion a believer's gifts. That's what I experienced.

In order for this to occur, women must be invited and welcomed into areas of service in the church. The body benefits when pastors recognize the gifts of their members and deploy them to build up the church. Recognizing the gifts of an administratively gifted woman, a pastor might seek her help to organize church events or retreats. Pastors might ask for insight on tone and application from a woman for an upcoming sermon on a passage specifically related to women (for example, 1 Pet. 3:1–7). Women possessing gifts to lead with vision and wisdom may be tasked to lead a ministry team under the care and oversight of the pastors.

Like every believer in Jesus, women deeply love the church and want to see her healthy, mature, and thriving. Because we love the church and because we desire to serve in areas of need, women can often overcommit themselves, sometimes to the neglect of their primary responsibilities if they are wives and mothers. Pastors and ministry leaders can help relieve pressure by asking about their home life, encouraging women to examine their schedules and keep their priorities in the right place, and providing an off-ramp in service if she needs to give more attention to the needs of her home. While all Christians are expected to use their gifts to build up the church, women will have seasons when our demands and responsibilities will influence the amount of time we're able to give.[6]

---

[6] Some seasons of life are more demanding than others, but some seasons carry demands on our time and attention by the result of our own choices. Believers should prioritize service to the church over optional commitments that detract from their service such as their child's dance class, travel team, etc. For more examination of this topic, see Donald Whitney, *Spiritual Disciplines Within the Church: Participating Fully in the Body of Christ* (Chicago: Moody, 1996).

When the gifts of women are utilized well in the church, the overall health of the church will flourish. Families will be strengthened, children will be discipled, and men will be encouraged to serve in their areas of gifting.

Give Strong Support

On the first page of the Bible, God created woman and gave her the descriptor ēzer or "helper."[7] This description is applied to God Himself in the Old Testament. The term refers to a deliverer, sustainer, shield, and comforter. A "helper" is someone who lends strength, comes to the aid of another, or gives hope and blessing.[8] When women possess the spiritual strength to live out this created design, they become a force for the good of the church because they give strength to all that the church does.

Consider Priscilla in Acts 18. Aquila and Priscilla met Paul and invited him to live with them during his time in Corinth. Imagine the conversations they had as they worked their tent-making trade by day and ate meals around the dinner table at night! Surely they heard him teach and share the gospel. As they spent time with him, they were discipled to more faithfully understand God's Word and work in the world. After staying with them for some time, Paul took this couple with him on his journey to Ephesus, presumably to help him in his work. He ultimately left them in Ephesus while he continued on to Jerusalem. Priscilla and Aquila

---

[7] *Strong's Concordance*, H5828.

[8] See Ex. 18:4; Deut. 33:7, 26, 29; Psalm 54:4, 70:5, 86:17, 115:9-11, 121:1-2; 146:5.

then met Apollos, who taught eloquently in the synagogue and earned the hearing of the people. He spoke accurately of what he knew, but Priscilla and Aquila recognized that there was more for him to learn. Instead of berating him or criticizing him, they both took him aside and explained what he was missing. Priscilla was an important part of this interaction, so much so that she's named first in the text as she recognized the need to come to the aid of Apollos and, therefore, the church, so that the whole counsel of God could be taught. She strengthened Apollos and explained the way of God more accurately. Then Priscilla and Aquila sent Apollos on to Achaia where he was a great help to the church, vigorously refuting the Jews and demonstrating through the Scriptures that Jesus is the Messiah (Acts 18:27–28).

The church is strengthened and people are helped when women fulfill their created design as *ēzers*. Their hope and faith in God strengthen their brothers and sisters in the church. They give courage to (literally, *en-courage*) the church to live in hope that God's promises are true and can be counted on, and that His Word brings life for those who live by it. Women partner with men in this battle for hearts and souls, contending for the faith as they stand on the truth of Scripture and call others to stake their lives on the solid ground of the gospel.

Your church plant may not have a formal women's ministry, but you can be sure that women's ministry is happening from the earliest meetings of your core team as women serve, care for needs, and counsel each other. These are the basics of ministry.

A formal women's ministry can be a tool to equip women to minister effectively and biblically.[9] It should work in tandem with the pastors and the preaching ministry of the church as it trains and deploys women to use their gifts to help meet the needs of women in the church and the church as a whole. Women's Bible studies provide a context for women to work out specific applications to their lives as they learn to read, understand, and obey Scripture together. Women's gatherings cultivate connection between diverse groups of women so that discipleship relationships can form and women can obey Titus 2 to teach and train younger women in Christian distinctives. What a joy it is for a pastor to have women capable of handling the Scriptures. As women are strengthened in their faith, they can faithfully serve as meaningful partners who support the work of the church to multiply mature disciples of Christ.

There is a key way that a sending church can help here. In the early days of planting, it may be difficult for a new church to have a robust ministry to women. While women's ministry is happening informally, the church may not have a building for mid-week groups to meet, or it may lack the leaders necessary to support such a ministry. If the sending church and the church plant are in the same region, then the

---

[9] I highly recommend *Word-Filled Women's Ministry: Loving and Serving the Church* edited by Gloria Furman and Kathleen B. Nielson (TGC; Wheaton, IL: Crossway, 2015) to help church leaders consider how a Bible-centered women's ministry can bolster the health of the church. Similarly, Charles Simeon Trust workshops have served to equip the women in our church with the tools they need to effectively and accurately teach the Bible in women's Bible studies. See www.simeontrust.org for courses and workshops near you.

sending church should consider inviting the women from the church plan into whatever women's ministry initiatives the sending church already has—weekly Bible studies, annual retreats, and so on. Or the women's ministry team from the sending church could seek out a few key ladies on the church planting team and work with them on the practices essential for starting a healthy women's ministry.

What if the churches are not in the same city? If Covid taught us anything, it is that we can use technology to disciple others from a distance. Monthly calls between ladies from the sending church and the church plant can go a long way to empower them for ministry. Also, distance doesn't mean they can't come together for an annual retreat. Churches could select a location that allows all the ladies to be included. Even over two or three days, investing in these ladies could have a significant impact on the church plant.

Hopefully, your church plant sees growth as people place faith in Jesus. Anyone might share the gospel and see someone come to faith, but capable women are needed to spend the time required to faithfully disciple new believers. Similarly, anyone might invite a believing coworker or neighbor to church, but doctrinally sound women are needed to walk through the doctrinal convictions of this church so those women can become faithful members of the church. The same is true for various counseling issues that women bring to the church. For example, a pastor may struggle to give careful help to a woman struggling with postpartum depression, but another woman who has walked that path can give personalized care. Similarly, a woman in the church might refrain from describing her difficult marriage to a male pastor but open up to another woman who is in a position to sympathize and help.

A few months ago, a young Christian woman visiting our church reached out to meet with me to understand more about why we believe that membership is only for baptized believers. She was baptized as an infant in the Lutheran church. Over coffee, I explained our position and, as I asked more questions, I realized she had more doctrinal confusion than just baptism. She was also confused about God's work in salvation, church polity, membership, and discipline. She's continued attending services, and we've spent time together regularly for months, discussing what Scripture teaches on each of these issues. Our male pastors are wise to pass regular one-on-one meetings like these to capable women in the church, but that necessitates that there must *be* capable women in the church to take on this responsibility.

Early in a church plant, qualified women should be identified and provided with pathways to develop those gifts so they can fulfill their roles as partners in the work. These qualified women are those with Titus 2 character and knowledge. They have teaching and counseling gifts, and the time and desire to cultivate them. A pastor's encouragement to women—calling out their giftedness, character, and strengths—can be the spark that sets aflame a pursuit that will benefit the entire church. Even more, a church can develop an internship or residency to train leaders in the church that is open to women, instead of restricting these to men. This creates a pathway of learning, growth, and maturity that will build a force of women who will then teach and train other women and the next generation in gospel living.

Share the Gospel

One final way women strengthen a new church is by sharing the gospel. Jesus' famous Parable of the Sower (Matt. 13) describes the indiscriminate sowing of gospel seed. Not all of that effort produces spiritual fruit—God is the one who brings the growth. But our task is to faithfully share.

While the discussion of women in ministry often revolves around what women cannot do, consider that women can faithfully proclaim the gospel 24-7 through the natural rhythm of their lives. Women are positioned to share the gospel in places, and among certain groups, that are difficult for men to access. When we send missionaries to evangelize in overseas contexts, we expect them to learn the language and know the culture so that they can effectively communicate the gospel to specific people in a new context. These efforts lead to national converts, and every missionary knows that nationals who understand the gospel are more effective in teaching it to others in their own country. They understand how their countrymen think, the narratives that drive them, and their unique obstacles or longings. Similarly, there are experiences common to women that make them uniquely gifted to share the gospel with other women.

A classic example of this would be the neighborhood playground—a spot that's frequented by young moms and little children. If a guy goes to the playground and hangs out, even with one of his children, it can be tough to strike up meaningful conversations with the other people there. But not another mom. She's got easy access to the people around her.

A woman doesn't have to be married or have children for this to be true. A single lady at a local coffee shop or out on a walk is going to have access to a circle of relationships that are limited for men. Simply by being attentive, women can start conversations and begin to share about who Jesus is and why He matters. While the door is open for these gospel conversations, evangelism doesn't come naturally for most, especially those who have been Christians for a long time. This is where mentorship is so critical. Mature women who demonstrate evangelistic intentionality—either in the church plant or from the sending church—can take women under their wings to help them learn and grow in confidence. Older women should meet up with younger women—at coffee shops, restaurants, and family rooms everywhere. Sure, they can meet in homes, but they can also go on a walk together and talk about what God is doing in their lives. Who knows who they might run into along the way who might be open to hearing about Jesus?

There are two other critical contexts for evangelism that are easy to overlook—one in the home and one in the church. If God has given you children, don't overlook their need for the gospel. Some of our most important work in evangelism is to share the gospel with our own children day after day. Want to shape the future of your church plant? Raise up godly, faith-filled kids who love Jesus and the church. It's easy to lose sight of this opportunity when we have our head down in the trenches of domestic life. We can think the win is simply getting our kid to pick up his shoes or brush her teeth before bed. Yet the daily rhythm of talking about Jesus, reading the Bible, praying together, and applying gospel truth to heart issues is the real work of parenting. As we are faithful here, we are doing critical work to build God's church. This task is important for all women, but especially for those who are married to pastors. Pastors' wives support their work by making the home a place of peace, love, and joy.

Finally, consider evangelism in the church. By this, I mean the gathered people of God on a Sunday morning. There you will find women at all places of spiritual maturity, including two types of women that you should not overlook. First, be attentive to women who attend church and think they are Christians but they're not. This reality is true for virtually every church and even more so for church plants. Women will show up who've previously been in churches with anemic or absent gospel messages. They may have attended church for a long time, and yet they have never heard the gospel or genuinely been converted. At the same time, curious women will show up when the church gathers. They'll come for various reasons. Perhaps they know someone in the church or are interested in spiritual matters. Maybe a neighbor or coworker invited them to come and check out the new church in town. Whatever the reason they attend, God has positioned these women alongside Christian women in the church who can take initiative to seek them out.

For this to happen, women must act with evangelistic urgency on Sundays. Rather than simply circling up with preexisting friends or other mature ladies, women can survey the gathered church to notice women on the margins, women who are new or seem to be drifting away. As they do, mature women can seek out these ladies throughout the week to hear more of their story and share the gospel with them.

One of my standing habits is to keep a list of people I meet on Sundays. In fact, our church has a running message board where all the pastors and wives post the names and basic biographical information of new people we meet. From that list, I'm able to see the names of women new to the church and can prioritize my time throughout the week to seek them out. The fact that they've already attended our church and have heard a gospel sermon makes it easier to start gospel conversations with them. As I listen to their stories, I'm able to hear and discern if they are truly converted or merely have some type of moral compass guiding their lives. Just last week, I met a woman who has visited our church three weeks in a row because she was invited by another church member. She is not a Christian, but has questions about God, the Bible, and the church that I was happy to answer. She's reading through the Gospels and we're continuing to meet to discuss what she's read. Others may have noticed her at church and assumed she was a Christian because of her presence in the service but praise the Lord that He draws unbelievers near His people so they can see and hear the beauty of the gospel displayed in their gatherings!

Women matter in multiplying other churches. In this chapter, I've attempted to show how women who use their gifts, give strong support, and share the gospel are a vital means that God uses to build His church. This is the answer I tried to give to the college girl in my car, and it's one I hope will echo in the lives of many other women as we labor together for God's great mission of multiplication.

CHAPTER 11

HOW DO YOU FUND A CHURCH PLANT?

Nathan Baumgartner

As a child, I aspired to become a professional musician. In high school, I spent hours each day practicing the piano, played music in church and at concerts, and declared music as my college major. While I was convinced that music performance would become my primary vocation, the Lord had other plans. Unexpectedly, as I sought to find a job to pay the bills while pursuing college and music, an opportunity arose for a job as a bank teller. Initially attracted to the possibility of "banker's hours" that would allow sufficient time to pursue music on nights and weekends, I quickly realized that the Lord had much to teach me in this new environment.

In bank teller training, leaders shared with bank employees about the task of handling carefully and effectively significant amounts of money every single day. Bank employees must recognize that this money does not belong to them but to their clients. Employees must steward these funds well, they insisted, to ensure that funds are used as the client directs. When this care is neglected, the temptation to become lazy surfaces. When the employee does not view his or her role as a steward of client funds, temptation may lead to carelessness, greed, or theft. Unfortunately, many bank employees have lost their jobs due to these wrongful actions.

Often, churches face similar temptations. It is all-too easy to assume that money management is a non-spiritual but necessary administrative activity. On the other hand, a church may believe that all funds it receives should be completely dedicated to serving the needs of the local congregation without regard for the spread of the gospel beyond its four walls. Yet, a biblical foundation for stewardship recognizes that all resources on this earth ultimately belong to God (Ps. 24:1). And God has called His church to advance the Great Commission, taking the gospel to the ends of the earth (Matt. 28:19–20). As stewards of monetary resources, healthy local churches seek to give generously to support gospel work, and this includes church planting—a key activity to obey Jesus' commission to his church (Matt. 16:18; 28:19–20).

This chapter focuses on how a local church can financially support church planting on a sustainable and scalable basis. We have the people in place. Now it's time to make sure we have the finances to support their work. Pastors should cast a vision of the Great Commission to be pursued through church planting. Church budgets should give generously to planting and provide the foundation for ongoing funding for planting. Churches should regularly communicate the impact of church planting and reinforce a culture that desires to see the gospel flourish. The remainder of this chapter will explore each of these three key activities.

Casting a Great Commission Vision

Jesus did not give the Great Commission to pastors. Jesus gave this mission to the church. However, pastors bear significant responsibility to teach their congregations that the Great Commission is essential to the church's mission. Churches in The Pillar Network (Pillar) believe that churches—not agencies or even well-intentioned individuals—plant churches. And the financial reality is that churches require money to operate. Although a pastor can share the importance of church planting, he must also connect this work to the responsibility of his local congregation to support such effort sacrificially and generously.

In 2 Corinthians 8, Paul unashamedly speaks about financial support for the church at Jerusalem, recognizing the generosity of the churches of Macedonia who gave even out of their extremely limited resources (2 Cor. 8:1–3). Paul continues to explain: "They begged us earnestly for the privilege of sharing in the ministry to the saints, and not just as we had hoped. Instead, they gave themselves first to the Lord and then to us by God's will" (2 Cor. 8:4–5). This description is emblematic of churches that understand the Great Commission so well that their people give sacrificially and joyfully. The congregations "gave themselves first to the Lord." They recognized that their resources were not ultimately for their own benefit but for God's work. They stewarded resources for the kingdom of God rather than for their own financial comfort. Paul compares these churches' generosity to the example of Jesus, who through giving up His riches became poor for the benefit of the church (2 Cor. 8:9). A big vision of God and His plan for the church will lead congregations to give generously and joyfully for the good of other local churches across the globe.

How does a church catch this vision? While this fundamentally flows from knowing and obeying the Word of God through faithful preaching, shepherding, and discipling, the vision must be regularly communicated. Effective leaders communicate effectively.[1] They communicate with precision, clarity, conviction, and frequency. Many leaders assume their message is sufficient if they say something once. But repetition and consistency are critical to lead cultural change. The church planting vision should be communicated through multiple channels and multiple times over a long period of time. Senior or preaching pastors should consider including regular highlights of a church planting vision as they preach through texts. The elders should intentionally speak of the importance of church planting in their areas of shepherding. Members' meetings and newsletters may provide another forum to share this vision. Guest speakers, particularly those with church planting experience, can testify to God's work in and through other likeminded churches (like Paul's example

---

[1] For an insightful and practical resource on effective leadership communication of vision, please see chapter seven of Justin A. Irving, *Healthy Leadership for Thriving Organizations: Creating Contexts Where People Flourish* (Grand Rapids: Baker Academic, 2023), 127–145. This chapter covers communication of vision and ongoing reinforcement of the vision, among other topics for leaders.

of the generous churches of Macedonia in 2 Corinthians 8). Whatever channels are available for consistent and regular communication provide opportunities to share the mission for church planting.

Cultivating a vision is necessary to engage the congregation in adopting a missional culture that prioritizes healthy church planting. Pastors should lead in this communication and share a biblical vision for the Great Commission and their local congregation's pursuit of it. When the church catches the vision and recognizes Christ's plan to build his church through local churches, this sets the stage for the next important step: budgeting for church planting.

Budgeting for Church Planting

Healthy budgets directly align with any organization's vision. For a church with the vision to make disciples of all nations, a budget provides the mechanism to exercise generous and wise stewardship as they obey the Great Commission. Cheerful giving toward the church's budget occurs because members believe in the purpose of their giving.[2] No greater mission exists than the expansion of Christ's kingdom! Unfortunately, some church leaders and members view a budget as a necessary but generally uninteresting document. Sometimes elders delegate budgeting solely to an administrative team. The Bible, however, explains that giving and finances

---

[2] David Dockery explains the importance of connecting vision and mission to giving for donors of any organization. David S. Dockery, ed., *Christian Leadership Essentials: A Handbook for Managing Christian Organizations* (Nashville: B&H Publishing Group, 2011), 125. See chapters six and seven for resources on budgeting and communication about giving.

are deeply connected to obedience to God. The love of and pursuit of money can easily lead to sin because it reorients a person's heart towards the wrong master (Matt. 6:24; 1 Tim. 6:10). Therefore, pastors should take an active role to establish the church's financial priorities.[3]

A budget is one of the most important organizational documents for a healthy church. Since Jesus gives the Great Commission to the church to make more disciples through planting more churches, church budgets should encompass a regular commitment to this mission. Consider the following four aspects in budgeting in order to prioritize church planting.

Operating Budgets

Churches generally assemble and approve an annual operating budget. This budget supports the core expenses of the church, and it's typically funded by tithes and offerings from its members. From women's ministry to insurance, children's ministry to communion supplies, staff salaries to missionary support—operating budgets provide a roadmap to pay ongoing expenses. However, churches that are serious about church planting should consider a line item specific to this purpose.

---

[3] Jamie Dunlop argues that budgeting is spiritual work that necessitates spiritual leadership. See chapter two of the following resource for more information on this argument and practical application considerations: Jamie Dunlop, *Budgeting for a Healthy Church* (Grand Rapids: Zondervan, 2019), 35–49. The entire book provides frameworks for building and communicating a budget that reflect biblical priorities for a healthy local church.

A few years ago, in the Pillar church where I serve in Minnesota, we restructured our budget to reflect several core expense categories. In addition to categories such as operations, ministry, and personnel, we created a major expense category called missions and church planting. We placed this expense group on the first line in our annual budget presentations and regular financial reporting. This serves multiple functions: (1) It provides an opportunity for leadership to regularly discuss the importance of church planting and missions as connected areas of obedience to the Great Commission; (2) it visually demonstrates primacy by placing this at the top of all the budget priorities; and (3) it creates a mechanism where the congregation can clearly see how commitments to this line item change over time. As the church's budget adjusts year-over-year, leadership explains proposals for how total budgeted giving will directly affect missions and church planting.

Potential uses for a church planting line item abound. These may include direct financial support for a new or existing church plant, funding a church-planting residency, or allocating money to a dedicated fund (see below for more details on dedicated funds). Creating budget visibility for church planting builds muscle in the congregation to prioritize and increase their giving for this purpose. Some may argue that a church's budget can barely cover its basic, internal operating costs, let alone provide for outside purposes such as missions and church planting. In such a case, consider starting small. Recall that the churches of Macedonia gave "according to their ability and even beyond their ability, of their own accord" (2 Cor. 8:3). A small dollar amount or percentage signals the priority of future planting. Church plants may consider building this discipline into their operating budgets long before they are ready to become a sending church. Preparation for the day when the church becomes a sending church leads to joy and faithfulness in present sacrificial giving (Prov. 6:6–8; 2 Cor. 9:6–8).

Another way the operating budget can serve to invest in church planting is through giving to denominational efforts and the Cooperative Program of the Southern Baptist Convention. Yes, church to church partnership is ideal, but the dollars invested in giving through the Cooperative Program are important as well. We don't want to lose sight of the fact that our collaboration through denominational funding streams is instrumental in supporting many valuable catalysts to church planting work around the world.

Dedicated Funds

In addition to the operating budget, some churches provide designated funds for benevolence or other ministry efforts. These funds enable church members to give directly to a fund or for a specific purpose rather than the general operating fund. While sometimes effective, this model also carries risks. It may undermine the importance of giving to the purposes advocated by leadership and approved for the church through the operating budget.[4] The presence of a designated

---

[4] This is not always the case, particularly if designated funds are used under certain circumstances or positioned as giving above and beyond regular tithes and offerings. However, churches should carefully consider whether the existence or use of designated funds threatens the efficacy and primacy of the operating fund.

fund may signal that the church leaders endorse giving to alternative funds rather than to regular tithes and offerings. It may also create a substitutionary effect, where people give to a designated fund rather than the operating budget, which may contribute to the church's inability to meet its basic financial commitments.[5] Although designated funds work effectively in certain contexts, leadership should evaluate the wisdom of allowing people to give directly to purposes other than the operating budget on an ongoing basis. It may be better to restrict designated giving for specific, time-bound opportunities.

But funds can be established for dedicated purposes even if they function subordinate to the operating fund. For purposes of definition, this chapter refers to these as *dedicated funds* (also known as *sinking funds*). Dedicated funds support future efforts when the budgeted expenses will not be realized in the same year as the budget. For example, imagine an established church plant. This church desires to begin investing in church planting but does not yet have a defined plan. Perhaps resources are limited, or the right people are not in place to send. Yet leadership emphasizes a vision of church planting even in the early years of the congregation. The next practical step is to begin aligning resources to support this vision. As a very small step, leadership proposes a $1,000 allocation in the upcoming budget year for future church planting. The church could establish a fund where $1,000 from yearly giving is deposited and separated for fu-

---

[5] More discussion can be found on the substitutionary effect in Dockery, *Christian Leadership Essentials*, 107.

ture use. Then, the following year, the church increases its allocation to this fund to $2,000. At the conclusion of two years, $3,000 will be available for future efforts.[6] In this case, the church budgets for church planting in its annual budget and yet holds on to the funds until needed. This is a very simple example to demonstrate how a church can prioritize planning for a church plant even if an opportunity is not immediately available.

Although dedicated funds allow aggregating money for church planting from the operating budget over time, consider a word of caution. If a church holds money in a designated church planting fund for an excessively long time, aggregating increasing balances without deploying funds for church planting purposes, the church may miss the aim of this fund. These funds should support church planting. Simply holding on to these funds indefinitely could signal passivity or a lack of commitment rather than a lack of opportunity. There may be an opportunity within Pillar or other church planting networks, for example, to financially support another church plant in a different region of the world. Perhaps this potential church partner is limited in resources yet could benefit from prayer, encouragement, relationship, and funding from your church. Even if small amounts are given initially, progress happens.

If church-planting money sits in a dedicated fund for a long period of time, this may work against the vision cast for

---

[6] Churches may consider a high-yield savings account to hold these funds and earn interest yet be accessible for needs when they arise. Alternatively, internal bookkeeping may be employed to ensure the funds remain earmarked for future church-planting purposes.

church planting. Churches may miss the vast opportunities that exist across the globe. Elders should actively and regularly consider opportunities for church partnership. These opportunities will demonstrate to the congregation the commitment to church planting. Even if financial support is limited, actively seek partnerships where funds can be deployed for the advancement of Christ's kingdom through starting and strengthening healthy, gospel-preaching churches.

Church Planting Residencies

This section will not serve as an apologetic for church-planting residencies but rather will explain how residencies can serve as a mechanism to regularly invest in church planting.[7] A church may not yet be ready to plant because the right team is not in place, but opportunity to invest in church planting may still exist. Church planting residencies allow a potential church planter to gain practical experience in the operations and ministry of a healthy church under the leadership of gospel-minded elders. Residencies are often structured as one- or two-year periods where the planter serves full-time, part-time, or as a volunteer on staff at a church. He participates in the daily life of ministry and learns from pastors and staff how a healthy church functions. A residency provides practical, hands-on training for someone who may

---

[7] For more information on establishing residences, see Matt Rogers, *A Workman Approved: Developing Future Pastors in the Local Church and Seminary* (Nashville: Rainer Publishing, 2018); Phil A. Newton, *The Mentoring Church: How Pastors and Congregations Cultivate Leaders* (Grand Rapids: Kregel Ministry, 2017).

play a major role in planting another church. In the latter stages of the residency, the planter may prepare for a specific opportunity by developing a plan, assembling a team, and identifying funding for the plant.

To give a potential church planter the opportunity to invest his time to learn and prepare for ministry, a full-time or part-time salary may be necessary. This type of role is sometimes devalued by a church because a resident will not serve that specific church long-term. But the Great Commission–motivated church with a vision for church planting should not share that perspective. A residency invests time and money in church planting by raising up a future minister who can be sent. The church may only be able to afford a part-time, modest salary for a resident, but even a part-time salary may allow him to reduce outside commitments and allocate more hours to serve and learn in the church.

One useful piece of this residency could be helping the future planter learn to raise money. While some may resent having to raise money, I've found that the work of fundraising closely resembles casting vision for the church plant or even evangelizing the lost. The more we are comfortable communicating a compelling vision and asking for investment, the better prepared we will be to do so in every area of life. Matt Rogers, who authored several chapters in this book, has written a simple tool called *Funding Your Vision* that contains a play-by-play guide for raising support. It also has built-in spreadsheets for planters to keep track of their work.[8]

---

[8] Matt Rogers, *Funding Your Vision* (Pastor's Notes; Equipped to Grow, 2016).

Throughout The Pillar Network, pastors report the value of residencies in a variety of contexts. Residencies occur in large and small churches, established and new churches, and in diverse geographies across the globe. Another way for churches to support church planting is to financially contribute to another church's residency. In the network, some churches have given funds sacrificially to enable another church in a different context with limited financial resources to hire a church-planting resident. Stories abound of residents who have grown in their pastoral leadership, ecclesiological convictions, and ministry experience who then transitioned to lead a church plant or revitalization. If your church is not yet ready to start a residency, or if you have reached your capacity to manage in-house residencies and are seeking other opportunities to allocate funds, you may be able to help another church accomplish this important task.

Campaigns and One-Time Efforts

Campaigns and one-time fundraising efforts have been intentionally left to the end of this section. The reason for this is that regular allocation of budgeted funds to church planting prioritizes this mission, recognizes it as a core part of the local church's focus, and builds the discipline for sustainable financial commitment.[9] However, periodically, an unexpected opportunity may arise where a specific need exceeds budgeted resources. In this case, a campaign or one-time offering may be appropriate. Giving campaigns like the Annie

---

[9] For more information on why special campaigns present risk, see Dunlop, *Budgeting for a Healthy Church,* 111, 145.

Armstrong Easter Offering or the Lottie Moon Christmas offering have fueled the work of our denominational agencies for decades.

A time-bound campaign allows a church to intensely focus on funding a specific effort. In the past year, Pillar churches have given to support other network churches in ways ranging from contributing to a building purchase to gifting a trailer. This generosity reflects dependence on the Lord and a desire for his glory to spread to the ends of the earth. Sharing stories of God's providence and work through church planting—specifically from the generosity of your church—will fuel excitement for continued engagement in this Great Commission work. This leads to the next critical section of a feedback loop of creating sustainable and scalable church planting funding models within your congregation.

Sharing Stories of God's Work

After casting a compelling vision and giving funds to support church plants, the leaders' work remains incomplete. It is important to regularly share stories of God's work through church planting efforts with your congregation. Consider Philippians 4 as Paul shares with the church at Philippi his personal gratitude for the congregation's sacrificial support of his ministry. Their giving enabled Paul to continue his work in the early church in a season of distress. Paul pointed out the benefit as not only his financial support but also God's provision for the church's needs (Phil. 4:14–19). Individuals and churches give not because God needs their money; everything in heaven and on earth already belongs to Him. Instead, our giving demonstrates joy and dependence on him;

it should all be counted as a privilege (1 Chron. 29:11–17). This was the motivation of the churches of Macedonia and Philippi who gave to support the church at Jerusalem and Paul, even when they had little to give. God used their giving for gospel work, and Paul wanted the supporting churches to know this.

Pastors in Pillar churches often reinforce the vision for church planting and the results of giving to church planting by regularly sharing stories with the congregation. These may include an update on a church plant partner in a members' meeting, a video from another pastor to be shared in a service or newsletter, or even a visit from pastors or members from the partner church plant. These stories and regular updates demonstrate to the congregation the real impact of a commitment to church planting. Planting partnerships involve real people in real churches who can be known, loved, and encouraged by their sending church.

Sharing these stories fuel a greater zeal for church planting and foster enthusiasm for giving toward that mission. This continues a cycle as shown below:

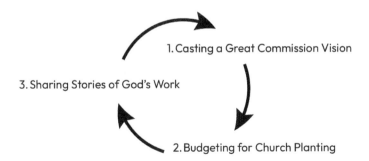

1. Casting a Great Commission Vision
2. Budgeting for Church Planting
3. Sharing Stories of God's Work

Framework for Sustainable Sending Church Communication

This image depicts how casting a Great Commission vision for church planting leads a church to gladly and generously give as part of its ongoing commitment to this mission. Sharing stories of how partnering church plants experience God's kindness rightly excites the congregation to embrace the vision even more tightly—and the cycle continues. This does not happen by chance; it requires intentionality and communication from leaders who want to guide the congregation toward sustainable commitment to start and strengthen other churches.

A Final Word About Sustainable and Scalable Financial Models

As a church seeks to implement financial structures to support church planting, the church should carefully consider how these structures contribute to a sustainable model of commitment. Although adjustments and modifications to any financial plan are expected, leaders wisely lead their congregation to give in a way that prioritizes church planting for the long haul. If the operating budget is tight, this may require starting with a small financial commitment to a partnering church plant. It may include a reevaluation of the budget to determine what can be trimmed to allow the church to hire a church planting resident. The church that is blessed with excess resources may be able to pursue a number of these tactics simultaneously. Regardless, each church should consider what can be sustained on a long-term basis. But they don't need to wait for the seemingly perfect time.

Starting sooner and smaller is often better than waiting indefinitely.

Scalability also matters, though it will look different for each church. Your church may start with budgeting to support a single church plant. Over time, as the Lord blesses and as resources grow, your church may be able to increase funding to that church plant or begin supporting a second plant. Because the vision for each church plant is ultimately to become self-sustaining, support for a specific church plant may decrease over time, freeing up funds that can be redeployed to another planting effort. Each year during the budget process, consider how even modest increases of the budget in dollars or percentages can be allocated to support these Great Commission efforts. In challenging financial seasons, be careful about the complete removal of giving toward church planting. As Paul exclaimed to the Philippian church considering their faithful and sacrificial giving, God will supply all their needs "according to His riches in glory in Christ Jesus" (Phil. 4:19). This is not a license for irresponsibility but rather a recognition that God is the sustainer of His people.

Jesus gave the Great Commission with a clear vision of church multiplication. He calls His church to prioritize this mission to plant healthy churches all around the world. This call includes stewardship of finances and giving generously to support the growth of Christ's church. Each healthy church should recognize that all they have comes from the Lord. So we submit to His vision for the expansion of His kingdom and the building of His church. This recognition and submission will lead churches to give generously to gospel work. It involves the entire congregation through regular communication and engagement with church planting partners. Finally, a commitment to sustainable and scalable funding models exercises a mission-oriented stewardship that enables a local church to contribute to the spread of the gospel across the globe.

CHAPTER 12

WHAT NON-BIBLICAL DETAILS ARE ESSENTIAL TO CHURCH PLANTING?

Phil A. Newton

You've felt a deep burden to plant a church. By God's grace, you are part of a healthy sending church that has trained, honed, and prepared you to pastor a new church. Slowly, you build a team that will join you in using their gifts, offering their prayers and time, and gathering to prepare for the first Sunday. You host Bible studies and team meetings in which you discuss the gospel and ecclesiology. You seek to identify gifts of team members. Alongside potential elders, you study the area where you plan to launch the church. You get to know its twists and turns, meet people from the community, and frequent local businesses to get to know your future neighbors. You pray and plead for the Lord to enable you and your team to reach people with the gospel.

You look for a meeting place that will serve your goals and accommodate your ministry. With trepidation and excitement, you make the first phone call to a potential landlord to rent space. The landlord has questions about money and what you will be doing in his property. Who will be paying the rent? Will it come out of the church planter's pocket? Are there funds budgeted to cover the expense? Does the church have a bank account? Can you prove this organization is really a 501(c)(3) religious, tax-exempt organization? Does the church have insurance to cover any damages? Does the church have documents to assure the landlord of who the congregation is, what they believe, and how they will function? Are there officers legally established to take care of financial matters? These questions may seem inconsequential, but they are essential for our subject in Part 3.

Though it's not glamorous, legal, organizational, financial, and structural details must be part of the planning before the church begins.[1] We're no longer in the Wild West where a cowboy church planter can round up a few people on his circuit ride every four weeks. We live in nations governed by laws meant to prevent abuse and fraud while maintaining peace in the community. Not all countries hold the same views for the establishment of churches.[2] Some coun-

---

[1] I'm grateful for Matt Rogers offering good insights on the processes discussed in this chapter. Without his expertise, I'm afraid this chapter would be deficient.

[2] This chapter will focus on church planting legalities in the U.S. After communicating with some pastors outside the U.S., I realized attempting to footnote (my original desire) the variety of legal necessities in other countries would become unwieldy. Nevertheless, I hope the outline of

tries do not recognize gospel-proclaiming churches. But for those planting churches where it's legal, knowing the landscape and abiding by it upfront will save a lot of headaches, money, and red tape.

This chapter seeks to identify some important details and legal structures necessary to establish a new church.[3] I will utilize footnotes to point to further research on various topics. Where do we begin? In the spirit of Romans 13:1–7, we're attempting to establish an outline that will serve as a checklist to make sure your church is *legal.*

Statement of Faith

Before starting the legal and structural details, work to adopt a statement of faith. Your theological beliefs will identify you and biblically anchor you to the historic Christian faith. A statement of faith identifies what you believe the Bible teaches about ecclesiology, worship, the ordinances, salvation,

---

details may serve as a reference point if you're outside the U.S. If your church is part of a national denomination, they may aid with your country's details. With networks, associations, and partnerships in nations where evangelical churches exist, there should be a good collective of information that will assist in church plants following legal regulations.

[3] Caveat: this chapter does not claim total familiarity or authority with your country, state, or community laws, nor does it substitute for an experienced attorney familiar with non-profit organizations, nor does it offer legal counsel. It attempts to offer suggested guidance for church planters to take care of legal and structural details. The authors and publisher do not warrant this chapter's counsel to comply with every law or code in your context. We recommend checking with local, state, and national authorities regarding matters of incorporation, tax-exemption, non-profit compliance, and other regulations affecting Christian churches.

mission, and other theological issues. It should be comprehensive, but concise. It's easily located on the church's website and available to all seeking membership. For a Christian church, doctrine matters. These doctrinal statements should include the biblical foundation for each declaration.

Nate Akin helpfully explains, "Confessions are statements of belief that guide biblical interpretation for cooperation and identity. They serve as a way for us to say to a confused world, 'This is what we believe.'"[4] Sending churches may offer guidance in choosing a doctrinal statement for the church plant. They will recommend a faithful confessional statement that has its moorings in historic Baptist confessions.[5] Akin offers three rationales for using Baptist confessions to ensure we have robust doctrinal convictions: "First, confessions are used to express our unity with broader, historical Christianity. . . . Second, confessions express our uniqueness or distinctives as Baptists, which particularly relate to our ecclesiological convictions. . . . Third, confessions act as a rallying point for cooperation and missions that seek to combat heresy, error, apathy, and pragmatism."[6]

---

[4] Nate Akin, *Convictional, Confessional, Cheerful Baptists* (Greenville, SC: Courier Publishing, 2024), 29.

[5] It's obvious that this chapter and the book focus especially on Baptists. If you're from another Christian tradition, then be sure your confession of faith is historically rooted. The language may be updated but the doctrine needs historic anchors.

[6] See Akin, *Convictional*, 35–43 for the full explanation.

It's generally wise for new churches to align with an historic statement of faith.[7] This anchors the new church in the long stream of biblical orthodoxy. In addition to an older statement of faith, many churches also identify with more recent biblical statements concerning pressing issues of our day They include *The Chicago Statement on Biblical Inerrancy*, *The Danvers Statement on Biblical Manhood and Womanhood*, and *The Nashville Statement* on biblical sexuality.[8] Older confessions don't address these issues that are under attack today.

Articles of Incorporation

The sending church should carve out ample time with the planter to work through legal and structural documents *before* the core team holds the constituting service. These include a statement of faith, articles of incorporation, the constitution, and the by-laws.

Just the term *Articles of Incorporation* may take your breath away. Having gone through this process, however, I can attest that it's not as difficult as it sounds. Articles of incorporation give the new church a legal identity as a church and state the distinct purpose and various responsibilities within the organization. This formal document will be filed with your state. With it, you'll be able to buy property, work

---

[7] The most frequently used were *The Baptist Faith & Message 2000*, *The New Hampshire Confession of Faith* (1853); *The Second London Baptist Confession* (1689), and *The Abstract of Principles* (1858), not necessarily in that order.

[8] See the following links to read these statements: https://www.thegospelcoalition.org/themelios/article/the-chicago-statement-on-biblical-inerrancy/; https://cbmw.org/about/the-danvers-statement/; https://cbmw.org/the-nashville-statement/.

with contractors, set up accounts with business vendors, open a bank account, and be recognized as a legal entity by the Internal Revenue Service (IRS). The articles have nothing to do with preaching or evangelism, but they are still important. To get this document, you will need an attorney familiar with incorporation and tax-exempt organizations, even if he or she holds different theological convictions.[9]

Who?

What will be your church's name? That's not an easy question. Here are a few things to consider:

- Choose a name that's recognizable. I don't mean something like *The Church of Jesus Christ who Alone Saves Sinners by Grace through His Imputed Righteousness*. While true, it's a bit cumbersome. I would opt for a name that is memorable and recognizable, and not too odd.

- You may choose a name that identifies your church's location. But you probably only want to do that if you know your location won't change. You may choose a name that expresses your purpose or explains your values. You may choose a name with biblical language. Be careful about that. If the church name is difficult to

---

[9] Not to advertise any group, but I did check with an online legal service website. They offer help for nonprofits, but for a fee, of course. Unless your sending church, or perhaps a team member, has an attorney who would like to help, you'll be helped by hiring an attorney so that you don't miss any details. Our sending church had an active layman who took care of this *gratis*.

pronounce or understand, then it might be a hindrance in the early stages.

- See if the name you've chosen is taken by a neighboring church. It can be confusing if you have multiple *Hope* churches in the same community. Also, make sure the name you're considering doesn't have negative connotations nationally.[10]

- Consider the prudence of your church name identifying with a denomination. A trend started several decades ago for church plants to obscure any reference to a denomination with their name. But there seems to be a growing perception that openly identifying with a denomination might prove beneficial. After all, you don't want inquirers guessing if your church belongs to a denomination. Those looking for a church might wonder what the church is hiding by not including their affiliation in the church's name. Theological clarity is valuable. It seems prudent to me to clarify your stance on issues related to baptism and governance by including a denominational marker in your church's name.

- When the church I planted prepared to incorporate, we let core team members suggest names, sifted out some that wouldn't work, and then let the church vote.

Another "who" question in your Articles of Incorporation will be names of the church's initial leadership structure

---

[10] I'm thinking about the Westboro Baptist Church that has been in the news during political seasons.

including elders, deacons, and potential trustees. It's best if you can begin with an initial team of elders, but if not, you will need a few people to serve as a board of directors or trustees for legal purposes. The Secretary of State will accept your application for incorporation along with the appropriate fee. While the church core team or the sending church can appoint and vote on the legal purposes group, I'd recommend that the initial church plant members vote on elder candidates.[11] Once you're incorporated, you will need to file for an Employee Identification Number (EIN) with the Internal Revenue Service.[12]

What?

This is your *legal* purpose statement. Remember, articles of incorporation are not the same as your by-laws and constitution, so you need not overdo it. This isn't the catchy statement you'll have on your church's website. For instance, your purpose statement might be something like: *Oak Street Baptist Church exists in the historic tradition of the Christian Church, to confess belief in the historic confessions and creeds of the Christian Church and Southern Baptist Convention, to teach and to learn the doctrines of the Bible, to disciple mem-*

---

[11] It's recommended, if possible, that the sending church send one or two elders or elder-qualified men to be part of the church plant. In such case, the sending church's elders along with the planting pastor (assuming he's an elder in the sending church) can examine and recommend to the core team the initial elder team. The core team can then approve these men in the constituting service or initial members' meeting.

[12] Apply online at: https://www.irs.gov/businesses/small-businesses-self-employed/get-an-employer-identification-number.

bers, to build fellowship, and to carry on the mission of Jesus
Christ's kingdom. Legal entities want to know that you are a
genuinely religious organization with clearly identified religious purposes.

Where?

Where will you receive correspondence from legal entities?
Even if you'll be moving to different locations for meeting
space, you still need to provide a permanent address to receive correspondence. You can always change the address later but start with a post office box or the sending church's address if it's convenient. I'd caution against putting the church
planter's address as the permanent address.

Why?

Articles of incorporation in the state where the church exists provide the beachhead to secure tax-exempt status.
While churches technically fall under U.S. code as tax exempt, the assumption of non-profit status as a church and
the legal standing as a non-profit organization according to
IRS guidelines may not be clear without the 501(c)(3) document. Tax free contributions may be challenged without the
official 501(c)(3) non-profit status, so it's best to have this
legal designation from the outset.[13] Some states require legal
documentation or registration before the planter can solicit
donations.[14]

---

[13] See https://www.501c3.org/does-a-church-need-501c3-status/.

[14] See https://www.501c3.org/501c3-services/charitable-solicitations-regis-

Southern Baptist Convention churches fall under the Convention's 501(c)(3) tax exemption status covering all SBC churches. Therefore, if you're an SBC church, you do not need to go through the 501(c)(3) application. But the Convention recommends that churches request a copy of the *blanket* 501(c)(3) status from the SBC Executive Committee in case other organizations, like banks, require the paperwork.[15] The new church plant is technically under the sending church's exemption status until they constitute. If necessary, in official paperwork, the church plant can use the legalese-sounding "Doing Business As XYZ Church" under the sending church's name (DBA church plant's name) until they hold the exemption status.

If the church plant needs to secure property or execute contracts, they will have a legal right to do so once they have the Secretary of State's incorporation document and the 501(c)(3) certificate. Otherwise, the company, individual, or vendor they're seeking to do business with as tax exempt may be put at risk. Plus, from a practical standpoint, it keeps the church plant from appearing to be a shady organization trying to avoid legal standing. Having the Employee Identi-

---

tration-2/ for more information, as this site identified 40 states that require 501(c)(3) non-profit organizations to register prior to receiving donations.

[15] The SBC FAQs explains: "Churches that choose to cooperate directly with the SBC are covered by the SBC group exemption and may request a copy of the Convention's group exemption letter once they have completed a credentialing process through the SBC Executive Committee and are identified as a cooperating church with the Convention." See https://www.sbc.net/about/becoming-a-southern-baptist-church/faq/.

fication Number (EIN) will be necessary for payroll, so apply for it at the IRS website.

Constitution and By-Laws

A church's constitution and by-laws clarify its purpose, governance, mission, membership process and expectations, titles and responsibilities of officers, process for selecting governing offices, and authority held by the officers and congregation. These documents provide a legally binding agreement that states how the congregation and its officer's function. They give both the congregation and its leaders tracks to run on that guard against authoritarianism, confusion, and costly decisions. They safeguard the church if any legal issues arise. The initial constitution and by-laws can be simple, as these documents will likely be amended in the church's first 10–20 years. For this reason, consult churches less than 5–10 years old as you write your own.

Constitution

The constitution should include the church's statement of faith, providing biblical anchors for its understanding of what the church is, who can be part of it, and how it conducts its mission. Constitutions give a blanket sweep through biblical ecclesiology, explaining how the church will function and how its members relate to one another. The details come later in the statement of faith and by-laws. The constitution may be a good place to identify ministry philosophy and the church's affiliations. It also establishes lines of authority for decision making, even though more details will be found in the by-laws.[16]

By-laws fill in the details the constitution introduces. By-laws define processes for membership, discipline, and restoration; processes for calling pastors and appointing elders and deacons; responsibilities of officers; removal of officers; members' meetings and the extent of congregational authority; and a statement of indemnification. The church will discover other areas that will need to be amended to the by-laws. Don't attempt to write the end-all document since you know it can be changed. Instead, keep to the essentials that you know you're happy to live with for a while.

Church historian Greg Wills notes that Baptists have long believed that "correct polity fostered true spirituality." He further explained, concerning 18th and 19th century Baptists, "Correct polity protected orthodox belief . . . promoted discipleship . . . and was foundational to evangelism. . . . They held that church polity was an intrinsic part of Christianity."[17] The by-laws should seek to be comprehensive, but that

---

[16] Jonathan Leeman has served churches well in his thoughtful books addressing congregationalism and authority: *Don't Fire Your Church Members: The Case for Congregationalism* (Nashville: B&H Academic, 2016) and *Authority: How Godly Rule Protects the Vulnerable, Strengthens Communities, and Promotes Human Flourishing* (9Marks; Wheaton, IL: Crossway, 2023). I've found that like-minded churches are generous in sending links to their polity documents to help fill gaps in how you should proceed. See also Benjamin L. Merkle, *Authority in the Church: Exploring the Roles of Congregation, Elders, and Deacons* (Nashville: B&H Academic, forthcoming in 2026). Ben Merkle's book will be an enormous help as you spell out details for church officers in by-laws.

[17] Greg Wills, "The Church: Baptists and Their Churches in the Eighteenth

doesn't mean every detail must be imagined. Think broad categories with shallow dives into most areas (elder and deacon responsibilities, pastor's duties) and deep dives into a few areas (membership, discipline). The congregation and leaders do not need to be boxed into restrictive frameworks since there's no way to know which decisions or actions will need to be made. Neither should they be given free rein over their areas of responsibility. Find a good balance.

For instance, the by-laws may spell out regular duties for a pastor to maintain a godly personal and family life; shepherd the congregation; preach and teach God's Word; equip, mentor, and disciple members; provide leadership; oversee staff; and participate in associations with like-minded pastors and churches. That covers a lot of ground without narrowly identifying how each area must be done.

Additionally, many churches add a child protection policy in the by-laws explaining the congregation's position to safeguard children and volunteers who work with children in the church's gatherings. This policy should list qualifications for who can serve with children, the process for screening workers, limitations on how workers interact with children, and processes for anything that veers from these standards, including what to do when suspicion of inappropriate behavior arises.[18]

---

and Nineteenth Centuries," in Mark Dever, ed., *Polity: Biblical Arguments on How to Conduct Church Life* (Washington, DC: Center for Church Reform, 2001), 19–20. A new, expanded edition of this book is forthcoming.

[18] Reading Deepak Reju, *On Guard: Preventing and Responding to Child Abuse at Church* (Greensboro, NC: NewGrowth Press, 2014) is a must when preparing the church's statement.

Church Covenant

A church covenant puts into clear, concise language what the corporate body expects of its members. The church covenant encourages holiness by setting forth the corporate body's responsibility to live holy lives and the church's responsibility to exercise formative and corrective discipline.[19]

The church planter and other core leaders, with guidance from the sending church, should develop the church covenant. Remember: this document states what typifies Christian practice in this particular church. It should be broad enough to cover personal, family, church, business, and community life without slipping into legalism. It should guard against narrow restrictions which are not clearly stated in Scripture.

I've found that asking potential members to agree with and sign the church covenant helps to reinforce the seriousness of church membership.[20] A pastor can be fairly assured that if church members lack clarity on what's expected of them as members of the church, they will underperform—not intentionally but due to a misunderstanding of what membership means. Additionally, those with a low view of membership often resist efforts to implement corrective church discipline. Reading the church covenant together at

---

[19] See Jonathan Leeman, *Church Discipline: How the Church Protects the Name of Jesus* (9Marks Building Healthy Church Series; Wheaton, IL: Crossway, 2012).

[20] See Brandon Langley, *Devoted Together: How to Find and Join a Church* (Greenville, SC: Courier Publishing, 2025) for a helpful discussion on church membership, as well as a guideline for training new members.

members' meetings or during the observance of the Lord's Supper will reinforce the serious nature of church membership.[21]

As Greg Wills reflected on 18th and 19th century Baptists, he noted, "When persons joined a Baptist church, they subscribed to its covenant, which summarized Christ's commission to the churches. In it they declared that they intended together to be a church of Christ. . . . Church membership meant pledging to be a church of Christ according to his rules."[22] Since each community has a unique context, pastors and elders can strive to develop a church covenant particular to their congregation, even while they'll likely borrow substance and phrases from other church covenants—historic and present day.

Details for the New Church

About five years after planting a church in Memphis, a seminary student who helped lead worship and work with students asked a simple question, "What's the most important word you would say for church planting?" I didn't hesitate, "Details." Having previously pastored three established churches, I had walked into settings where others handled details to get the church off the ground and running. I still

---

[21] See Jonathan Leeman, *Church Membership: How the World Knows Who Represents Jesus* (9Marks Building Healthy Churches series; Wheaton, IL: Crossway, 2012).

[22] Wills, "The Church," 23. See an early 19th century explanation of "The Duties of Members Towards Each Other," in Samuel Jones, "Treatise of Church Discipline (1805)," in Dever, *Polity*, 150–51, for an outline that can help shape a church's covenant.

paid attention to details but did not need to deal with legal matters or establish structures or write a constitution and by-laws.

Not so when I planted a church. I wasn't aware of how many details I missed in the first few years of the church's existence. Yet I discovered much later, how you begin sets a trajectory for years to follow. That's why we encourage sending churches to teach church planters the full range of local church life, including the not-so-glamorous matters addressed in this chapter. Attending these details before the constituting service will allow the pastors to focus on more important matters.

To help with this process of attention to details, I'll offer a checklist with an occasional comment.

- Choose a legal name for the church.

- Read the available historic confessions of faith. Choose one and add any additional clarifying statements to address contemporary moral and ethical issues.[23]

- Develop the Articles of Incorporation, consulting with an attorney in the process.

- Register with your Secretary of State as an incorporated non-profit religious entity. The attorney can help with this initial process. You will need to renew yearly with the Secretary of State.

---

[23] At this point, church planters often, with guidance from their sending church, initiate application for membership to The Pillar Network. See www.thepillarnetwork.com/join.

- Develop a constitution and by-laws. Make sure there is a statement of indemnification to protect members and officers. Include the statement of faith in the constitution.

- File for 501(c)(3) non-profit status.[24] If you're a Southern Baptist Convention church plant, then contact the SBC Executive Committee about the process to receive the blanket 501(c)(3) certificate held in trust by the Convention for all SBC churches. With this certificate, you will not need to do a separate 501(c)(3) application with the IRS.

- Apply online for an Employer Identification Number (EIN). You'll need this for payroll and other financial matters.

- Upon constituting, become part of the Southern Baptist Convention through the local association, state convention, or the credentialing process through the SBC Executive Committee.[25]

- If you're an SBC church, contact LifeWay for your unique SBC ID number. This seven-digit number is assigned by LifeWay Christian Resources for all "co-operating churches." It will be necessary to have this

---

[24] See: https://www.irs.gov/charities-non-profits/how-to-apply-for-501c3-status.

[25] See https://www.sbc.net/about/becoming-a-southern-baptist-church/faq/.

number when your church registers messengers for the annual meeting each June.[26]

- Open a bank account. For financial transparency, require two signatures for all checks. The church planter should have someone else handling the banking. Appointing a treasurer early on will be critical.

- Establish a budget.[27]

- Keep good records. Appoint a church clerk for this process.

- Develop and immediately implement (upon congregational approval) a child protection policy to ensure the safety of children in the church before the first service (see Deepak Reju's *On Guard*). Explain this policy in every new members' class. Develop a summary document of these standards that you can make available to those bringing children into the church's care. These standards must give information on the vetting process for those who serve in the children's area and define what can be expected of workers.

- Make sure you have appropriate insurance: tenant, liability for the church, liability for pastors, employee health, abuse and molestation, theft and vandalism.[28]

---

[26] See https://www.sbc.net/about/becoming-a-southern-baptist-church/faq/.

[27] See Jamie Dunlop, *Budgeting for a Healthy Church: Aligning Finances with Biblical Priorities for Ministry* (9Marks; Grand Rapids: Zondervan, 2019) for a very helpful guide. Nathan Baumgartner's helpful chapter on church finances provides an excellent overview.

[28] I found the following blogpost helpful in detailing insurance issues. It's

- Implement the membership process stated in the by-laws.

- Find a meeting place. You may have already worked on this before working on some of the other details. Here are ten considerations:

  1. Understand how your ministry will use your space.

  2. Know you can get a Certificate of Occupancy.

  3. Don't forget about fire sprinklers. Will they be required for a church meeting in the space? Will you have to pay to provide them?

  4. Create some margin in your budget.

  5. A seven-day-a-week building may not be the answer.

  6. Keep good financial records.

  7. Make sure the pastor does *not* co-sign or guarantee a lease.

  8. Know whether the lease rate is monthly or annual.

---

from an insurance company but please understand that I'm not advertising for them, nor do I know them. But their information will be good to know in planning for insurance needs: churchpropertyinsurance.com/blog/2023/01/how-to-start-a-church-plant/. Meanwhile, find your own local insurance agents whom you can trust with these details. You may not need all the types of insurance noted above. Check with other churches in your region to find out which companies service them, and if they've had a claim, how the company responded. Rates are often competitive, so shop around but choose a highly rated company. Also, make sure to have adequate liability insurance in today's litigious society.

9. Know what type of lease you are signing.[29]
10. The leasing agent you call about the property represents the Landlord.[30]

While any church planter worth his salt wants to dive into the work, he must pay attention to details. Some of the details aren't very exciting but are certainly necessary. Some dear brothers may say they don't like or want to do anything that involves administrative details. Like it or not, you must take care of these legal and structural details. The longevity, health, and effectiveness of the new church's ministry often depend on a good start. Here is another place our denomination can help us. Many state conventions have staff who are trained to help new pastors develop these documents and they know the rules in their state. We'd be wise to use their help. Deal with details from the early days of planning, assign responsibilities for core team members, and build a comprehensive checklist of what needs to be done. When these details are considered, the church plant will be able to give far more time to preaching, teaching, worshiping, discipling, evangelizing, and fellowshipping down the road.

---

[29] These include *gross leases* in which the landlord covers most of the building's operating expenses; *net leases* put some of the operating expenses on the tenant; *variable leases* make some adjustments on raising or lowering rental costs.

[30] This article goes into more details, so do check it out: "Top Ten things to Know When Finding a Facility for Your Church Plant." https://www.newchurches.com/resources/.

CHAPTER 13

HOW MIGHT ASSOCIATIONS FOSTER COLLABORATIVE PLANTING?

Liam Garvie

Jack Johnson is no theologian. But as his mellow voice drifted out of the Marshall speaker and across the sun-soaked Italian patio, the refrain struck me: "It's always better when we're together." You probably know it. It's a laid-back love song about how companionship betters lonely pursuits, and shared experiences make even small, everyday things more enjoyable.

As Johnson's subtle instrumental left room for the lyrics to sink in, I looked across that patio at my wife engrossed in her book, my two oldest kids rowdily playing Monopoly, and my youngest chasing lizards, "Better Together" drew out from me a very contented wee amen.

But very quickly, I started thinking about how the sentiment holds for churches, too. A flurry of churches that belong to The Pillar Network came to mind. These were *Baptist* churches—churches that cheerfully maintained a strong conviction regarding the independent autonomy of the local church and other baptistic ecclesiological distinctives. Yet these were *partnering* churches, churches that actively sought to do more for God and for the gospel than they could manage on their own through collaboration with each other. My mind lit up like a flight radar, tracing a line from a church in Colombia to a church plant in Cameroon, one that was planted by a separate church in the United Arab Emirates. By associating through The Pillar Network, these churches connected and collaborated in ways that bore fruit on the ground.

It's in this sense that "Better Together" isn't just a lyric, it's a conviction, a conviction among Baptists who see in Scripture, history, and practice that associating for the sake of Christ's Kingdom is not merely aspirational, but crucial for the spread of the gospel across the world.

Is it really though? Some of you are humming along already. But some are only hearing fret squeaks and feedback! So let me adjust the levels. I want you to hear this.

Some of you are getting *theological feedback*. You think I'm overstating the case. You're thinking, "Churches can plant churches on their own. It is entirely possible to do that without any associational partnership at all. Thousands have and thousands will." I hear you, and I agree. Churches can plant churches on their own. That's our strong conviction. But independence doesn't equal isolation! Indeed, as Stephen Wellum reminds us, "There is a New Testament precedent for churches working together to advance the gospel."[1] We'll get to that in a second.

Others are getting *experiential feedback*. Past experience yells, "Don't do it! It wasn't a great success. It slowed things down and sucked the life out of your church's planting ambitions." That happens. Maybe collaboration cost you more than it delivered—on that occasion. But don't be deterred! For others, it's "present experience" that puts them off. You're probably thinking, "I don't have the calendar space or the head space for partnership meetings or associations." Listen, "Cooperation among churches is not optional for gospel faithfulness. . . . If we love Christ's kingdom, we will help others establish more gospel-preaching outposts—other churches—where Christ is rightly known and worshipped."[2]

That's why, despite the low-grade feedback, it really is "better when we're together." Let me show you that by starting with some biblical examples of partnership. After that, we'll trace how the instinct for cooperation for Christ's sake became part and parcel of what it means to be Baptist. From there, we'll explore practical ways churches associate together for the gospel so that we can wrap up this part on implementing a church plant by showing how churches can do that work together.

---

[1] Stephen Wellum, Lecture on Ecclesiology, Southern Seminary, 2019 (class notes).

[2] Mark Dever, *A Display of God's Glory* (Washington, DC: 9Marks, 2001), 53.

Churches Collaborating in Scripture

The New Testament doesn't give us a single text on church-to-church partnership. There's no, "For I received from the Lord what I also passed on to you" on collaboration and association. But there's plenty of evidence that churches in the New Testament collaborated, resourcing and strengthening the cause of Christ together. Let me give you just two examples, one church-to-church and one church-to-church-planter.

Jerusalem and Antioch

When news that a church had been planted in Antioch among the Greeks reached the church in Jerusalem (Acts 11:19–21), they rejoiced. But they also wanted to do something. They demonstrated an instinct to partner by sending Barnabas to encourage the believers and strengthen the work (Acts 11:22). He did, and together with Paul whom he recruited, taught great numbers and saw the church grow.[3] You know what happened next! God used Antioch as a launchpad for missions, for the making and maturing of disciples and the planting of churches in cities and regions beyond the reach of the members there. And the Jerusalem church was every bit part of that through their gospel partnership.

But the relationship wasn't one-sided. Later, when news of famine-induced hardship experienced by churches in Judea reached Antioch, the church in Antioch demonstrated

---

[3] Luke uses the word *church* (*ekklēsia*) in Act 11:26 to describe the community of Christians in Antioch. Luke has not used the word church (ekklēsia) since Acts 9:31 (cf. 13:1; 14:27).

the same instinct. They sent financial relief (Acts 11:27–30). Their aim wasn't just to sustain the lives of the believers in the church in Jerusalem, but to sustain the spreading of the Word of God in that region. Later still, when doctrinal distortions created confusion around what a person needs to do to be saved, the church in Antioch appointed Paul and Barnabas to visit the apostles and elders about this issue (Acts 15:1–5). The representative churches agreed on their shared gospel convictions and clarified the mission of the churches represented.

That's a scant summary, but do you see what I see? In this one example of church-to-church partnership, we see a mutual concern for the strengthening of gospel churches that not only serve as cities on their respective hills, but as launchpads for the planting of gospel churches. Partnership is neither paternalistic nor denominational. It's relational, mutual, and focused on maintaining theological clarity and missional ambition.

Philippi and Paul

Collaboration for the gospel isn't just for existing churches. It's for the churches that we want to see brought into existence. That's the kind of collaboration you see between the church in Philippi and the Apostle Paul. Paul's letter to the Philippians is one big thank you letter for ten years of gospel partnership (Phil. 1:5). They've sent finances (Phil. 4:18) and a friend (Phil. 2:25) to underline their love for Paul and their commitment to help him start and strengthen churches all over Europe.

Fly through Philippians and you discover quickly what resulted, by God's grace, from their partnership: churches were planted, leaders were trained, and funds were raised. Even while in chains, Paul testifies that the Philippian church's gifts served to advance the gospel in Rome, including to the palace guard and people throughout Rome (Phil. 1:12–14). And who can measure what fruit came from the quilling of the letters to the Ephesian, Colossian, and Philippian churches? Do you think they regretted collaborating with Paul? Not on your life!

Note one more thing about the collaboration of Paul and the church at Philippi. Gospel partnership doesn't just catalyze the spread of the gospel; it creates deep affection between partners. To share in God's work is to share a great bond. You hear it in Paul's voice, don't you? He has them in his heart (Phil. 1:7) and loves them with the very affection of Christ (Phil. 1:8). The feeling is mutual, hence the gifts. Such affection is so central to gospel partnership that he informs them of his prayers for them—that their love would keep on growing in discernment, with gospel-shaped priorities (Phil. 1:9–11), that it might demonstrate once more that collaborating for the cause of Christ in the New Testament isn't merely transactional, but relational. It involves the hands *and* the heart, which is another reason why it's better when we're together.

Do you see? Though there's no explicit passage on collaboration in the New Testament, it's there. Independent churches enjoyed interdependent partnerships. Churches prayed, sent pastors, gave money, encouraged one another, clarified doctrine, stood side by side in suffering, and linked arms to take the gospel to unreached places. As a result, disciples were made, churches were planted, and existing churches were strengthened. Churches voluntarily collaborating can do more together than they could ever achieve alone.

Churches Collaborating in Baptist History

The instinct for cooperation wasn't just for Bible times. It's an historic instinct in Baptist churches, too. As John Hammett writes, "Baptists, from the earliest days of their history, have evidenced an associational impulse."[4] They recognized that while local churches are fully autonomous, they are also joyfully interdependent when it comes to advancing the gospel. Across centuries, this impulse has been expressed in three primary ways: confessions, associations, and missions.

Confessions

Two of the earliest and clearest signals of this instinct are found in the First London Confession (1644) and the Second London Confession of Faith (1677, republished in 1689). Each version neatly compresses vital doctrines that we cheerfully uphold and fiercely defend, such as the doctrines of grace and the nature of the church.[5] But we sometimes forget that "the First London Confession of 1644 urged local churches to *associate* with other like-minded churches 'as members of one body in the common faith un-

---

[4] John. S. Hammett, *Biblical Foundations for Baptist Churches: A Contemporary Ecclesiology* (Grand Rapids: Kregel Academic, 2005), 143.

[5] Stephen J. Wellum, *Systematic Theology: From Canon to Concept*, vol. 1 of Systematic Theology (Brentwood, TN: B&H Academic, 2024), 520.

der Christ their only head.'"[6] In other words, local churches collaborated in ways that gave expression to their unity without surrendering their autonomy. Back then, local churches were associated through their doctrinal alignment and their shared mission. That continues today. The associational impulse is written into the Baptist Faith and Message 2000: "Christ's people should as occasion requires organize such associations and conventions as may best secure cooperation for the great objects of the Kingdom of God. . . . Members of New Testament churches should cooperate with one another in carrying forward the missionary, educational, and benevolent ministries for the extension of Christ's Kingdom."[7] In other words, from 1644 to 2000 to today, the principle remains: we happily and voluntarily partner to spread the news about Christ.

Associations

Churches can collaborate *informally*. Association doesn't *need* to be formal. How many of us know the joy of gospel partnership with like-minded pastors who are dear friends? The Pillar Network was born out of such friendship.[8] Throughout Baptist history, such friendships have been the seedbed of ambitious and effective gospel endeavors. Tom Nettles writes, "Fuller, Sutcliff, Pearce, Carey, and

---

[6] Hammett, *Biblical Foundation*, 144, italics mine.

[7] Baptist Faith and Message 2000 (Nashville: Southern Baptist Convention, 2000), Article XIV.

[8] To hear the origin story of the Pillar Network, listen to episode 2 of this Podcast - https://pillar.squarespace.com/pillar-articles/ep2.

Ryland exemplified a God-centered vision for missions that was sustained by cooperative pastoral friendship and ecclesial partnership."[9] Baptist historian Michael Haykin agrees, "Church history teaches us that the most fruitful efforts in evangelism . . . were the result of deep friendships and intentional collaboration among churches. Not hierarchical control, but mutual commitment for the sake of Christ's name among the nations."[10]

But as is often the case, friendships formalize when they widen and more churches agree with the vision to do more together and want to link arms. *Formal* associations provide a structure that sustains and multiplies gospel collaboration. In England, as the Particular Baptist movement grew, they formed associations even before they penned their Confession.[11] The same was true for Scotland into the 1800s. Christopher Anderson, who planted Charlotte Chapel in Edinburgh, wrote that "churches sought communion with one another, not as an act of necessity but of love, and that love expressed itself in mutual labour for the kingdom."[12]

---

[9] Tom Nettles, *The Baptists: Key People Involved in Forming a Baptist Identity*, Vol. 2 (Fearn: Mentor, 2005), 222.

[10] Michael A. G. Haykin, *Rediscovering the Church Fathers*, (Wheaton: Crossway, 2011), 121.

[11] By 1651, thirty General Baptist churches in the Midlands region of England had formed an association. They produced a confession called "The Faith and Practice of Thirty Congregations, Gathered According to the Primitive Pattern," quoted in Hammett, *Biblical Foundations*, 94.

[12] Christopher Anderson, *Historical Sketches of the Native Irish and Their Descendants: Illustrative of Their Past and Present State with Regard to Literature, Education, and Oral Instruction* (Edinburgh: John Johnstone, 1830),

The latter point is crucial. These weren't fraternals. They weren't hangouts for theological eggheads or guys who liked to do lunch. The history of Baptist associationalism in the United Kingdom was unapologetically kingdom-minded, existing to extend gospel witness. Haykin confirms this when he writes, "Particular Baptists were not simply content to meet for fellowship—they sent missionaries, pooled resources, and planned together for gospel advance."[13] Mission drove their methods. They recognized that shared theology ought to take shape in shared strategy. Churches in the United States of America followed suit. Nettles explains, "The Philadelphia Association drew on the model and experience of the English Particular Baptist associations, demonstrating that from the beginning, Baptists understood associationalism not as a threat to autonomy but as a means of doctrinal stability and missional advance." Wills adds that associations that sprang up like the one in Philadelphia "multiplied the influence of churches, provided for the education of ministers, and expanded missionary efforts far beyond what any church could accomplish alone."[14]

"Mmmmm, it's always better when we're together." And nowhere is that more evident than in the arena of missions.

240, italics mine.

[13] Anthony L. Chute, Nathan A. Finn, and Michael A. G. Haykin, *The Baptist Story: From English Sect to Global Movement,* (Nashville: B&H Academic, 2015), 70.

[14] Gregory A. Wills, *Democratic Religion: Freedom, Authority, and Church Discipline in the Baptist South, 1785–1900* (Oxford: Oxford University Press, 1997), 42.

Missions

The standout example of ecclesial partnerships enabling churches to do more together is William Carey's planting endeavors in India. He was sent not by an agency or an institution, but by an association of churches. When you read what happened before he set foot on the ship's gangplank, you quickly rule out any notion that this is one man going it alone. Andrew Fuller preached and fundraised. John Ryland, John Sutcliffe, and others wrote circular letters to the churches urging them to weep and pray over the plight of the lost.[15] Together with Carey, they embodied what Nettles called "cooperative pastoral friendship and ecclesial partnership."[16] These churches didn't just *talk* about missions. They did it. They sent Carey and others—and from Serampore, India, Carey, William Ward, and Joshua Marshman articulated one of the clearest biblical philosophies of modern gospel partnership that we know. They believed the churches in their association had three continuing roles:

- **Hold the rope** (financial and prayer support),

- **Tell the stories** (encourage others through reports),

---

[15] For an outline of the details of associational involvement, see L. Waite, & M. A. G. Haykin, *May I Again Taste the Sweets of Social Religion: The Story of William Carey's Devotion to the Local Church* (Eugene, OR: Pickwick Publications, 2023) 250 or M. A. G. Haykin, *The Missionary Fellowship of William Carey* (A Long Line of Godly Profile; Orlando: Ligonier, 2018).

[16] Tom Nettles, *The Baptists: Key People Involved in Forming a Baptist Identity* (Vol. 2; Fearn Roth-shire, Scotland: Mentor, 2005), 222.

- **Send more workers** (sustain the work through collaboration).

That they did. And the result? Carey made disciples, just as his Master instructed and his association churches prayed. But more than that, he planted churches, the first in Mudnabati, Dinajpur, Northern Bengal. In a moving report to the Baptist Missionary Society written in December 1795, Carey said, "I can with pleasure inform you . . . that a Baptist church is formed in this distant quarter of the globe."[17] And that was just the first. Churches were established across India, Scripture was translated into Bengali, and church-centered missions was modeled. And it all started in an association of Baptist churches who in their heart of hearts were convinced that they could do more together than they could on their own.

Do you hear it yet?

Churches Collaborating Today

The instinct to associate for the sake of the gospel didn't stop with Carey. Today, alongside a recovery of the importance of ecclesiology, we're seeing a recovery of Baptist associationalism. Friendships formalize and networks take shape. Those are often local and regional, ambitious in disciple-making and church planting locally. But in some cases, they are national and international, zealous to make Christ known around the globe.

---

[17] Carey, quoted in Waite & Haykin, *May I Taste*, (digital edition).

That's true of The Pillar Network, church planting through denominations, and other networks committed to church planting.[18] The Pillar Network is an association of churches worldwide who are doctrinally aligned, missionally driven, and committed to equipping, planting, and revitalizing churches together. By God's grace, the churches in this network are applying what we've seen both biblically and historically. They leverage the benefits of partnership for the sake of the kingdom of God. This partnership provides a context for collaboration, built on the belief that elder-led Baptist churches, committed to confessional clarity and the Great Commission, can do more together than they ever could apart.

It's true. I've seen it with my own eyes. Let me offer some personal testimony since there are two hats I have had the joy of wearing. The first, as one of the pastors at Charlotte Baptist Chapel. In a five-year timeframe in which we thought we might be able to plant one church, God has enabled us to plant/revitalize two. How? Through a church-to-church partnership with another Pillar church in South Carolina. Like Philippi, this partnering church provided finance and friendship. God helped us do more to reach the lost in two towns in Scotland through our gospel partnership.

The second testimony I'll share is one given while wearing the hat of Director of International Ministry for Pillar. I've seen a church plant in Cameroon started by a church in the United Arab Emirates and aided by another collaborat-

---

[18] Pillar Network is comprised of Southern Baptist churches in the US and baptistic churches around the world.

ing church in Colombia. That's tri-continental collaboration right there! I've seen a church in the Far East planted because a regional group of Pillar churches chipped in (I'm talking finance, not golf) to make it happen. I've seen the Pillar region of churches in the Carolinas send a planter to Thailand and help a church in Tucuman, Argentina build a facility for worship.

These stories don't just illustrate the principle; they prove the point. We really are better together. I'm a firm believer that Christ is worthy of the effort collaboration takes.

Make the Most of Associational Partnerships to Plant Churches

If your church isn't part of a like-minded association, join one. That means overcoming your aversion to partnership, or your anxiety about the head and calendar space that belonging to one will necessitate—and it does take time, especially if you want to make the most of it. It may mean putting in the hours to convince your church family of the importance of joining. If this book finds its way into the hands of a member or pastor of a Baptist church, consider Pillar or any network that expedites the spread of the gospel through partnership with like-minded churches.

If your church is already part of a like-minded association, leverage it. I'm talking now to members and pastors of Baptist churches, especially churches that associate together under the Pillar banner. Connect to cooperate. How? Let's get practical. When churches collaborate, it tends to take shape in four main ways. Rooted in Scripture and affirmed by experience, these *Four Ps* give structure to how churches can work together for gospel advancement.

Pray

Partner with other churches by praying with them for their own planting ambitions or for churches that are planting presently. Paul's letters are saturated both with gratitude for the prayers of partnering churches (Phil. 1:19) and requests for boldness in disciple-making and church planting (Eph. 6:19–20). This isn't just the pastor's privilege. Multiply the number of pray-ers by including partner churches in your gathered Sunday prayers and midweek prayer meetings. International churches in Pillar are sent prayer points from a different church in a different part of the world each week. As a result, our churches gain new insight into global mission opportunities. And thanksgiving is multiplied hundreds of times over when God, who is good and kind, answers (1 John 5:14–15).

People

It's easily overlooked by church members and pastors, but one of the greatest things a church can do for the cause of Christ is to send members—the faithful ones, not the ones you secretly pray to relocate—to strengthen the work of churches elsewhere. A couple of years ago, I visited a church plant in Rome. The pastor is godly, and the members are terrific. But it's small and the work is hard and slow. I've gone back to my own church family in Edinburgh and gone hunting for Italians! I've encouraged them to consider if they could move to

Rome and help. I did the same for a Telugu speaking church in Abu Dhabi, saying to Telugu speakers at Charlotte Chapel that they could do their job from Abu Dhabi and strengthen the witness there. You see it in Scripture, mostly in passages we tend to speed-read, the ones at the end of Paul's letters. Some move for a time, like Epaphroditus. Others stay for longer, like Timothy. Make the most of your association by asking: Who could we send and how could we help? Or, who do we need and how can we find them?

Pastors

Training and sending pastors are primarily what I have in mind. Acts 13 reminds us that the Holy Spirit sets pastors apart for gospel endeavors. Acts 20 adds that Christ Himself appoints shepherds. But Acts 16 and 2 Timothy 2:2 add two vital components: identifying and commissioning. In the case of Timothy, Paul spots his potential, the church affirms his character, and together they train a guy who serves several churches throughout his ministry. Every healthy church should be a greenhouse for future leaders who are biblically qualified, theologically sound, and missionally minded. Associations flourish when churches think beyond their own pulpits and invest in the next generation of church planters and pastors. At the same time, associations like Pillar create a context where churches needing pastors can find trustworthy ones. Whether a church is revitalizing, replacing, or reproducing, being part of a doctrinally aligned network increases the chance of finding the right shepherd for the task. The shared convictions, mutual trust, and rigorous assessments make all the difference.

Pounds[19]

Let's not be shy about it: gospel work requires gospel-motivated giving. The early church understood this instinctively. Paul went to great lengths in his letters to encourage generosity between churches, not as a burden but as a joyful investment in gospel advancement (2 Cor. 8–9). The Jerusalem church benefited from the Gentile churches' sacrificial giving. That wasn't pity; it was partnership. Associational life like that found in Pillar allows churches to invest financially in kingdom work around the world, confident that their giving is going to doctrinally aligned and missionally fruitful gospel ministry.

Through Pillar, churches are planting churches across Africa, Asia, Europe, and the Americas—not because they have endless funds, but because they believe it's better to send it than to have it sitting in the bank. But financial partnership isn't one-directional. Churches that give one day may receive the next. We've seen it: young planters funded by churches across the globe; revitalizations made possible by gifts from partner congregations; struggling works helped through one-off gifts from friends they've never even met.

If your church has resources, use them to bless others. Add a planting or partnership line to your annual budget. Support a plant or planter directly. Match gifts when another church is planted. Contribute to shared funds within your network. You don't need to be big to be generous. And if your church is in need, ask away! Without any hesitation. God often answers prayer through the generosity of other

---

[19] The money kind, not the calorie kind.

churches. Let it never be the case that an opportunity to proclaim Christ is missed for lack of funds. Pounds—or dollars, euros, shillings, dirhams, pesos, and so on—in the hands of gospel-hearted churches, eager to maximize kingdom-minded work through collaborating, can fuel the kind of advancement none of us could accomplish alone.

I know I mentioned *Four Ps* but I've got a bonus one. *Prudence.* Don't be daft or haphazard when looking for churches to partner with. I'm not commending *any-old* collaboration. I'm commending *wise, intentional, gospel-shaped* collaboration. Partnership is too precious, and too powerful, to approach casually. So here are a few additional words of counsel:

- *Choose Partners Wisely*: Look for churches that share your *theological convictions, ecclesiological instincts,* and missional priorities. Partnering doesn't require uniformity on every detail, but it does require *doctrinal clarity* and relational trust. Don't rush it. Ask good questions. Read their statement of faith. Talk to their pastors.

- *Invest in Relationships*: Partnership isn't just about strategy, it's about relationship. So treat it like one. Make the most of opportunities to talk, to visit each other's churches, and to get to know each other's people and priorities. Remember, friendship fuels fruitfulness.

- *Anticipate Disagreement*: Even likeminded churches disagree. Don't be surprised if hesitation or strain develops when talking about methods, timelines, budgets, and personalities. And don't ghost each other when it gets awkward. Build in structures for honest conversation. Commit to gracious, truth-filled dialogue. The health of your gospel partnership is in part seen not in how well you *agree*, but in how well you *disagree*.

- *Celebrate and Evaluate*: Don't just plant and forget. Celebrate what God is doing! Share stories of gospel fruit. Let your churches hear about answered prayers and new disciples. But also evaluate. Is this partnership still serving the mission? Are we aligned in our aims and methods? Wise churches know when to press on, when to pivot, and when to part ways with grace.

Whatever you have—prayers, people, pastors, or pounds, put it to work prudently. Leverage associational partnerships, whether with Pillar or whomever, to make ministry happen that wouldn't without your cooperative effort. Likewise, make the most of collaborative opportunities to find what you need. Let other churches help. Leverage everything God gives churches in the Pillar Network for the sake of Christ's name among the nations. After all, it's all His anyway.

Now are you singing along?

I know, I know. Jack Johnson's lyric wasn't written for the church, but "It's always better when we're together" nutshells a biblical principle that has been lived out in Baptist history and is eagerly applied today for the sake of the gospel. "It's always better when we're together" because together we do more for Christ's kingdom and for the lost than we could do on our own.

Maybe you're still not convinced. Goodness! I hope not! But if you are, or if you need a little more encouragement to maximize the potential associational partnerships that exist in The Pillar Network, let me leave you not with a laid-back lyric of Jack Johnson, but with the stirring prose of Christopher Anderson. Anderson planted the church I now serve way back in 1808. He believed partnership should be driven by more than a simple desire for efficiency or strategy. He believed it should be fueled by *brotherly love, Christ-honoring courage, and missional ambition.* He wrote:

> In order to much good being done, co-operation, the result of undissembled love, is absolutely necessary; and I think that if God in his tender mercy would take me as one of but a very few whose hearts he will unite as the heart of one man—since all the watchmen cannot see eye to eye—might I be but one of a little band of brothers who should do so, and who should leave behind them a proof of how much may be accomplished in consequence of the union of only a few upon earth in spreading Christianity, oh how should I rejoice and be glad! . . . Such a union in modern times existed in Fuller, Sutcliff, Pearce, Carey, and Ryland. They were men of self-denying habits, dead to the world, to fame, and to popular applause, of deep and extensive views of divine truth, and they had such an extended idea of what

the Kingdom of Christ ought to have been in the nineteenth century, that they, as it were, vowed and prayed, and gave themselves no rest.[20]

---

[20] Originally published in Christopher Anderson, *Annals of the English Bible*, vol. 2 (London: William Pickering, 1845), 355 - https://archive.org/details/annalsofenglishb00ande/page/n5/mode/ cited in M. A. G. Haykin, "As the Heart of One Man," in https://christianhistoryinstitute.org/magazine/article/as-the-heart-of-one-man. I am grateful to Nate Akin for bringing this quote to my attention.

PART 4

DEVELOPING A CHURCH PLANT

CHAPTER 14

WHAT TEAM MEMBER EXPECTATIONS MUST BE ESTABLISHED AND MAINTAINED?

Steven Wade & Ben McRoy

What does it mean to be a planting team member? In Part 3, we described where a church planting team member might come from (Chapter 8). But it's not enough for us to simply get people on the planting team or core group. We want to help them last.

Establishing and maintaining realistic expectations for the core team builds confidence to venture from the sending church into uncharted waters. As in any relationship, expectations set a foundation for trust, harmony, and momentum. Without a clear understanding of what is expected of them, team members may grow frustrated and discouraged or get distracted and veer off course. This can lead to abandoning the team—or, worse, the team member may cause damage to the team and the mission.[1]

On the other hand, church planters typically exude zeal and deep commitment to the plant, often assuming the same level of zeal and sacrificial commitment from every team member. The planter may be disappointed and irritated with team members who—whether in reality or perception—don't live up to expectations.

To avoid this danger, it is vital for a church planting team to communicate clear expectations for team members. "Clarity is kindness" is an oft-quoted maxim, and in this case, it is indeed. Clarity about team member expectations helps those considering joining the team make an informed decision; it helps those already on the team focus their efforts on what is expected of them; and it helps church planters set the trajectory of the work. This chapter offers some realistic expectations that sending churches and planters should have for core team members. Then it will address how these expectations can be established, and how they can be maintained as the church plant begins.

Foundation: Healthy Expectations for Team Members

Church planters usually invest significant time and energy in the plant before it begins. They've spent time discerning and

---

[1] In Paul David Tripp, *What Did You Expect? Redeeming the Realities of Marriage* (Wheaton, IL: Crossway, 2015), he makes the point that most marital discord, especially in the first few years of marriage, is over unmet expectations. Therefore, he encourages engaged couples to be clear about their expectations from the start. The same point holds here for sending churches and church plants.

wrestling with God's call to plant a church. They've prepared for the by growing in knowledge about planting through books, conferences, and most likely attending seminary.[2] Additionally, many planters must participate in some sort of training or residency that assesses their readiness. In short, church planters have thought a lot about church planting by the time they begin to recruit core team members. And as a result, they want the best of the best to join their team. They have lofty expectations for all their team members and can be guilty of assuming team members are as committed and involved as they are. And yet, that is rarely the case.

Those who join a church planting team may have given little thought to the work. They do not know what is involved with church planting, or the hardships and challenges common to it. They have never considered the level of flexibility and endurance needed to see a church plant thrive. They've never read a book or even listened to a podcast about church planting. They are just faithful followers of Christ whose hearts have been captured by the idea of seeing the gospel advance in a new place. They are willing to be part of the work, but don't know what will be expected of them.

Sending churches play a vital role in setting realistic expectations for team members. Their pastors should help

---

[2] Obviously this book is written mostly by Southern Baptists. While other denominations strive to plant churches, we are grateful to advocate for planting through the SBC. And one of the key reasons for that is the Cooperative Program, which fuels six healthy, conservative seminaries. Several of the authors of this book teach at Southeastern Baptist Theological Seminary. We would welcome readers to check out what that school has to offer by way of training for pastoral ministry and church planting. See www.sebts.edu for additional information.

church planters set realistic and achievable expectations. Of course, these expectations differ based on where the church is being planted. For example, if we are asking team members to join a core team for a plant across town in the community where they already live, there's going to be one set of expectations. On the other hand, if we are asking them to uproot their lives and move from rural North Carolina to Salt Lake City, then the expectations will differ considerably.

Sending churches should consider the need to prepare the latter group for cross-cultural challenges as well as the predictable issues associated with starting a new church. Consequently, they also encourage potential team members to count the cost of participating in a plant and encourage them toward spiritual growth throughout the process. Sending churches can foster team health and unity by establishing clear expectations for those considering the call to join the core team.

Here are five expectations we suggest for healthy core team members.

Personal Spiritual Growth

Participating in a church plant is a step of faith. Team members leave a church family they have loved for a long time. They are asked to leave the familiar and to begin—in faith—something new and unknown. The call to leave and embark on this journey with a new shepherd and a new fellowship provides opportunity for spiritual attack *and* for spiritual growth (see Eph. 6). It is often in the crucible of the unknown that God calls us to a deeper love and trust of Him. It's also in that crucible where Satan often makes his most intense attacks. So spiritual growth must be a priority for every team member during the preparation and planting of a new church.

While core team members add the duties, meetings, and various tasks that the church plant requires, it is important that they not neglect the most important thing: their own walk with the Lord (John. 15:1–8). Team members should commit to grow in the practice of the spiritual disciplines. Growing in Christlikeness doesn't happen by accident. For that reason, core team members should be both taught and expected to practice spiritual disciplines. We suggest working through a book like Don Whitney's *Spiritual Disciplines for the Christian Life* and communicating the clear expectations of the ongoing practice of the disciplines.[3] While we cannot address every spiritual discipline here, let's consider three of the primary foundational disciplines for spiritual growth.[4]

God's Word. Spiritual growth happens as the Spirit of God works in us primarily through the Word of God given to us as we live in community with the people of God (John 17). Because of this, disciplines like Bible intake and prayer are crucial to our growth on both personal and corporate levels. The Bible is God's Word (Ps. 19, 119; Heb. 4:12; 2 Pet. 1:21–22). When we read, meditate on, memorize, speak, or

---

[3] Donald Whitney, *Spiritual Disciplines for the Christian Life* (Carol Stream, IL: Tyndale House Publishers, 2014).

[4] Of course, these disciplines are key for every Christian at every stage of life, but there's something to the faith and risk inherent in a church plant that provides a unique opportunity for some Christians to shake off stagnation and apathy and give themselves wholeheartedly to these means of grace.

teach the Bible, we are reading, meditating on, memorizing, speaking, and teaching the very words of God.[5]

Prayer. In addition to hearing from God through his Word, God has invited and even commanded us to speak to Him in prayer (Heb. 4:16). Prayer is the means God has given through which we seek His will, His intervention, and His assistance in our pursuit of His mission. God promises to respond to the prayers of his people. Prayer is perhaps the greatest regular display of our dependence on the Lord to do the work in us and through us. No strategy, plan, or event will ever be as effective as prayer in advancing God's kingdom through church planting.[6]

Community. While spiritual disciplines are vital for spiritual growth, God intends our growth to occur as we live in community with other believers. I've been helped here through James Wilhoit's *Spiritual Formation as If the Church Mattered.* Wilhoit takes the spiritual disciplines often mentioned in books like Whitney's and shows how they find their fullest expression within the community of the local church.[7]

---

[5] For additional study, consider D. A. Carson, ed., *The Enduring Authority of Christian Scripture* (Grand Rapids: Eerdmans, 2016); Matthew Barrett, *God's Word Alone: The Authority of Scripture–What the Reformers Taught and Why It Still Matters* (The Five Solas Series; Grand Rapids: Zondervan Academic, 2016); J. I. Packer, *God Has Spoken* (Wheaton, IL: Crossway, 2021).

[6] Consider the following: Joel Beeke and Brian Najapfour, editors, *Taking Hold on God: Reformed and Puritan Perspectives on Prayer* (Grand Rapids: Reformation Heritage Books, 2011); D. A. Carson, *Praying with Paul: A Call to Spiritual Reformation* (Grand Rapids: Baker Academic, 2015); Paul Miller, *A Praying Life: Connecting with God in a Distracting World* (Colorado Springs: NavPress, 2017).

[7] James Wilhoit, *Spiritual Formation as If the Church Mattered* (2nd ed.;

To be clear, Christians grow and mature as they live out their lives with other believers. One of the expectations of core team members is that they commit to treat other team members as their spiritual family.[8] The "one another" statements of the New Testament describe how church members should relate to each other. Christians should love another (John 13:34), be devoted to and live in harmony with one another (Rom. 12:10), care for one another (1 Cor. 12:25), forgive one another (Eph. 4:2), bear with or be patient with one another (Col. 3:13), comfort one another (1 Thess. 4:18), and submit to one another (Eph. 5:21).[9] This commitment is lived out through both the formal gathering times (i.e., worship gatherings, small-group meetings, etc.) and the informal relationships we experience throughout the week.

Team members need accountability in their spiritual journey in which they are confessing sin (James 5:16; 1 John 1:9), putting to death the deeds of the body (Rom. 8:13), and growing "in the grace and knowledge of our Lord and Savior Jesus Christ" (2 Pet. 3:18). If team members are unwilling to fight against sin or pursue holiness, they severely handicap the fruitfulness of the church plant. While no team

---

Grand Rapids: Baker, 2022).

[8] This is one of the main reasons that documents like a church covenant truly matter. Phil established that point in his chapter in this work on the value of critical documents like a church covenant (See chapter 12).

[9] For a list of the New Testament "one another" passages, see Phil A. Newton and Rich C. Shadden, *Mending the Nets: Rethinking Church Leadership* (Greenville, SC: Courier Publishing, 2024), 60–61.

member will be without sin, it's essential that they all seek to honor the Lord in all they do (1 Cor. 10:31).

Unity Not Uniformity

Jesus commands His disciples to follow His example of love and love one another (John 13:34). In John 13:35, he adds, "By this everyone will know that you are my disciples, if you love one another." Love for one another results in unity of spirit, unity of purpose, and unity in our testimony. Later in John's Gospel, just before He goes to the cross, Jesus prays: "May they all be one, as you, Father, are in me and I am in you. May they also be in us, so that the world may believe you sent me" (John 17:21). Unity must be present in a church planting core team. It is our love for God and one another that leads to unity, and unity leads to effective witness to a lost world. Every team leader knows that without unity, a team cannot succeed.

If the enemy can turn team members against one another, the team will lose its effectiveness for gospel advancement and the church plant will be doomed to fail. For that reason, Paul reminds the church in Ephesus, "For our struggle is not against flesh and blood, but against rulers, against authorities, against cosmic powers of darkness, against evil, spiritual forces in the heavens" (Eph. 6:12, CSB). God reminds the church through the Apostle Paul that the war against the church is spiritual, and even the people who sow division and strife are only tools in Satan's hand. They are not the enemy; they are succumbing to the enemy. As the team works to plant a new church, there will be ample opportunity for differences of opinion, frustration, and division. So the team must pursue unity.

However, in the pursuit of unity, it's imperative to acknowledge that unity does not mean uniformity. In God's providence, He brings together a team made up of all kinds of people, with all kinds of backgrounds, and all kinds of gifts. As a matter of fact, church planters often marvel at the diversity that God puts together in a core team. This diversity should be celebrated, not minimized. Uniformity attempts to squeeze everyone into a small box of personality and practice. Yet, when the Bible speaks of the healthy function of a church, we are reminded that the diversity of peoples and gifts are a glorious testimony of the gospel and an effective means to accomplish the mission of the church. Paul speaks of the church as a body that has many parts (Rom. 12 and 1 Cor. 12). Each part is necessary. No one body part can do the work of the other body part. Rather, there is a beautiful tapestry, a body, or as Paul describes it in Ephesians 2, a building that functions as God's temple, when every part is working according to their measure of faith and the gifting of the Holy Spirit (Eph. 2:18–22; 4:11–16).

So, as you develop the expectations of core team members, remember that unity is vital, but unity doesn't mean uniformity. There are a variety of personalities, opinions, strengths, gifts, and services that come together under the headship of Christ. This is a great benefit to the nature of interdependent team formation that Matt laid out in Chapter 7. Here we are applying the same idea to the whole team. Pursue unity in Christ and celebrate the diversity Christ gives. In this, Christ will be magnified.

Commit to the Mission

Every core team member must have a strong commitment to the mission of the church. Planters cannot assume that everyone who shows up at an interest meeting understands what a church is or what a church does. A core team member should clearly understand the Great Commission and their church plant's vision for fulfilling it.

It is not enough for core team members to commit to their own discipleship; they must be committed to making new disciples. Many core team members should be experienced in evangelism and discipleship enough to lead others. To put it bluntly, if a person is not sharing the gospel in their current assignment, they will not likely start sharing the gospel in a new assignment. If a potential team member is not already discipling others, then they will not likely disciple others just because they join a church plant.[10]

Further, while the primary concern is that a person be committed to making disciples, team members must also understand and commit to the church plant's vision for making disciples. For example, most church plants develop language to talk about discipleship. The church we are part of uses the following language: "We are committed to making disciples who know Christ, grow together, serve others, and go to our neighbors and the nations with the gospel." We talk about evangelism as helping people find new life in

---

[10] See the following resources: J. Mack Stiles, *Evangelism: How the Whole Church Speaks of Jesus* (9Marks Building Healthy Churches Series 6; Wheaton, IL: Crossway, 2014); Mark E. Dever, *The Gospel and Personal Evangelism* (9Marks; Wheaton, IL: Crossway, 2017).

Christ. And we call our groups Faith Groups. Joining the core team requires commitment to both the language and the practice of the church.

Additionally, and perhaps more significantly, every church has some discipleship pathway. Some plants meet on Sunday morning, some in the evening. Some have groups focused on growth while others emphasize groups focused on outreach. Whatever the practices of the church in their chosen discipleship pathway, core team members should be expected to walk in that pathway. Every core team member must commit to fulfill the Great Commission in the way that the church plant intends.

Servant Mentality

Church planting is hard work. While we are certainly dependent on God to bring the increase, the work of plowing and planting, of fertilizing and watering is hard work. This reality should not be minimized when establishing expectations for team members. Peter, Paul, and James introduce themselves in their letters as "servants of Christ." They all willingly sacrificed for the cause of King Jesus. Likewise, church plant team members must share this servant mentality.

What is a servant mentality? First, a servant mentality means that we put others before ourselves. Philippians 2:1–4 provides a great framework for how team members are to view one another. In this passage, the Apostle Paul describes an others-centered approach to life in which we all follow Jesus in counting others as more significant than ourselves. For this to happen, team members must set aside their own desires and ambitions and humbly consider the needs of others—including team members, guests, neighbors, and even the nations who have yet to hear the good news.

Second, a servant mentality means always looking for a place to be useful. Paul encourages Timothy to purify himself so that God can make him "a special instrument, set apart, useful to the Master; prepared for every good work" (2 Tim. 2:21; CSB). This mentality gives core team members an expectation to always be looking for a place to use their gifts and abilities to further the mission of the church. God is the one who placed this team together to accomplish His will in this church plant, and He has uniquely prepared each member to step up and serve.

Finally, this servant mentality means team members have a "whatever it takes" attitude. Not only are there tasks that God has uniquely gifted each member to accomplish, but there will be tasks that many team members could do, but no one really wants to do. Some tasks will be menial while others will be important; some will never be seen by others while some will be visible to all. In every case, a servant mentality means stepping up and stepping in to do what needs to be done. This may mean jumping in and helping a team set up chairs or pack up the nursery items even though they were not "assigned" that duty on a particular Sunday. Or it may mean volunteering to do what no one else wants to do.

Perseverance

The final and fundamental expectation we suggest for planting team members is perseverance. Too often, core team members have not been adequately prepared to commit to the new work and persevere. The months leading up to the public start are exciting, the first weeks afterward are filled with new faces and learning experiences. But then, the new wears off, and the grind of every-week rhythms begins. Perhaps there is a week with no new guests. Summer comes—or, football season comes—and the numbers fall back a bit. Perhaps an outreach ministry you started months ago fizzles out, or a family that you tried to reach decided to join another church. Whatever the cause, the excitement and momentum everyone once had subsides, and team members begin to feel the weight of the work. In those moments, it is vital that core team members have a commitment to persevere.

Eugene Peterson's book *A Long Obedience in the Same Direction* reminds readers through the liturgy of the Psalms of Ascents (Psalms 120–134) that everyday persistence in the pathway of discipleship brings lasting change. God's extraordinary work in and through us is often accomplished in our obedience and service through the ordinary things we do over the length of our lives. In other words, God is at work in Week 32 just as He was on the day the church started. For teams to experience this, they must be committed to persevere.[11]

While it is sometimes necessary or providential for a team member to step away, leaving the team should be the exception rather than the norm. In almost every case, when a core team member leaves, it harms the team. It stifles momentum, increases workload, and often has other negative effects. So, church planter, communicate the time commit-

---

[11] Eugene Peterson, *A Long Obedience in the Same Direction: Discipleship in an Instant Society* (Downers Grove, IL: IVP, 2024; commemorative edition).

ments clearly. Of course, there's no magic number here, no binding contract. But committing to at least one year seems to wise, unless a member is providentially hindered. In any case, when a person or family commits, they will often push through difficult situations to see God move in ways they never expected. As the Apostle Paul states, "Let us not get tired of doing good, for we will reap at the proper time if we don't give up" (Gal. 6:9).

From the Beginning:
Establishing Team Member Expectations

The first part of this chapter suggested five team member expectations that will prepare a church plant to work together to accomplish God's call to plant a church. Your team may choose different expectations or articulate the ones offered here differently. That's fine. But if your expectations for team members are not clear from the beginning, then they will most certainly not be met. As in any partnership, expectations are only as good as the communication.

This section offers four suggestions on how to establish clear expectations with the team.

Be Candid

Many pastors have experienced being called to a church only to find that his expectations of his role were not the same as the church's. Sometimes, the two are so far apart the pastor leaves. To avoid this unfortunate situation, we suggest taking time to think through core team member expectations and to communicate them from the beginning. It is helpful to talk with other planters to find out what they did well and what they wish they could do again. Sending churches should do their best to make sure conversations like these happen.

Once the expectations are identified, make sure to communicate them from the beginning—even at the very first interest meeting. No, you don't need to have a detailed answer to every question. But clarity from the start will help people their possible role in the church plant.

Be Specific

As you move forward, be as specific as possible when communicating team member expectations. For example, it is one thing to say a team member is expected to be growing spiritually. Someone who hears that may have their own perception of what that means and think they've mastered that one. But you want to be more specific on what spiritual habits core team members should practice. These disciplines may vary from person to person. Being specific on what you mean by each expectation is helpful for all.

Ask for Commitment

Once you have determined the core team member expectations, it may be helpful to formalize the commitment. Asking someone to formally agree to the expectations can assure that they understand them and are serious about keeping their commitment. To that end, we suggest a Core Team Member Covenant that includes what they can expect from the sending church as well as what the sending church expects of them. A formal time of celebration and prayer for

God to help the team accomplish all that He desires them to accomplish can be a special time that solidifies calling and develops team relationships.

Follow Me

Peter exhorts his fellow elders in 1 Peter 5:3 to be "examples for the flock." Paul commends his own ministry as an example to the Ephesian elders in Acts 20 and tells the Corinthians to follow him as he follows Christ (1 Cor. 11:1). In the same way, pastors and church planters who establish team member expectations must model those expectations themselves. We have observed pastors who thought they were above particular tasks and called someone else to clean up a mess or fold chairs, as well as pastors who jumped in to work side-by-side with team members loading a trailer after a worship gathering. The ones who inspire and lead are those who lead like Christ, by example.

Keep It Going: Maintaining Team Member Expectations

Getting started may be half the battle, but the battle is not won if it is only half won. Establishing expectations is not enough. Church planting teams must have a plan to maintain the expectations. This section offers four practices that might help.

Affirmation: Celebrate What You Value

We have two statements that are often repeated in our staff meetings: You celebrate what you value, and you repeat what you celebrate. In terms of team member expectations, this means we celebrate those who are living out the expectations of the team. Do this on a corporate level and on an individual level.[12] One church plant even gave the "Above and Beyond" award regularly to a team member who went above and beyond in living out the team member expectations. However you do it, remember, your people repeat what you celebrate. One caveat is necessary. If your team doesn't naturally celebrate those who are exemplary in living out team member expectations, either your expectations or your values are off. Consider changing the expectations to match what you value or begin truly valuing what you expect of team members.

Set a Reminder

Some habits require a regular reminder so that we don't neglect them. Right now, there is a red light blinking on my refrigerator to remind me to change the water filter in the water dispenser. If I fail to do so, I will not see any immediate changes. My water will not suddenly taste bad or become discolored, but over time the quality of the water will deteriorate and eventually even be dangerous to drink. In the same way, maintain healthy habits in the church plant team by setting reminders to regularly revisit the expectation. You may not notice any immediate effects if you fail to do so, but eventually the habits and practices of the team will deterio-

---

[12] See Sam Crabtree's helpful book, *Practicing Affirmation: God-Centered Praise of Those Who are not God* (Wheaton, IL: Crossway, 2011), that gives biblical rationale and clear examples for why we need to offer this kind of praise.

rate. Remember, drift always happens away from discipline, never toward it.

Imitation: Do As I Do

I was talking with a friend today who said that the only time he ever told his sons "Do as I do, not as I say," was in reference to his driving. How do you think that worked out? *Exactly!* He reported that his sons, now grown, drive just like he does. In the same way, pastors and church planters must exemplify the expectations we have for team members.

While we addressed this before in reference to establishing expectations, here we want to make a different point. In establishing the expectations, it is important to show team members a good example. But in maintaining them, we suggest you live out the expectations particularly toward the team members. For example, if our expectation is for team members to serve others, then take time to serve core team members. Host a celebration dinner in which you can serve them. As you model the expectations to your core team, you give your people a sense of the impact that their service might have on others.

Teach It

It has been said, "If you can't do it, teach it." No doubt in some cases this is true. But in ministry, I have observed that you really know how to do something when you can teach others to do it. While team members can hear about the expectations, they really grasp them and begin to live them out as they are challenged to show others how to live them out.

Give team members the opportunity to teach newer team members or members of other ministry teams the expectations they have learned. As they teach others to practice spiritual disciplines or have a servant mentality or persevere through hardship, they will more fully grasp the idea and its importance.

While sending and planting pastors cannot change hearts, they can teach, model, and patiently train those who show interest in joining a church plant. All the while, as they faithfully seek to build expectations in their team members, they learn to trust the Lord of the church to shape, hone, and refine those who will partner together in planting a new church.

CHAPTER 15

HOW DOES THE CHURCH MOVE TO SELF-GOVERNANCE?

Victor Rodriguez

Every race starts with a signal. It doesn't matter if you're an Olympic athlete or a child running in your backyard. When you hear "on your mark," you know it's time to get into position. "Get set" is the final warning before that last word: "Go!" That's the moment when all the preparation is put into action, and the race begins.

Many pastors have established their churches at the "on your mark" stage. They've built them on strong biblical convictions and sound theology. Others are already at the "get set" stage. They've established meaningful membership, prioritized the faithful preaching of the Word, and cultivated a solid culture of evangelism and discipleship.

But one of the last stops for a church plant is official-ly recognizing its first internal elders. That's the "Go!" that takes many church plants a long time. This makes sense. After all, there's no fast way to equip faithful men and to entrust them with pastoral ministry. So it seems difficult to cross that imaginary line between "Get set" and "Go."

Pastors often ask questions about raising up leaders from within their church. Where do I start? What if I don't have any qualified candidates? I'm a bi-vocational pastor—how will I find time to train others for pastoral ministry? How do I handle the discouragement of having invested what little time I had in someone who turned out either unqualified for or not interested in ministry? And, if someone manages to advance in the process, how will we know when they are truly ready? What if we make a mistake?

This chapter is written for pastors who are "on their mark" in doctrine and "set" in practical areas but who are not sure how to "go," that is, to develop a pastor from within the church. These men must be affirmed by the congregation itself, as seen in the New Testament. This is a key step—if not *the* key step—in setting a church up for long-term health. If the church plant develops healthy elders from within, it's far more likely that the church will last. In contrast, church plants that go years without raising up a new elder tend to stagnate or recede.

So, how should a church plant, and in turn the send-ing church, work toward appointing the first pastors from within?

Hold Biblical Convictions
about Church Leadership

Decades ago, getting directions was very different. You needed a map—or, in the early days of the Internet, at least a printer to print off the MapQuest directions. In either case, it was essential to know your starting point. Today, that's not as necessary since GPS automatically detect your location. One problem we face when appointing the first internal elders is that we know where we want to go but we're not necessarily clear about where we are. To identify our starting point, we must review key ecclesiological convictions. We'll move from the most basic to the more practical points.

First, the church belongs to the Lord. God purchased it with His own blood (Acts 20:28). This truth must anchor us lest we fall into the temptation of thinking that the church depends on our ability or wisdom to move forward. Though the church is to be led by pastors, it belongs to God—and He will provide everything it needs. God is the one who adds to the church those who are being saved (Acts 2:47), and He is also the one who provides pastors to equip the saints for the work of ministry (Eph. 4:11). God provides qualified pastors for His church who will care for, protect, and feed the sheep with the Word of God.

Second, God has shown us how to bring order to the church. In Paul's letter to Titus, the churches in Crete were disordered and functioning poorly. Paul commands Titus to fix the situation by teaching sound doctrine and appointing elders or pastors.[1] What was the specific issue in Crete? It was very similar to what we face today: a culture filled with lies, greed, sexual immorality, violence, and false teachers within the church. These false teachers produced false believers who look more like the world than Christ (Titus 1:10–13; 3:10–11). What was the solution? To appoint elders (pastors) to lead the church by faithfully preaching God's Word so that the church would reflect Christ to the world through their good works (Titus 1:5, 1:9; 2:1, 2:11–15; 3:8).

God brings order to His church—both in Crete and in your context—through sound doctrine and qualified pastors. There's a temptation for a church plant to press any man into service as a pastor. The planter may know that it's vital for the long-term health of the church and erroneously compromise biblical convictions about the qualifications for an

---

[1] The words *pastor*, *overseer* (or *bishop*), and *elder* in this chapter are interchangeable, based on the conviction that this is how the Scriptures teach it. John S. Hammett, *Biblical Foundations for Baptist Churches: A Contemporary Ecclesiology* (2nd Ed.; Grand Rapids: Kregel Academic, 2019) 191, describes it this way:

> The evidence for the interchangeability of the three terms is most clearly seen in Acts 20 and 1 Peter 5. In Acts 20, Paul summons the elders of the church in Ephesus (v. 17). When they arrive, he tells them that the Holy Spirit has made them overseers of the flock (v. 28) and charges them to shepherd the church of God. In 1 Peter 5, Peter addresses the elders (v. 1), telling them to shepherd the flock and to serve as overseers (v. 2).
>
> The synonymous use of these terms seems evident and has been widely recognized as such by exegetes. Baptist confessions of faith use all three terms to refer to this office in the church. Clearly, the specific term used for church leaders was not a primary concern for the biblical writers. Their greater concern was with what those leaders *do*.

elder in order to rush the process. Be warned—it is far more difficult to remove an unqualified elder than it is to wait and appoint a qualified man in due time.[2]

God's Word outlines these qualifications in 1 Timothy 3:1–7 and Titus 1:5–9, and offers examples in 1 Peter 5:1–5 and Acts 20:18–38. These qualifications emphasize character, spiritual maturity, and the ability to teach and lead the church faithfully. They don't focus on skills, charisma, or talent. As D. A. Carson famously said, "The most extraordinary thing about these qualifications is that there is nothing extraordinary about them."[3]

Third, a plurality of elders is God's design for church leadership. The church should be led by more than one pastor or elder. In many church contexts, leadership centers around one man—a single leader who has a vision and a congregation fully submitted to his authority. In many cases, this lead pastor is a godly man seeking to honor the Lord in the way he uses his authority.

But it's not the biblical model. As Pastor Phil Newton writes in *40 Questions About Pastoral Ministry*, "The New

---

[2] This point has been made in premarital counseling by virtually every pastor. It is far better to wait and marry the right person than rush and marry a buffoon because you were lonely or felt that you needed a spouse to keep up with your friends or prove you were really an adult. Marriage is great. But it's really great if you marry well. The same is true for pastoral ministry. Having multiple pastors is great, but it's going to do you more harm than good if you put the wrong men in those roles only to have to remove them down the road.

[3] Phil A. Newton, *40 Questions About Pastoral Ministry* (Benjamin L. Merkle, series editor; Grand Rapids: Kregel Academic, 2021; Spanish Edition), 34. Kindle Edition.

Testament consistently shows a pattern of plurality among those who serve as pastors/elders/overseers."[4] Similarly, Alexander Strauch explains that in the local church, the New Testament clearly presents a consistent pattern of shared pastoral leadership.[5] Consider the following verses:

- "This is why I left you in Crete, so that you might put what remained into order, and appoint elders in every town as I directed you" (Titus 1:5).

- "And when they had appointed elders for them in every church, with prayer and fasting they committed them to the Lord in whom they had believed" (Acts 14:23).

- "Now from Miletus he sent to Ephesus and called the elders of the church to come to him" (Acts 20:17).

- "So I exhort the elders among you, as a fellow elder and a witness of the sufferings of Christ, as well as a partaker in the glory that is going to be revealed" (1 Pet. 5:1).

- "Is anyone among you sick? Let him call for the elders of the church, and let them pray over him, anointing him with oil in the name of the Lord" (James 5:14).

- "We ask you, brothers, to respect those who labor among you and are over you in the Lord and admonish you, and to esteem them very highly in love because

---

[4] Newton, *40 Questions About Pastoral Ministry*, 68.

[5] Alexander Strauch, *Biblical Eldership: An Urgent Call to Restore Biblical Church Leadership* (2nd ed.; Littleton, CO: Lewis and Roth Publishers, 1995).

of their work. Be at peace among yourselves" (1 Thess. 5:12–13).

These texts point to the reality that New Testament churches followed the model of pastoral plurality. This means that the church plant must do two things: 1) The church plant must be convinced that it needs multiple pastors; and 2) The church plant must be convinced that biblically qualified pastors are non-negotiable.

Having biblical convictions about ecclesiology is part of getting "on your mark." And in the case of the plurality of elders, it's not always easy to put that conviction into practice.[6]

Preach the Word Faithfully and Lead by Example

Now that we have the starting point in place, we are ready to toe the line and "get set!" That happens by keeping the role of pastoral ministry front-and-center in the life of the church.

In the introduction to *Finding Faithful Elders and Deacons*, Thabiti Anyabwile explains, "A church without godly leaders is a church in danger of extinction. And a church that

---

[6] The following resources are very helpful for deepening your understanding of the topic of pastoral plurality and its benefits: Alexander Strauch, *Biblical Eldership: An Urgent Call to Restore Biblical Church Leadership* (2nd ed.; Littleton, CO: Lewis and Roth Publishers, 1995); Jeramie Rinne, *Church Elders: How to Shepherd God's People Like Jesus* (9Marks Building Healthy Churches Series; Wheaton, IL: Crossway, 2014); Phil A. Newton and Matt Schmucker, *Elders in the Life of the Church: Rediscovering the Biblical Model for Church Leadership* (9Marks; Grand Rapids: Kregel, 2014); Phil A. Newton and Rich Shadden, *Mending the Nets: Rethinking Church Leadership* (Greenville, SC: Courier Publishing, 2024).

does not train leaders is an unfaithful church."[7] When a pastor—and therefore the church—fails to develop leaders, that church is only one generation away from ceasing to exist. That's why the Apostle Paul instructs his beloved son in the faith Timothy: "What you have heard from me in the presence of many witnesses entrust to faithful men who will be able to teach others also" (2 Tim. 2:2). This means that the best way for a church plant to move toward self-governance is to raise up pastors from within, rather than trying to hire from the outside.

Paul charges Timothy to entrust what he received to others who will then entrust it to others. And what was Timothy to entrust? The preaching of the Word of God, the gospel of Jesus Christ. That preaching always came hand-in-hand with Paul's personal example.

Later, in 2 Timothy 3:10–11, Paul says, "But you have followed my teaching, conduct, purpose, faith, patience, love, perseverance, my persecutions, and sufferings—such as happened to me at Antioch, Iconium, and Lystra. What persecutions I endured! And the Lord rescued me from them all." Timothy had followed Paul's example in Antioch, Iconium, and Lystra. What happened in those places? Acts 13 and 14 tell us that in Antioch, Paul preached the gospel and was persecuted and expelled. In Iconium, he preached the gospel, and there was a plot to kill him. In Lystra, unsurprisingly, he preached the gospel again and was dragged out of the city and left for dead.

---

[7] Thabiti M. Anyabwile, *Finding Faithful Elders and Deacons* (9Marks; Wheaton, IL: Crossway, 2012), 15.

The next day, Paul left with Barnabas for Derbe. Acts 14:21 tells us that Paul preached the gospel there, made many disciples, and then—astonishingly—returned to Lystra, Iconium, and Antioch. Why would he return to places where his life was at risk? Because strengthening new believers and appointing elders in every church was more important to Paul than his own safety. Paul was a man of conviction who faithfully preached the gospel and lived it out by example.

Why did Paul mention these cities to Timothy? Acts 16:1–2 tells us that it was in Derbe and Lystra where Paul first met young Timothy. Even in Iconium, people spoke well of Timothy. It's as if Paul is saying, "Timothy, do you remember that even though they tried to kill me, I kept preaching? You saw my example!" Just as Paul charged Timothy to entrust the gospel to faithful men, every pastor must do the same. They must preach faithfully and lead a holy life.

This is the not-so-secret sauce for raising up future leaders from within. The pastor, even if only one pastor at the time, must give himself to investing in other men. This may mean these men go on to become pastors in the church. Other times, this life-on-life investment will result in mature members for the church. Either is a huge win!

A Word of Encouragement to Pastors Invested in Discipling

Brothers, it can be tempting to lose heart in the work of developing others. We hold to pastoral priorities and seek to give our lives to help others move toward leadership. Sometimes:

- The person flames out,

- The person is flaky,

- The person moves on to another place or another church,

- Or the person doesn't embody the potential you thought they might have.

Other times,

- You have limited time amid all the other tasks of pastoring,

- You are bi-vocational and just don't have time to invest in more than one or two people,

- You get frustrated because the person isn't doing what you want.

Pastors, let's not lose focus. Stay faithful to preach the Word—it is the primary means by which the next generation of pastors will be trained. "Be diligent to present yourself approved to God, a worker who does not need to be ashamed, accurately handling the word of truth" (2 Tim. 2:15).

And remember, even though we've been called to the honorable office of pastoral ministry, before we are pastors, we are sheep—we are children of God, called to persevere in holiness. As the Puritan pastor Thomas Watson once said, "A minister must be both a burning lamp and a shining light; he must shine in doctrine and burn in holiness."[8] God calls us

---

[8] Thomas Watson, *Heaven Taken by Storm, or, The Holy Violence the Christian is to Put Forth in the Pursuit After Glory* (London: R.W. for Tho. Parkhurst,

to be examples, to show what it means to follow Christ and to preach the Scriptures faithfully. That way, the men in our congregations can imitate us, even as we are being formed in the image of Christ.

When you faithfully preach God's Word week after week and when you model Christlike character, you are helping your church learn to self-govern. You're giving them a living example of what it means to follow Christ. You're strengthening the congregation's faith by consistently preaching the gospel. You're helping faithful men grow and explore whether they may have a pastoral calling. And you're teaching the whole church how to recognize the pastor that God may be raising up from among them. This might mean that the church planter has to do the work alone longer than he would like, but if that's the case he can trust that his faithful investment will reap a harvest in due time.

Seek Pastors from within the Congregation

I'm not very good at finding things. But I certainly have a better chance of finding something when I'm actually looking for it. Still, even when I am looking, I often struggle. My wife has a phrase she repeats every time I'm searching for something in the fridge. She says, "It's right in front of your nose—look carefully, I put it there." And I believe her! I have the conviction, but I just don't know how to find it.

The same thing can happen when we try to identify a pastor within the church. We know God sends pastors—and

1670), n.p. University of Michigan Digital Library. http://name.umdl.umich.edu/A65299.0001.001.

sometimes, they're right in front of us. But even if we are actively looking, we might not recognize them.

Just because we believe that God sends pastors to His church does not mean we expect Him to send fully finished products. That's not how it works. God is indeed sending pastors to His church, but they come as men who need to be developed, and in some cases, still need to be saved! It's common for pastors and church planters to evaluate someone for pastoral ministry based on the level of maturity or experience the existing pastors have. We sometimes forget how much growth and change the Spirit produced in us, even after we became pastors. We must lean to thread the needle so that we don't lessen pastoral qualifications but also don't hold up an impossible standard.

That means every man God sends to the church is a potential pastor who must be discipled so that he becomes:

> above reproach, the husband of one wife, temperate, self-controlled, respectable, hospitable . . . not given to drunkenness, not violent but gentle, not quarrelsome, not a lover of money. He must manage his own family well and see that his children obey him, and he must do so in a manner worthy of full respect . . . not a recent convert . . . and have a good reputation with outsiders.

Do those words sound familiar? They should. They're the qualifications for pastoral ministry listed in 1 Timothy 3, and they apply to every believer.[9]

Seeking the pastors that God is sending to the church means discipling every man who joins the congregation so that he is exemplary in all these areas. In the process, some of them will begin to desire pastoral ministry and demonstrate teaching ability. God's plan has always been to raise up faithful men from within, men whose faithfulness has already been tested among the flock. That's how it worked in the churches of the first century, and that's how it should work today. So where do you look? Here are ten practical tips for identifying future pastors within your church:

Stand Firm in Your Convictions

Do you firmly believe the church belongs to the Lord? Great! Do you recognize that God brings order to His church through the preaching of His Word and the appointment of pastors? Excellent! Do you believe God has designed His church to be led by a plurality of male elders? Wonderful! Then keep growing in these convictions by continually studying how God governs His church. The more you reflect on these themes, the more apt you'll be to see the men God is raising up.[10]

---

[9] I'm excluding the qualification that distinguishes elders from the congregation: he must be "able to teach" (1 Timothy 3:2).

[10] Here are a few books on the subject for your continued study: John S. Hammett, *Biblical Foundations for Baptist Churches* (Grand Rapids: Kregel Academic, 2005); Gregg R. Allison, *Sojourners and Strangers: The Doctrine*

Commit to Grow in Your
Preaching and Personal Holiness

Never allow complacency in these two areas. If you are already preaching faithfully every week, keep going—and strive to improve. If you're pursuing holiness now, do so even more fervently. Pastors must always be growing in these areas. Of course, there will be bad sermons and moments of failure. The goal isn't perfection on this side of eternity, but don't settle for good enough.

Let me suggest that you register annually for preaching workshops or mentorships.[11] Ask fellow pastors or leaders for constructive feedback on your sermons. Don't neglect accountability. Connect with a trusted brother with whom you can share your struggles and receive encouragement in ministry and personal life. Sometimes, we can so hyper-focused on finding fellow pastors that we forget to strive to be faithful pastors, even if we are doing it all alone.

Pray Intentionally for Workers for the Harvest

As the Puritan pastor John Owen once said, "A minister without prayer is like a soldier without weapons."[12] No list of pastoral recommendations should ever leave out prayer,

---

of the Church (Foundations of Evangelical Theology; Wheaton, IL: Crossway, 2012); Mark Dever and Jonathan Leeman, editors, *Baptist Foundations: Church Government for an Anti-Institutional Age* (Nashville: B&H Academic, 2015).

[11] Visit these websites for more information: simeontrust.org; christcenteredandclear.com; predicafiel.org.

[12] Quote attributed to John Owen; source not located.

especially when it comes to identifying, developing, and appointing godly men to pastoral ministry. Jesus Himself urged us to pray to the Lord of the harvest to send out workers into His harvest field (Matt. 9:38). I'm often amazed at the way prayer gives me eyes to see what God is doing around me. The more I pray, the more often I ask, "Is God raising that man up?" when I meet with someone or see them in the church on Sundays.

Teach the Congregation Patiently

Preach expositionally through Acts, Paul's letters to Timothy and Titus, and Peter's letters. Teach in detail the qualifications of a pastor and the responsibilities pastors have before God and the congregation. Also, teach the responsibilities of church members toward God and their pastors. Use Sunday School or small groups to solidify your church's understanding of what a biblical church is and how it should function. Include ecclesiology in your membership classes. Whenever possible, bring these topics up when discipling new believers. And when you think you've taught everything there is to teach—teach it again. Be patient with those who have never heard of meaningful membership, and also with those who have never been part of a church that practices it seriously.

Remember: people are always coming in, and repetition helps the congregation stay alert in identifying the fruit of godly men that God may be raising up among them.

Identify Godly Men in Your Congregation

Don't look for finished products. Look for signs of godliness in the men whom God has already brought into your church. Keep 1 Timothy 3 and Titus 1 close. Ask yourself: Who is showing evident spiritual growth? Who asks thoughtful questions about your teaching? Who takes notes during sermons? Who reads books you recommend quickly and eagerly? Who is growing in knowledge and love for God's Word? Who shows concern for members who missed service? Who pays attention to the sick and the needy? Who is teachable? Who receives correction humbly? These questions can serve as a good starting point to identify men in whom you can intentionally invest more time. It may not mean that the man in question is ready to be appointed as a pastor, but it can serve as a guide for those in whom the pastor invests extra energy.

Involve the Church in the Process

Just as the Holy Spirit worked through the church in Antioch to identify Paul and Barnabas for a specific mission (Acts 13:1–4), He continues to work through the church today to identify, develop, and affirm pastors from among the congregation. Prepare your church to recognize what a godly man looks like. Regularly ask in members' meetings, "Is there someone you believe God may be raising up for pastoral ministry? Is there someone the Spirit might be calling to this role?"[13]

---

[13] Here the nature of the church and church size play a key role. You can only ask these questions in a congregation where people know one another

Keep the church informed about leadership training programs and pastoral development efforts. Ask members specific questions about the preaching and the Christian walk of the men in training. Try to discern their leadership qualities and their reputation in the congregation. Ask yourself: Who is starting to be recognized as a spiritually mature believer? Who do the members see as a leader? Who do they already view as a pastor? There may be times when it's wise to put men forward for a more public and formal assessment process. Many of our churches recommend candidates for pastoral ministry far in advance so that the members of the church have time to get to know the pastor, have him over for dinner, watch his marriage and family life, and discern if he is indeed a good fit for the role.

Don't be Afraid to Ask and Invite

Some time ago, I joked with another pastor that if I had to send one of my church members to a "Best Christian Competition," I would send Brother Paul (this is a real story but that is a fictitious name). He's godly, kind, and faithful. He leads his home well and has a great reputation with those outside the church. But no one had ever asked him if he had considered pastoral ministry. A couple of years ago, I asked him directly, "Have you ever considered pastoral ministry?"

---

and where they feel comfortable coming to pastors to make recommendations. It's important that we keep in mind the myriad of ways that our ecclesiology will shape our practice. Meaningful membership and faithful pastoral ministry provide the grounds where future pastors can be seen and affirmed.

He responded, "That thought has never crossed my mind. But if the Lord calls me, I'll be available." Later I asked his wife, "Have you ever considered being a pastor's wife?" She answered similarly, "Honestly, I've never thought about it. But if the Lord calls my husband, I'll gladly support him." Today, this brother leads the church's hospitality team, teaches regularly, and is beginning a pastoral training program.

Give Potential Pastors Access to Your Life and Delegate Responsibilities

As the saying goes, "More is learned from watching the pastor than from listening to the sermon." It's crucial that the men you disciple and train have access to your life. Let them hear your teaching and see how you treat your wife and children. Let them watch you preach both publicly and privately. Let them accompany you to ministry appointments, counseling sessions, and pastoral visits. Afterwards, ask them about what they observed. Also, delegate real responsibility. Let them lead a small group, preach a midweek service, or oversee a ministry area. Then ask: Do they take initiative to solve problems? Are they clear in communicating expectations to those they lead? Do they care more about results or people's souls? When they teach, are they faithful to the text? Are they open to feedback on their preaching? Do people remember what they preached?

Develop a Training Program for Those You've Identified

Build a program that facilitates the development of the men God is calling to pastoral ministry. Consider the work of the North American Mission Board, the International Mission Board, and many state conventions who have labored to develop tools for just this purpose. You may not always use the tools exactly has they are built, but they will provide you with basic scaffolding that you can adapt to serve your church's needs. Many churches today have created pastoral training curriculum or a residency program. These usually include reading books to deepen understanding, and hands-on training. The trainees begin ministering while they are being developed. Every program should be adapted to your specific context and address the needs of the individual, the congregation, and the surrounding community.

Don't Reinvent the Wheel

Seek counsel and mentorship from pastors and churches who've been where you are. You can be certain someone has done this before you. As you work to identify, train, and appoint pastors within your church, seek the advice of pastors and churches that already done what you want to do. In my case, our pastoral training program is a hybrid from three or four sister churches who shared their materials with me. Whether you're just starting to train leaders or are preparing for the final steps of ordination, get help from those who've already walked this path.

I thank God for The Pillar Network—a network of doctrinally aligned churches committed to equip leaders, plant, and revitalize churches—so I don't have to walk this road blindly.

Two Important Warnings

First, watch the temptation to rush the process of appointing someone from within. The longer you go as a solo pastor, the more you just want someone else to carry the weight with you. But needing help in your life or ministry is not a reason to speed up the evaluation process. We can also be tempted to speed up the process when we have a charismatic or someone who has pastored before. Neither charisma nor public speaking ability nor personality are mentioned in the New Testament's qualifications for ministry. A man who doesn't meet the biblical requirements is not qualified—no matter how likable or gifted he may seem. Remember Paul's words to Timothy: "Do not be hasty in the laying on of hands, and do not share in the sins of others. Keep yourself pure" (1 Tim. 5:22).

Second, don't be overly rigid or restrictive. I come from a church background where I was named youth leader just three months after my conversion—without anyone even asking me. Maybe your context is similar—or maybe you've heard stories of unqualified men being appointed as pastors and seen the devastating consequences that followed. Stories like these often cause churches and pastors to create an overly rigid evaluation process—so strict, in fact, that they go beyond what Scripture requires. And this can be just as harmful as moving too fast. This creates a license-legalism dynamic. On one side, people remove biblical requirements and rush into appointing men. On the other, they add extra-biblical barriers that prevent qualified men from being recognized.

Let us guard ourselves from both extremes and strive to be faithful to God's Word. It is my prayer that in the "on your mark, get set, go" of our pastoral ministry, we would remain firm in our biblical convictions and committed to grow in our preaching and personal holiness. We must run this race with our eyes fixed on Jesus, trusting that He gives His church everything it needs to move forward.

CHAPTER 16

HOW CAN DEACON MINISTRY IMPACT CHURCH PLANTING?

Brandon Langley

Deacons are the unsung heroes of multiplying churches. I write this from an airport terminal, occasionally glancing out the window to watch the hustle of trucks, planes, carts, and conveyor belts. The logistical complexity and diverse roles necessary for flying from one city to the next is striking. No matter how prepared a pilot may be, he needs all the pieces to come together. In a somewhat comical display of divine providence, after writing that last sentence, a voice came over the loudspeaker to notify us that our flight is delayed because the cabin crew hasn't arrived. No cabin crew, no flying. The mission is delayed, if not terminated, unless the whole team shows up.

Like the airline industry that gets you from one city to the next, church planting is God's plan for getting the gospel from one city, town, or village to the next. Church planting may not be quite as logistically complex as air travel, but there are a lot of moving parts. Pastors who are constantly treading water to keep up with the day-to-day are not likely able to lead church multiplication efforts in addition to their sermon writing, pastoral counseling, and ministry oversight. Like a pilot in the cockpit, they need a team to load the luggage, refuel, and welcome the guests.

Looking up to the horizon for sending opportunities requires some breathing room, but where does that breathing room come from? More than that, the work itself is beyond what any one man can do. By God's design, the church is a multiplication mechanism, fully operational when three essential parts are working together: the members, the elders, and the deacons.[1]

In his greeting to the church at Philippi, the Apostle Paul references three distinct roles of ministry in the local church. He addresses, "The *saints* in Christ Jesus who are at Philippi, with the *overseers* and *deacons*" (Phil. 1:1). This is the only New Testament letter to reference overseers and deacons in the greeting. Different commentators have sought to explain this anomaly,[2] but I find the hypothesis of com-

---

[1] See Benjamin L. Merkle, *Authority in the Church: Exploring Congregation, Elders, and Deacons* (Nashville: B&H Academic, forthcoming 2026).

[2] For example, Joseph H. Hellerman argues that Paul purposely omits his own title "apostle" and refers to himself and Timothy as "slaves" while elevating the titles of his recipients so as to model how to elevate others over self. Hellerman writes, "Paul began, at the outset of his letter, to challenge

mentator Walter Hansen convincing. Hansen sees a connection between Paul's thanksgiving for missionary support and Paul's understanding that both overseers and deacons made the support possible. Hansen writes, "Paul's reference to his partnership with the Philippians at the beginning (1:5) and end (4:15–18) of his letter indicates that this letter serves as a 'thank you' for their financial support. Paul addressed the leaders of the church because they were the ones who administered this support and sent Epaphroditus bearing the gifts of the church to Paul (4:18)."[3]

The church at Philippi supported the missionary work of the Apostle Paul while he was imprisoned in Rome over 800 miles away. Though transportation was slow, difficult, and expensive, the Philippian church found a way for gospel partnership. This would have involved arranging travel, lodging, and the security of funds in a world without Airbnb, bank transfers, or airplanes. Getting support to Paul was a complex missional operation—one made possible by all the offices of the church working together in Philippi.

---

the fixation on titles and status that was so prevalent in the colony, by practicing in his greeting the very relational ethos he would enjoin later in the epistle: 'in humility consider others as more important than yourselves' (Phil. 2:3)." Hellerman's book is fantastic and I wholeheartedly recommend his work, but I do think there is more going on in Paul's motivation for addressing both overseers and deacons in this letter. Joseph H. Hellerman, *Embracing Shared Ministry: Power and Status in the Early Church and Why It Matters Today* (Grand Rapids: Kregel Ministry, 2013), 128.

[3] G. Walter Hansen, *The Letter to the Philippians*, (PNTC; Grand Rapids: Eerdmans, 2009), 195.

The Saints

Paul first recognizes the saints in Philippians 1:1. Every local church is fundamentally made up of saints—those whom God has made holy by grace through faith in Jesus. Saints are given a new identity in Christ, and they band together to carry out the work of the ministry in and through local churches. Ephesians 4:12 explains that God has given spiritual leaders not to *do* the work of the ministry for the saints, but to *equip* the saints for the work of the ministry. Every individual saint, therefore, is responsible for building up the whole through their unique gifting, spheres of influence, and opportunities. Paul describes the local church saints in this way, "For as in one body we have many members, so we, though many, are one body in Christ, and individually members of one another. Having gifts that differ according to the grace given to us, let us use them" (Rom. 12:4–6).

Without uniquely gifted saints giving, praying, and discipling, the Philippian church could not have maintained their own ministry in Philippi, much less steward a healthy and generous gospel partnership with Paul in Rome. For Paul to be provided for, some faithful saints stewarded their businesses well and generously gave toward the work while encouraging fellow saints to do the same. The multiplication ministry is an every-member-ministry. Dietrich Bonhoeffer offers this strong but helpful warning, "The chain is unbreakable only when even the smallest link holds tightly with the others. A community which permits within itself members who do nothing, will be destroyed by them."[4] The multi-plication mission is fueled by church members who gather regularly and do the work of the ministry together in a way that overflows to the ends of the earth.[5]

The Elders

All organizations need leadership. Armies need generals, teams need coaches, and sheep need shepherds. The position of leadership God designed for the church is the office of shepherd/ elder/overseer (Acts 20:17, 28; 1 Pet. 5:1).[6] The church in Philippi had become more established since the early days of ministry in Lydia's house. They now had a plurality of overseers teaching, leading, and shepherding. According to Paul's letter to Titus, a church is "out of order" until this leadership structure is put into place (Titus 1:5). This plurality of leadership no doubt played an essential role to lead the way for the whole church's partnership with Paul. The overseers must have been teaching the congregation to

---

[4] Dietrich Bonhoeffer, *Dietrich Bonhoeffer Works,* Volume 5, (Minneapolis: Fortress Press, 2005) 96.

[5] For a clear and thorough argument for church-centered missions see two volumes: Aaron Menikoff and Harshit Singh, *Prioritizing Missions in the Church* (9Marks Church-Centered Missions; Wheaton, IL: Crossway, 2025) and John Folmar and Scott Logsdon, *Prioritizing the Church in Missions* (9Marks Church-Centered Missions, series ed. Jonathan Leeman; Wheaton, IL: Crossway, 2025).

[6] For a detailed breakdown of each title and how they are used interchangeably in the New Testament see: Phil A. Newton and Matt Schmucker, *Elders in the Life of the Church: Rediscovering the Biblical Model for Church Leadership* (9Marks; Grand Rapids: Kregel Ministry, 2005), 45.

cherish Paul's message and missionary work. They must have been leading their congregation to give sacrificially and strategically. They must have led the way in discipling those who could go and represent the church. Without leadership, teaching, and oversight, the kind of gospel partnership Paul deems praiseworthy doesn't happen. Elders set the trajectory, but there are practical limits to what a group of shepherds can do.

The Deacons

Beyond the Word ministry, prayer, and leading of the elders and the everyday disciple-making, evangelizing, giving, and serving of the members, church ministry requires significant logistical and practical administration. Who collected, counted, and protected the money for the Philippian church while they raised funds? Who arranged the travel and did the hard work of carrying the support such great distances amidst the many dangers? When Paul was arranging for believers to carry financial support from Corinth to Jerusalem, he wrote to the Corinthians asking for individuals whom they "accredit" for the task (1 Cor. 16:3). Those kinds of accredited servants would need exemplary character and a servant's heart. Beyond this missional project, who helped organize all the other ministries on the home front in Philippi while support was being taken to Rome? There must have been a robust deacon ministry built after the pattern of Acts 6.

Deacon Ministry: The Origin Story

In Acts 6, Luke emphasizes that the disciples were increasing in number. This rapid growth brought new levels of complexity to the ministry.[7] More people in the church means more needs. More people mean more sinners attempting to work together. A notable percentage of the growth came from widows who no longer had means of supporting themselves, but who had found refuge in the Christian community. Daily allocations were distributed from the common fund to meet the need, but as the need grew so did the logistical burden.[8] Land, animals, money, and personal possessions were donated, sold or traded, and then the proceeds were used to purchase supplies that had to be distributed.

The already-daunting task of food distribution became even more difficult when accusations arose over presumed injustice. A group of Hellenist widows complained that the Hebrew widows were getting special treatment. This injustice was more than an administrative issue. The unity of the church was in danger. Two groups of women from rival cultures were now in a conflict so intense that it threatened the Word ministry of the apostles. John Stott explains, "The apostles discerned a deeper problem, namely that social ad-

---

[7] Darrel Bock comments on Acts 6:1, "This verse presents the juxtaposition of two realities in the new community: a growth in the number of disciples and a management problem that this growth is producing among Hellenists and Gentiles." Darrell L. Bock, *Acts* (BECNT; Grand Rapids: Baker Academic, 2007), 257.

[8] F. F. Bruce, *The Book of the Acts*, rev. ed., The New International Commentary on the New Testament (Grand Rapids: William B. Eerdmans, 1988), 120.

ministration (both organizing and distribution and settling the complaint) was threatening to occupy all their time and so inhibit them from the work which Christ had specifically entrusted to them, namely preaching and teaching."[9]

There were certainly many instances worth reporting in the first century, but Luke chose to record this situation to show both the seriousness of the threat and the wisdom of the solution. Under the influence of the Holy Spirit, the apostles determined that the widow care ministry be delegated to a select group of servant leaders, thus laying the groundwork for a permanent ecclesiological structure.

Seven men were chosen from among the congregation. They were of good repute, full of the Spirit, and full of wisdom. They were Hellenists themselves, specifically chosen for the important task of restoring unity. From the listed qualifications, the apostles surely intended for these servants to do more than just serve tables. A hostile situation was brewing, and they would need relational skills to navigate the waters of conflict and accusation.[10] Additionally, the task of collecting, organizing, and distributing food would have been beyond the scope of what these men could accomplish alone. They would have needed to organize and oversee the ministry while mobilizing the church members to carry out the work alongside them. F. F. Bruce argues that the nature of the work tasked to these deacons demanded special qual-

---

[9] John Stott, *The Message of Acts* (BST; Downers Grove, IL: IVP Academic, 1990), 121.

[10] See Merkle's forthcoming volume, *Authority*, for a thorough explanation of diaconate ministry.

ifications. He writes, "They should be wise men, competent in administration and also qualified to deal wisely with a situation in which such delicate human susceptibilities had to be considered."[11]

Luke provides six growth summaries that function like snapshots of the missional progress in the book of Acts.[12] Each summary is strategically placed at a crucial point in the unfolding story to communicate how the church is multiplying.[13] Acts 6:7 tells us that it was after the appointment of these deacons that the Word of God continued to increase, and the number of disciples multiplied greatly in Jerusalem. The point is clear. Deacon ministry makes multiplication possible.

Deacon Ministry and Church Planting Today

Some church planters reject the office of deacon because of their own bad experiences with deacon boards. I remember a story from Bible college about a deacon who threw a Bible through a stained-glass window in fierce opposition against his pastor. For many, the office itself has become associated with painful experiences. Church splits, divisions, and pastoral burnout have been attributed to unhelpful deacons. Ignoring or neglecting a biblical concept, however, is not the right response. We cannot throw out preaching just because

---

[11] Bruce, *Acts*, 121.

[12] Acts 6:7; 9:31; 12:24; 16:5; 19:20; 28:31; Richard N. Longenecker, *The Acts of the Apostles* (EBC; Frank Gaebelein, gen. ed.; Grand Rapids: Zondervan, 1981), 234, calls these verses panels or progress reports.

[13] Stott, *The Message of Acts*, 123.

we have heard bad sermons, and we cannot ignore a biblical office because of its distortions.[14]

If the Word increased and disciples multiplied because of deacon ministry in the first century, it's sensible to say that a church who lacks a deacon ministry may also be stunted in their multiplication. Let's consider all the practical and logistical responsibilities that go into pulling off just one Sunday gathering. A whole host of details must come together. Bills are paid, facilities are cleaned, the air conditioning is working (hopefully), technology is utilized, music is planned, childcare is coordinated, the ordinances are prepared, parking is managed, bulletins are printed, visitors are greeted, offering is collected, announcements are made, and the list goes on. We haven't even begun to discuss what it takes to operate other ministries throughout the week. Additionally, God has called us to more than just the Sunday gathering. We are commanded to be salt and light in the world (Matt. 5:13–16). We are called to care for the impoverished, the helpless, and the hurting (James 1:26–27). Consider ministries that care for the drug addict, the homeless, the orphan, the widow, the homebound, the grieving, and the sick. Consider ministries that provide counsel and guidance for the broken family, ministries that evangelize the lost, and ministries that disciple children and youth.

What about church planting and church revitalization efforts? What structures and systems need to be in place to

---

[14] "How Are Deacons Misunderstood?" *Devoted Together (blog)*, August 25, 2021, https://devotedtogether.com/2021/08/25/how-are-deacons-misunderstood/.

recruit and train future planters? What is the plan for maintaining close relationships and providing support to those planters already sent? Consider the logistical details that are involved with sending missionaries and maintaining gospel partnerships among people groups that have no access to the message of Jesus around the world. If pastors are left to coordinate all of this, they may sell the church short in the weekly teaching of the Word, they may have to punt on leading the church into missional endeavors, or they may try to do it all and they won't be pastors for long. Deacon ministry changes the game for overwhelmed pastors and underserved communities. It can free up multiplication bandwidth in a sending church, and it should certainly be a factor while assembling a church planting team. If possible, church planting teams should seek to appoint deacon-qualified members to lead areas of service from the beginning. The spiritual qualifications and expectations for each role will positively impact the culture of the whole church.

Deacon Ministry Implementation

The airline industry operates with all its moving parts working together because a group of people came together to create, execute, and oversee a plan. On a smaller scale, but of greater significance, someone did the same for the missionary enterprise of getting support and encouragement to the imprisoned Paul. Creating a robust deacon ministry for the needs of your church will require some hard thinking, planning, and strategizing on the front end with the possibility of a big kingdom pay-off in the long run.

One of our lay elders works for a metal roofing company. They bend, sell, and distribute metal roofs all over the southeast United States. Our lay elder is the general manager who oversees the day-to-day operations and watches for ways that he can make processes more efficient. Their company recently embraced a philosophy of business called lean thinking famously embraced by Toyota. The basic premise is to lead your team to take ownership of the company's efficiency by cutting waste and improving processes. The key to the business philosophy is ownership. Everyone must own their part in the ecosystem. One of the practical encouragements for every company overseer is to slowly work through every single process and system where product moves from one stage to another, stopping to ask who owns which part of the process and what can be improved to cut waste so that employees can spend time accomplishing what is most valuable.

Now, I don't believe churches should be built on big business principles. But occasionally a well-run business stumbles across godly wisdom. As an exercise, let's think about your current church. Let's follow the footsteps of potential visitors who live near your church's gathering place. When they arrive in your church parking lot, what do they see? Do they see trash in the parking lot, uncut crass, or a full lot with no one to direct them or greet them? Whose responsibility is that? Who owns this part of logistical responsibility? Was the pastor supposed to do a parking lot sweep that morning before Sunday service? Is he to walk out into the parking lot during the first five minutes of the gathering to make sure people find their way? Or could this be the responsibility of a qualified deacon? We have had visitors pull into our packed parking lot before, unable to find a spot, and then pull right back out onto the road. A deacon of parking who mobilizes a parking team could have changed that reality.

Let's keep following our guests. They enter the foyer. Who greets them? They try to find the nursery. Who oversees that? They sit down, fill out a welcome card, and drop it in a box before leaving. Who is going to follow up? If someone does follow up, what does the process look like to assimilate them into the life of the church? Over the years, I realized that as the lead pastor, I take ownership directly over too many things at our church. There are too many tasks that fall upon me only because I have not done the hard but important work of recognizing deacon-qualified people and empowering them. My hope is to appoint deacons for every aspect of our church's ministry. I want a deacon of welcome and hospitality, visitor follow-up, audio/video/tech, member care, missionary care, children's discipleship, youth discipleship, bus ministry, women's discipleship, and more. I want to cast a vision for these faithful church members not only to take ownership of their area of service, but to model Christ-likeness, mobilize members to do the same, and even to disciple someone to do what they do.

Work through everything your church does from the time visitors show up to your church gathering until they are sent out years later on a church-planting team. Be as detailed as possible, stopping along the way to ask, "Who owns this part of the process? Can a deacon role be utilized here?"

As qualified members take ownership of each step, the pastors will be free to preach, pray, and lead the church into more faithful and fruitful missional engagement. More creative deacon roles may even emerge that will lead to more planting. Maybe a deacon of ESL ministry will lay the foundation for a church plant among a particular people group. Perhaps a deacon of church planting could be developed who will coordinate planter care and connection efforts with your sent ones. The point is, deacon ministry will help your church focus on multiplication. Before you set out to plant a church, take some time to strategically implement the ministry of deacons. You will not only make your church healthier, but you will be freer to plan, pray, and lead toward church planting both locally and globally.

Deacon Ministry and Spurgeon

Geoffrey Chang served the church well with his book on Charles Spurgeon's biblical and theological vision for ministry.[15] Spurgeon is well-known as the Prince of Preachers, and rightfully so. But Chang helps us to see that Spurgeon was far more than a preacher. He was a real pastor of a real church who took seriously both the Bible's teaching on ecclesiology and the Great Commission task of planting churches.

To say that Spurgeon was an ambitious and hard-working pastor is an understatement. His kingdom impact and legacy are a miraculous display of the Spirit's work. If you want to gain credibility or a hearing in your writing or speaking, just quote Spurgeon and ears perk up. The scope, breadth, and depth of his ministry is staggering, but he didn't

---

[15] Geoffrey Chang, *Spurgeon the Pastor: Recovering a Biblical and Theological Vision for Ministry* (Nashville: B&H Publishing Group, 2022).

accomplish that ministry alone. He had elders and deacons in the trenches with him.

By 1868, The Metropolitan Tabernacle had ten deacons. Spurgeon writes of their ministry:

> Their duties are to care for the ministry, and help the poor of the church, to regulate the finances and take charge of the church's property, seeing to the order and comfort of all worshipping in the place. The work is divided so as to secure the services of all and prevent the neglect of anything through uncertainty as to the person responsible for its performance. One honored brother is general treasurer, and has been so for many years - long may he be spared to us; another takes all out-door work, repairs of the exterior, keeping the gates, appointing doorkeepers, etc.; another has all indoor repairs; while others watch over the interest of the new churches which are springing from our loins; and one brother as a good steward sees to the arrangement and provision of the weekly communion, and the elements required for the Lord's table; thus with a common council we separate duties.[16]

The Metropolitan Tabernacle saw an incredible increase of the Word in their day as disciples and churches multiplied. Honestly, it sounds a lot like Acts 6:7. If you want

---

[16] Chang, *Spurgeon the Pastor*, 161.

your church to become a multiplying church, heed the wise warning of Spurgeon, "Deprive the church of her deacons, and she would be bereaved of her most valiant sons; their loss would be the shaking of the pillars of our spiritual house and would cause a desolation on every side."[17]

---

[17] Chang, *Spurgeon the Pastor*, 162.

CHAPTER 17

HOW CAN I TRAIN THE CHURCH PLANT IN EVANGELISM?

Karson Douglas Merkel

Why are you planting a church anyway? If you polled your pastors and your church planting core team, would they have similar answers? Perhaps some are excited to be part of the "adventure," whatever happens. Maybe others are tired of fighting for parking spaces and cushioned seats in your crowded meeting place. Some who are going simply want a shorter church commute. Hopefully, whatever side benefits may come, your people have bigger, God-sized goals in mind—seeing another place in the community transformed by the gospel's power, seeing broken lives restored by the patient and loving witness of a body of believers, and co-laboring to establish a new outpost of heaven to the glory of

God. These goals establish a church plant. It's easier to get a few people gathering in a new place under a new leader. It's much harder to root missionary DNA in the life of those people such that they give themselves to this work until Jesus returns.

If you want to see that other neighborhood or city reached with the gospel, how do you expect that growth to happen? There are a few possibilities. The growth might happen *through transition*. Christians in the vicinity of the new plant will likely hear about it and some may join. Sometimes this is good, particularly if they're coming from unhealthy churches or places with no healthy churches nearby. But growth through transition should not be our primary goal. Too often, church plants unintentionally weaken other churches by drawing away members. We want to see growth through conversions, not just transition.

Church growth might happen *through addition*. This could also be called "pulpit growth." As we preach God's Word, we pray that it would pierce hearts and lead the lost to repentance and faith. Paul charged Timothy to "preach the Word" and to "do the work of an evangelist" (2 Tim. 4:2, 5). Peter preached at Pentecost and about "three thousand souls" were "added" (Acts 2:41). Imagine if God did that through your church plant! However, growth by addition centers around one person preaching and is limited to those in the room. We celebrate this kind of growth, but we need more than growth through addition.

Our church plants need growth *through multiplication*. As pastors and leaders of the sending church, God has given you to the congregation not simply to *do* the work of ministry but to *equip the saints* for it (Eph. 4:11–12). I assume that's largely why you've picked up this resource—you earnestly desire to equip your people for the work of ministry, especially evangelism. While growth through transition is inevitable, and growth through addition is essential, growth through multiplication is where our churches' greatest impact can be unlocked.

Now I'm not advocating a "multiplying movement" sort of missiology.[1] I don't think that church planters ought to have a "need for speed," so to speak. I'm simply saying that "two are better than one, for they have a good reward for their toil" (Eccl. 4:9). And yet, we can easily overlook this sort of organic growth by focusing on things like staffing or programs. Writing in 1960, missionary and missions professor J. H. Bavinck observed that nearly all sending churches have "from the outset failed to recognize and to use the tremendous power inherent in the ordinary believer."[2]

Just think of all the places that your people go in a week that you will never step foot in—workplaces and neighborhoods, doctors' offices and classrooms. Consider all the people represented through relationships and friendships with your church members. The opportunities are vast! If you can excite and equip your members for evangelism in their everyday lives, they'll not only go more places than a pastor or staff

---

[1] See chapter 3 in this book where Phil addresses movement methodology, showing its contrast with healthy evangelism and ecclesiology.

[2] J. H. Bavinck, *Introduction to the Science of Missions* (Phillipsburg, NJ: P&R, 1960), 214. See chapter 7 where Matt advocates for developing a planting team that has the church's mission at heart.

team could ever go; they'll be in all those places at once. And as God works through the faithful witness of normal believers in local churches, His Word "multiplies" (Acts 6:7, 9:31, 12:24). How can you help the church plant grow through the multiplication of each member engaging in evangelism? Well, in many ways, the work of training has already begun.

Your Work Starts Now

Missionaries don't learn how to share their faith while they're on the airplane to a foreign land, magically gaining clarity on the gospel and acquiring the boldness to share it while they're 30,000 feet in the sky. No, long before they leave their homeland, they've either learned those things or they haven't.

The same principle applies to a church plant. The planting team doesn't just "figure things out" once they get to where they're going. The men and women of the church plant will be discipled into faithful and fervent evangelism (or not) before they even set foot on the other side of town or in that other city or state. As Robert Coleman notes, Jesus began preparing His disciples long before sending them out: "Remarkable as it may seem, Jesus started to gather these men before he ever organized an evangelistic campaign or even preached a sermon in public."[3]

The goal of your church and the church plant is clear, but how can you ensure you are cultivating zeal and faithfulness for evangelism before they're launched? How can you

---

[3] Robert Emerson Coleman, *The Master Plan of Evangelism* (Grand Rapids, MI: Revell, 2009), 21.

make your sending church into a greenhouse for evangelism as you prepare to send out this plant?

Clarifying Evangelism

If you've ever gardened or owned a houseplant, you understand how important it is to know what you're trying to grow. The sunlight, soil, and water requirements vary from plant to plant, and if you get it wrong, you'll end up inhibiting the plant's growth, smothering it, or even making your garden into a haven for weeds.

In the same way, we need to be clear on what "evangelism" is if we want it to flourish. What counts as evangelism—and what doesn't? How specific and intentional do we need to be in our training? How do we know if we're doing something wrong or if we just need to be patient?

We often explain evangelism by saying it's "sharing the gospel," but consider Mack Stiles' slightly longer definition: "Evangelism is teaching the gospel with the aim to persuade."[4] You can break that definition down into four simple parts:

1. "Teaching" could be anything from a one-off conversation or Bible study to a Sunday morning sermon.

---

[4] J. Mack Stiles, *Evangelism: How the Whole Church Speaks of Jesus* (Wheaton, IL: Crossway, 2014), 26.

2. Our "aim" keeps us from being content with mere information-transfer or chasing rabbit trails in our evangelistic conversations.

3. "Persuading" comes from 2 Corinthians 5:11 and means we seek to convince others with grace and wisdom rather than manipulation or frustration.

4. Most importantly, "the gospel" is what we aim to teach persuasively. There are many methods to share this good news, but it always touches at least four points: God's holiness; our sinfulness; Christ's life, death, and resurrection; and the response required to receive the gift of salvation.

Evangelism isn't just for pastors or those with a "gift." All Christians are commanded to be prepared to share with others the reason (the *apologia* or substantial explanation) for the hope that's in them (1 Pet. 3:15). And every Christian is sent out and commanded to evangelize—to proclaim repentance and forgiveness of sins as Christ's witnesses, making disciples of all nations (Matt. 28:18–20, Mark 16:15, Luke 24:47–48, John 20:21, Acts 1:8). This is the central focus of the church's mission, and as members of the body of Christ, we must all be engaged in this mission.

We do well to think of evangelism as a team sport rather than an individual activity. God designed evangelism to include the whole church working together. The love and unity between a church's members are a witness to the watching world (John 13:35; 17:20–21). Robust evangelism needs a

church—a connected church, growing in Christ together—
to be an effective evangelistic witness.

Motivating Evangelistic Fervor

Often, when pastors want their churches to grow in evangelism, their mind goes first to programs. What kind of event
can we plan so that people can invite their non-believing
friends? Or what kind of training can we schedule to *really*
get people excited about evangelism? While programs have
their place, what a church needs is a heart for evangelism,
not just the tools to do it. The fastest car in the world is use-
less without a battery hooked up or gas in the tank. And we
desperately need our churches to be plugged in and fueled up
with the heart necessary for evangelism. So, what's the fuel?

The critical fuel for growing in evangelism is a love for
the gospel. Help your people to love Jesus more, and they
will grow in their evangelism. Love for others will spur them
on at times (1 Thess. 2:8). Pity and concern will motivate
them (Jude 23). So will duty and obedience (Matt. 28:18–
20). However, the most powerful and sustainable fuel for
growing in evangelism is growing in love for Jesus and what
He has done for us in the gospel. Stiles summarizes it this
way, "Be so in love with Jesus, so enamored with his sacrifice
for sinners, so grateful for the forgiveness of your sins, so
amazed with his grace that you can't help the gospel message
coming out of you."[5]

---

[5] J. Mack Stiles, *How Do I Get Started in Evangelism* (Wheaton, IL: Crossway), 23, Kindle.

If you or your people are lacking in evangelism, it may reflect a lack of joy in Jesus. Evangelism is a combination of zeal for what we believe, concern for our neighbor, obedience to our King's command, and love for our Savior because of what He's done. Love like this is contagious. The more you, as a leader and a sending church, lift high the beauty of Jesus Christ, the more your people will love Him as well and grow in their desire to obey His commands. As we obey Jesus in evangelism, we demonstrate our love for Him (John 14:21). Teaching your people to treasure Christ is the key to helping a congregation see that evangelism is a normal part of life for *all* Christians, not just the "professional" ones.

Measuring Evangelistic Success

In five years, how would you know if the church plant was faithful in its evangelism? Numbers? Movements? Revival? For the church planter and the sending church, it must be crystal clear that success is faithfulness, not "results." Faithfulness is up to us; the fruit is up to God. "Neither he who plants nor he who waters is anything, but only God who gives the growth" (1 Cor. 3:7).

As a sending church, watch your words and tone when asking for updates. You don't want to communicate an unbiblical expectation for the church plant to do what only God can do. Instead, your job is to constantly encourage. Use your words to put wind into their sails and help them to be gospel-driven rather than numbers-driven. Tell your church planting pastor(s) when and how you pray for them.

Trust that it's the Holy Spirit who "regenerates and draws sinners to repentance and faith in Jesus Christ as Savior."[6]

Developing an Evangelistic Culture

The best soil for evangelism is cultivated by a vibrant culture of evangelism in your church. Culture is believing "people like us do things like this."[7] If you can instill in your church beliefs like "Jesus followers like us talk about Jesus," then evangelism will become part of their DNA. The people in your church body will have different strengths and levels of experience, but they can work together and disciple one another to share the gospel with their neighbors and friends. Aim to develop and strengthen a culture of evangelism within your sending church now, while the church plant is still in its incubation stage. This culture will likely be the greatest tool God uses to stoke their fervent and faithful witness. Evangelistic strategies can be helpful, but "culture eats strategy for lunch."[8]

What does this kind of culture look like? It looks like coming to the gathering with antennas up—ready, expectant, and eager for gospel conversations. It looks like reaching out before gospel opportunities to ask for prayer or support. It looks like thinking first about the work of ministry starting

---

[6] Pillar Network, "Statement of Faith," accessed June 26, 2025, https://thepillarnetwork.com/beliefs.

[7] Seth Godin, "People like us (do things like this): Change a culture, change your world." Seth's Blog, accessed June 27, 2025, https://seths.blog/wp-content/uploads/2013/07/2017-people-like-us.pdf.

[8] Godin, "People like us."

with them, not about what church leaders will do to organize the people in evangelism. As Stiles reminds us, "A culture of evangelism is grassroots, not top-down."[9]

As the sending church, it's essential to be confident in those you're sending because the people you send will shape the culture of the church plant. The New Testament pattern was to send not just anyone, but their very best (consider the pattern in Acts 13, where the Antioch church sends out Paul and Barnabas). This principle has gained renewed attention in the missions' community, and we should adopt the same mindset for church planting. That doesn't mean every team member needs formal theological training or cross-cultural skills. But it does mean that we should be generous in our sending and intentional in our training, especially in teaching and discipling people on our core teams.

The weeds of nominalism and easy-believism can choke out a culture of evangelism. If your people don't know who "we" are—if there are no clear borders of meaningful membership—then a culture of evangelism will struggle to take root and flourish. At a basic level, church members must be able to trust that others in the body understand and can communicate the gospel. If I don't trust that the people at my church are clear on the gospel, why would I want to bring my non-Christian friends to be around them? So we must ensure that our church planting team is clear on the gospel and that they understand their evangelistic responsibility as Christians. A culture of evangelism doesn't require a team of Michael Jordans—elite evangelists with standout skill. It's

---

[9] Stiles, *Evangelism*, 65.

about having a *team*—a team with a shared understanding, a shared goal, and a shared willingness to grow together in gospel faithfulness.

Cultivating Faithful Evangelism

What does this look like on a practical level? Let me offer five applications to prepare your church plant for faithful evangelism.

Teach the Gospel Thoroughly and Plainly

The fountain of teaching in any church is the pulpit, and you can train your people well by modeling faithful evangelism in your sermons. Make the gospel thorough and plain in every sermon. Speak as if you expect non-Christians to be in the room, addressing them respectfully and directly. For instance, consider how a Buddhist would differ in his understanding of that point, and how Christianity offers a better answer. Over time, your faithful example of sharing the gospel from the front will equip your church and church plant with a great foundation. The apple won't fall far from the tree. The way that you value and practice evangelism now is likely what you'll see in this new plant.

Review the gospel in core team meetings. Encourage your church planter to walk through the gospel plainly with prospective members as they prepare to plant. Teaching Ephesians in bite-sized chunks would be a great start. As they explore the gospel and emphasize its priority, they could have their people practice sharing it with one another.

Get People Together

Talk to your church planting pastor about the team going to plant. Are there natural or gifted evangelists among them? Help them to get other members involved in the evangelism they're already doing. Challenge them to think not just about doing the work, but bringing other church members with them as they go. Coleman calls this "principle of association" an important part of the master plan of evangelism.[10] Good evangelism is contagious, and going together often disarms the fears that deter some church members from sharing their faith.

Give Away Resources

Encourage members of the church plant to read good books about evangelism together. At prayer meetings and core team meetings, give away books like *Evangelism* by Mack Stiles, *Gospel Fluency* by Jeff Vanderstelt, or *The Gospel Comes with a House Key* by Rosaria Butterfield.[11] There are also great resources for walking through the gospel with non-Christians that you could pass on to the church plant team.[12] If some-

---

[10] Coleman, *Master Plan of Evangelism*, 35.

[11] There are certainly more books we could list here, such as Will Metzger's *Tell the Truth* (4th ed. rev.; Downers Grove, IL: IVP) or J. I. Packer's *Evangelism and the Sovereignty of God* (Downers Grove, IL: IVP, 2012).

[12] *Christianity Explained* is an effective evangelistic Bible Study available for free online at christianityexplained.com. Greg Gilbert's books can also be useful in the evangelism process: *What is the Gospel?* (9Marks; Wheaton, IL: Crossway, 2010) and *Who is Jesus?* (9Marks; Wheaton, IL: Crossway, 2015). See also Phil A. Newton, *Are You a Christian? Many Opinions, One Truth* (Greenville, SC: Courier Publications, 2025).

one is apprehensive about evangelism, he or she can simply read through the pamphlet *Two Ways to Live* from Matthias Media or other good gospel tracts. Grease the wheels of good evangelism by generously giving away resources.

Platform and Encourage Good Gospel Stories

Take some time at your next prayer meeting or core team meeting to intentionally highlight effective evangelism or gospel stories. Here are some ideas:

- Ask someone to share his or her personal testimony. You can work with the person beforehand to ensure the gospel is clear.

- Invite members to share in a prayer meeting about recent gospel conversations they've had with people in their lives.

- Interview a member who's started an evangelistic Bible study in the workplace or who's been processing the gospel with a neighbor.

- Invite a member to give a recap of an evangelistic book you've handed out.

- Pray publicly for the specific evangelism efforts of people in your body and pray that the church would see themselves as partners in evangelism and gospel ministry.

By calling attention to these efforts, you're helping your people to see that evangelism is normal, and that "people like us do things like this."

Pray!

"Pray earnestly to the Lord of the harvest to send out laborers into his harvest" (Matt. 9:38). Pray privately and pray publicly for this culture to take root in your church plant. Pray for opportunities to present themselves and for your people to have the courage to jump into them.

Gather the planting team often to pray together for the work ahead. Have them pray for the specific neighborhoods or schools in the vicinity of the new church. This will put their minds in the right place, expecting God to work.

Pruning Common Pitfalls

Along with these practical applications, there are a few things we should avoid and even prune back as we cultivate faithful and fervent evangelism.

Focusing Too Much on "Adapting to the Culture"

When our church began its core group meetings before planting, our pastors were often asked about what they were going to do to reach the more artistic and liberal area they were going to. It's easy for church planters to look at their context and feel the pressure to become like the culture in order to attract people to Christ. But when Paul speaks of being "all things to all people" (1 Cor. 9:22), he's speaking of removing obstacles to the gospel message, not adding incentives.

Tim Keller explains that "to the degree a ministry is overadapted or underadapted to a culture, it loses life-changing power."[13] In our current cultural moment, the tendency is to overadapt. Yes, cultural particulars matter. But the most important aspects of our churches will make us look a lot like other churches throughout the world and across time. As your church plant seeks to adapt to the place they're going, encourage them to focus on the main things and not the flair. Help them consider that what you win them *with* is usually what you win them *to*. Focus on faithfulness, and don't make culture king.

Boxing Evangelism into a Specific Approach

The Roman Road, the Four Spiritual Laws, the Bridge Illustration, a 90-second testimony—there are many ways for your people to receive training in evangelism. Are some methods better than others? Of course! But as a pastor, or as a sending church, you'll do well to fan the flame of whatever faithful evangelistic methods your people pursue.

The danger comes when we turn one method into *the* method. When we start equating a particular method with sharing the gospel, we risk discouraging our people or distorting the riches of the gospel message. Paul, in his evangelistic speeches in Acts, doesn't say the same thing every time. Jesus didn't follow up his instructions on prayer in Matthew 6 and add, "When you evangelize, evangelize like this." Don't make your people think that if they didn't use method X, they haven't *really* shared the gospel. In my experience, sometimes the best approach is the simplest: ask someone to

---

[13] Tim Keller, *Center Church: Doing Balanced, Gospel-Centered Ministry in Your City* (Grand Rapids: Zondervan, 2012), 24.

read the Bible with you. As Coleman puts it, "The Master gives us an outline to follow, but he expects us to work out the details according to local circumstances and traditions."[14]

Relying Too Heavily on Programs

Programs are fun and they're usually easy to get people to rally behind. But in most cases, their impact is limited. They're often brief and non-relational; any fruit they bear typically comes through faithful follow-up or existing personal relationships. Programs often end up being like sugar for your congregation or church plant—they might provide a quick burst of energy, but too much will lead to bellyaches and malnutrition. A healthy diet of evangelism puts less confidence in exciting events and more confidence in the gospel.[15]

The aim of an evangelistic church should be to cultivate the right culture, not put on the right program. Remind your congregation or church plant that "the growth of the gospel happens in the lives of people, not in the structures of the church."[16] How do you know what programs to keep? The book *The Trellis and the Vine* offers a compelling illustration: our trellis-like programs are only valuable inasmuch as they help the vine of spiritual life to grow. It's worth it to constantly reassess the programs put on by your church and measure

---

[14] Coleman, *Master Plan of Evangelism*, 100.

[15] Stiles, *How Do I Get Started in Evangelism*, 24.

[16] Collin Marshall and Tony Payne, *The Trellis and the Vine: The Ministry Mind-Shift That Changes Everything* (Kingsford, N.S.W.: Matthias Media, 2009), 82.

their intent versus their impact. Just because your church has "always done" an evangelistic Christmas event doesn't mean you must continue to fund it or do it in the same way. Some "trellis" is necessary, but sending churches should encourage their planters to "make a conscious shift away from erecting and maintaining structures (programs), and towards growing people who are disciple-making disciples of Christ."[17]

There are so many ways for your church plant to be faithful in its evangelism. And the key to avoiding common pitfalls is to keep the gospel front and center. Preach Christ faithfully, love Him genuinely, pray for evangelism fervently, and encourage evangelism generously. May God give your church plant a healthy, lasting culture of evangelism.

---

[17] Marshall and Payne, *The Trellis and the Vine*, 17.

PART 5

CARING FOR
A CHURCH PLANT

CHAPTER 18

WHAT ARE THE TASKS AND TENSIONS OF SHEPHERDING THE SENT?

Dwayne Milioni

Launching a church plant is a lot like launching children into the real world. You use the same parenting principles, yet each child operates differently. Some kids leave the nest and immediately flourish, while others struggle to survive. The same is true of church plants sent by local churches. Due to the unique dynamics of each church plant, the task and tension of caring for those sent remains an ongoing and complex challenge for the sending church.

Like children, church plant teams come in various shapes and sizes. While the process of equipping teams is similar, and while they all share common doctrine and mission, the ongoing care for each plant or re-plant can vary according to unique factors. Having sent out twenty teams to plant or replant churches, I will attest that variability is the only constant factor in team make-up, location, and context. The key is the relationship between the sending church and the team being sent.

Some church plants hit the ground running. The team is solid, unified, and the lead planter fits naturally with his team and new context. The church finds a suitable place to meet, and from the beginning, the Lord blesses it with steady growth. But that's not always the story. Other teams face real challenges. Sometimes, team members move on, and the team feels unsettled. Some lead planters work to understand their new context and still find it challenging to lead. Finding a place to gather can be frustrating, and unexpected costs seem to pop up. Growth might be slow or not happen at all for a season. Every plant has its own story. And that's okay.

For sending churches, the mission is always the same: every church plant must become a gospel-centered, autonomous, and kingdom-minded church. Sometimes that happens sooner than expected; other times, it takes a bit longer. But during that in-between time—the season between when a team is sent and when the new church officially covenants—the sending church must answer critical questions. How involved should the sending church be? How much authority should it hold during the transition?

It comes down to finding the right balance. The sending church has a role to play in offering support, guidance, and oversight, but it must not hold on too tightly. The goal is to help the new church grow toward maturity without hindering its progress or overlooking immediate needs.[1] A clearly defined relationship between the sender and those sent is vital during this transition period.

Again, it's a lot like parenting. Initially, parents have full authority over their children. Over time, as children mature and prepare to step out on their own, the relationship shifts from one of authority to one of influence. The same is true with church planting. Initially, the sending church and its elders may hold authority over the team, but as the plant matures, the goal is to gradually release authority while continuing to offer wise and loving influence. The following chart illustrates the progression of this shift over time.

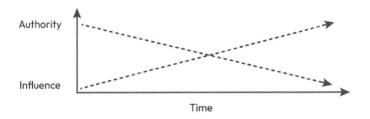

How does a sending church offer the kind of oversight that helps a plant grow toward healthy, Baptist autonomy? Every plant shares the same mission, but because each one is shaped by its own people and context, the sending church

---

[1] Aubrey Malphurs, *The Nuts and Bolts of Church Planting* (Grand Rapids: Baker Books, 2015), 17–26.

must remain relationally engaged yet flexible, striking a balance between control and enablement.[2]

Biblical and Theological Foundations for Sending Oversight

Biblical Foundations

From the beginning, The Pillar Network has focused more on the sending church than its church plants. We desire to be a growing family of multiplying churches. As such, the church at Antioch stands out in Scripture as the clearest example of what it means to be an equipping and sending church. The Antioch church, shaped by prayer and the leading of the Holy Spirit, offers a model for modern churches in gospel expansion through church planting. Their attentiveness to the Spirit's guidance made church planting a natural outflow of how they lived out the gospel. Their ongoing relationship with the church planters they sent paints a picture of faithful sending and oversight. As such, we encourage every local church to become an Antioch Church. When it comes to how the sending church relates to its church planting teams, their example provides a solid framework for faithful, hands-on, and relational oversight.

As the gospel spread beyond Jerusalem and Judea, the Holy Spirit began to move in the hearts of Gentiles. When the gospel was proclaimed to the Greeks in Antioch, many came to saving faith in Christ (Acts 11:21). From the mother church in Jerusalem, a missionary named Barnabas was sent

---

[2] Mark Dever, *Nine Marks of a Healthy Church*, 4th ed. (Wheaton, IL: Crossway, 2021), 201–225.

to help the new church at Antioch. Many others came to faith in Jesus (Acts 11:24). Barnabas recognized the need for discipleship among the new believers, so he left for Tarsus to find a former Pharisee named Saul, whom he personally discipled, and brought him to Antioch to help teach and equip the church. For an entire year, Barnabas and Saul (Paul) discipled new believers. These disciples were called Christians (Acts 11:26).[3]

A prophet from Jerusalem appeared at the church in Antioch to request financial assistance for the struggling churches in Judea, which were facing famine. In response, the church at Antioch raised money to support the need and initiated a cooperative effort for other churches to contribute (Acts 11:29–30). As time passed, Antioch began to raise up elders within the church, each reflecting the diversity of the city (Acts 13:1). As these elders ministered God's Word and prayed, they were led by the Holy Spirit to send out two of their leaders to go and replicate their church. So they appointed Barnabas and Paul to be their first church-planting missionaries.[4]

Antioch became a hub for church planting across Asia Minor and eventually into Europe. The elders at Antioch continued to oversee the missions and fundraising strategy. Paul continued to return to Antioch to deliver reports and

---

[3] Ed Stetzer and Daniel Im, *Planting Missional Churches: Your Guide to Starting Churches that Multiply*, 2nd ed. (Nashville: B&H Academic, 2018), 38–42.

[4] John B. Polhill, *Acts*, vol. 26, The New American Commentary (Nashville: Broadman & Holman Publishers, 1992), 290.

to collect love offerings from the churches that were working together in missions.

Here is a summary of Antioch serving as Paul's sending church, along with Paul's ongoing relationship to it:

- Acts 11:25–26. Paul's ministry begins alongside Barnabas, and both become leaders and possibly elders.

- Acts 11:27–30. The church at Antioch sends Paul with famine relief to Judea.

- Acts 13:1–3. Paul is commissioned by Antioch for his first missionary journey.

- Acts 14:26–28. Paul returns to Antioch and reports to the elders after his first journey.

- Acts 15:1–2. Antioch sends Paul and a delegation to the Jerusalem Council.

- Acts 15:30–35. Paul returns from Jerusalem with a letter of cooperation.

- Acts 15:36–41. Antioch sends Paul on his second missionary journey.

- Acts 18:22–23. Paul returns to Antioch after planting several churches.

Also, when we consider Paul's indirect references to Antioch in his letters to the churches in Galatia and in Acts, it's clear that Antioch remained his home base and a steady source of support and strategy (Galatians 2:11–14; Acts 15:2, 22). The elders at Antioch provided spiritual, relational, and missional oversight—not just to Paul, but to others they sent out to plant. The kind of partnership they shared with their church plants gives us a compelling model for church-centered cooperation that Baptists should emulate.

Theological/Missiological Foundations

A biblical understanding of missions involves healthy, gospel-centered local churches. Planting reproducible churches until Christ returns is the joyful purpose of church-centric missions. What does a reproducible church look like? I often answer this question by using the language of five "selves" that I adapted from some 19th-century missionaries.

In the early days of modern missions, as our first missionaries made converts, they often expected those new believers to adapt not only the gospel but also Western culture. Converts were regrettably told to leave their communities and move into mission compounds—essentially small fortresses—where they were taught to speak, dress, and behave like Western Christians. They were cut off from their own people and culture and became utterly dependent on the missionaries for survival, guidance, and direction.

This practice created an unhealthy dependency, not just spiritually, but practically because these young believers relied on Western missionaries and Western dollars for everything. Rather than raising up local leaders and sustainable communities of faith, the work centered around a few missionaries who maintained most of the control. As a result, while there were many converts, very few actual churches were being planted, at least not churches that could sustain themselves over time.

That began to change through the work of some missionaries serving in Korea and China. Learning from the exploits of Hudson Taylor, these men flipped the model.[5] Instead of pulling new believers out of their communities, they kept them rooted among their own people. They began multiplying churches within the new believers' culture and relationships. Their approach wasn't just missiologically sound—it was biblical.

These missionaries developed what came to be known as the "three-self" principles for healthy, indigenous churches. Their conviction was simple but profound: every local church should be *self-governing, self-supporting,* and *self-propagating.*[6] In other words, the church should raise up its own leaders, fund its own ministry, and multiply on its own, without being propped up indefinitely by outside missionaries or money. These principles freed local churches from foreign dependence, enabling them to stand and grow independently. Over time, these three-self principles gained near-universal support among missionaries and became a new standard for assessing church health and guiding church planting efforts.

A missionary named John Nevius built upon these principles, significantly influencing the growth of the new churches in China, and laying the foundation for an explo-

---

[5] See Howard Taylor, Frederick, and Geraldine Guinness Taylor, *A Biography of James Hudson Taylor* (London: Hodder & Stoughton, 1997).

[6] Joshua Bowman, "The Nevius Method: Retrieving Theological and Missiological Criteria for Money in Missions," *Journal of Global Christianity* 7, no. 1 (n.d.), accessed July 2025, https://trainingleadersinternational.org/jgc/april-2022.

sion of healthy churches in Korea. Nevius taught that new be-lievers should remain in their communities and apply the gos-pel within their own cultural context, rather than adopting foreign customs. He emphasized relational evangelism over programmed events and urged churches to prioritize disciple-ship from the outset. According to Nevius, every local church should be capable of training its own leaders and providing consistent opportunities for leadership development.[7]

Nevius didn't just offer good theory; his ideas yielded real, lasting results. He shaped a model of church planting that prioritizes local ownership, gospel contextualization, and sustainable growth—principles we rely on today. From this model, I have adapted and added two additional "selves" that I use to describe the characteristics of a reproducible church. Here they are, along with a brief explanation of each. The goal of every church is to become:

1) Self-theologizing
2) Self-governing
3) Self-supporting
4) Self-multiplying
5) Self-cooperating

1) Self-Theologizing

A gospel-centered church interprets the Bible correctly and communicates theological truth with clarity. The church can discern false doctrine, admonish when needed, and apply the

---

[7] See Joshua Bowman, "The Nevius Method."

Scriptures in their specific cultural context. Church members are equipped to make disciples.

2) Self-Governing

An autonomous local church consists of baptized believers who voluntarily covenant together as a congregation under the authority of Scripture and the lordship of Jesus Christ. Biblically qualified pastors or elders, typically selected from within the body, lead the church by equipping its members for ministry and guiding them in the regular practice of God's ordinary means of grace.[8]

3) Self-Supporting

A strong local church can financially sustain its ministries, support its pastors, and care for needs within its community. The church isn't dependent on outside funding. It gives generously to missions and mercy ministries as an overflow of its love for God and neighbor.

4) Self-Multiplying

A healthy church reproduces itself. It makes disciples, sends out leaders, plants, re-plants, and revitalizes churches through relational evangelism and intentional missions.

---

[8] Brian A. DeVries, *You Will Be My Witnesses: Theology for God's Church Serving in God's Mission* (Wheaton, IL: Crossway, October 15, 2024), 140–141.

5) Self-Cooperating

Mature churches don't just grow—they partner with other like-minded churches. They develop local mission strategies and work alongside each other and within their networks to advance the gospel beyond their own reach.

From the beginning, The Pillar Network focused on the sending church, not just the churches planted. We view Antioch as the biblical model of a church that embodies these "five selves," one that equips, sends, and remains connected. Paul didn't just get his start there; he continued to come back for support, strategy, and encouragement. What should the ongoing relationship be between the sending church and those it sends? The Antioch model offers a framework for healthy oversight and partnership, grounded in gospel clarity, trust, and long-term cooperation. Achieving this level of maturity may take years. Until then, there must be an intentional, ongoing relationship between the sending church and its plant.

What the Early Years Require

Now that we have considered the task of sending from a Baptist perspective,[9] how does the sending church shepherd its church plant until it reaches a state of multiplying maturity? It takes wisdom for the sending church to transition from authority to influence, particularly during the early stages of

---

[9] The authors of this book serve in Baptist churches. We anticipate that some readers will not be from our Baptist tradition. We hope that our contribution to the sending church will serve beyond our Baptist family for the good of Christ's kingdom throughout the globe.

a church plant. Here are several tips I've learned from the successful plants my church has sent.

Equip and Send Well

Effective equipping, planning, fundraising, team building, and church-wide praying will pay off. A successful church plant begins years before the team is sent and a church is launched. It is best to make the church plant an "All-in" endeavor by the sending church's congregation. By the time the team is commissioned and sent, the whole church should be engaged and excited to support the new work. The twenty "sending services" that my church has celebrated over the years have been some of my sweetest memories. A well-sent team will have a better chance of thriving.[10]

Establish Relational Accountability

Like parents raising a child, the sending church must have an ongoing relationship to its plant. We have found that establishing a five-year covenant with our church plant teams is a way to provide relational and fiscal accountability. This covenant defines the relationship with the church plant and explains the transition from operating under the full authority of the sending church and its elders to becoming an autonomous sister church. The agreement lays out the communication channel between the sending church and the church plant, typically a monthly conversation and update. It also

---

[10] Craig Ott and Gene Wilson, *Global Church Planting: Biblical Principles and Best Practices for Multiplication* (Grand Rapids: Baker Academic, 2011), 349–370.

describes the financial commitment of the sending church for the next five years. This plan can be adjusted depending on the growth and viability of the church plant.

Have a 1-3-5-Year Plan

Goals turn intentions into direction, and without them, a church plant will struggle to navigate all the challenges of forming or reforming a new congregation. The sending church should help the lead planter and his team establish a series of goals for years one through five. These goals help the team to focus its energy and limited resources. They also help to avoid mission drift. The goals should include dates and numerical achievements. I have found that having 1-3-5-year goals that are specific yet flexible helps the sending church leaders by providing an evaluative tool for their plant. Consider budgets, fundraising, ministries, events, meeting spaces, and numerical growth when making the plan. This plan should be more specific in the first year and can be adjusted in the future.[11]

Engage the Church Elders and Staff

A well-equipped team needs a holistic understanding of what makes a church thrive. One of the biggest fallacies I heard when I first started pastoring was, "Just preach expositionally and the people will come." While I believe that preaching and teaching God's Word is central to the life of the church, leading and growing a healthy church requires much more.

---

[11] Ott and Wilson, *Global Church Planting*, 371–394.

When our elders and staff are all invested in preparing the planting team, the team's training becomes more comprehensive and our oversight becomes stronger. I love seeing our church elders and staff use their gifts—not just in preparation, but in the ongoing care and support of our church plants. It encourages me every time they share conversations they're continuing to have with them.

Maintain Physical Presence

Successful church plants thrive when they stay closely connected to their sending church. Ongoing communication matters, but nothing replaces face-to-face fellowship. At our church, we highlight one of our church plants each month with a video update during our Sunday gathering. During their first five years, we aim to visit annually and often send teams to help with outreach events. I offer to preach for them and spend a weekend on-site. It's always encouraging for their team when my wife and I or someone from our church spend meaningful time with them. Without question, our most fruitful plants are the ones where we've maintained the closest personal connection.

Evaluate With Care

There's a steep learning curve for any church planter or re-planter. Ongoing evaluation is necessary, but it shouldn't get in the way of daily ministry. That's where the sending church comes in. We can offer encouragement and a steady, outside voice. A seasoned pastor can provide clarity when a young planter is navigating the deep waters of a brand-new church in a new context. That outside wisdom matters, but it must never create dependency. I've learned—sometimes the hard way—that offering counsel is helpful only as long as you avoid micromanaging. Early on, I crossed that line more than once. Eventually, I realized there are some lessons my teams needed to learn for themselves, even if it meant stumbling. Failure can be a great teacher. My job is to keep them from crashing, not to keep them from learning.

Healthy oversight means the sending church offers support without control—empowering church planters to grow through experience, not just instruction.

Models of Oversight Between the Sending Church and Its Plant

Every church planting team eventually asks: What kind of relationship should we have with our sending church once we're launched? This isn't just a governance issue—it affects trust, pace, and long-term health. For the sending church, the challenge is to provide guidance without micromanaging, care without control, and to do so while honoring our Baptist convictions. Below I will offer a friendly critique of several standard models.[12]

Elder Delegation Model

In this model, one or more elders from the sending church remain temporarily on the plant's elder team during the early stages. This fosters doctrinal alignment and leadership stability, which is especially helpful if the planting team lacks

---

[12] Stetzer and Im, *Planting Missional Churches*, 63–81.

seasoned elders. It's an effective short-term solution for en-suring plurality and avoiding mission drift.[13] However, the line between support and overreach can become fuzzy. I see value in this model for short-term help, but once the plant covenants to become a local church, the sending church el-ders should step away. Baptist ecclesiology doesn't support elders functioning across two separate congregations.

Campus or "Mission" Model

In this model, the church plant becomes a "campus" (a new term) or "mission" (an old term) of the sending church for a season. The sending church elders function like a governing board until the plant can establish qualified leaders and orga-nize itself. The sending church elders oversee the finances of the campus church, or the plant's finances are absorbed into the sending church's budget. This model is helpful for legal and financial accountability in the early stages. But if extend-ed too long, it creates confusion about spiritual authority and stunts local leadership. I tend to avoid this model because it puts the new congregation in a position of submitting to pastors who aren't truly among them. Shepherding from a distance is rarely effective and often leads to dependency.

Covenantal Partnership Model

This model relies on a written agreement that outlines mu-tual expectations, phases of oversight, and the path to full autonomy. The sending church offers care and counsel, but

---

[13] Malphurs, *The Nuts and Bolts of Church Planting*, 81–96.

not direct authority after the new church covenants as its own. The strength here lies in its clarity. It preserves shared doctrine and vision without crossing Baptist ecclesiological boundaries. It works best when a qualified team is already in place, and both churches are committed to a long-term partnership. This is my preferred model, but the plant should wait to covenant together until it has biblically qualified elders in place to lead. Once that happens, the authority to call and submit to their own elders belongs to the members of the new church.

Hybrid/Phased Approach

There can be a combination of the three models mentioned above. Many factors come into play when planting or re-planting a church. The hybrid approach gradually reduces oversight (e.g. reducing elder oversight from 100% in year one, 50% in year two, 0% in year three), with the goal of full autonomy. It allows space for leaders to grow while they are still receiving pastoral care and correction. The timeline is helpful, but it must be flexible. This hybrid approach is most useful for churches committed to long-term multiplication, but who will be careful with the stewardship of doctrine, resources, and leadership. Once the church officially covenants, its elders should be chosen from within, not borrowed from another church.[14]

---

[14] See the APPENDIX for a composite model of these approaches, identifying key features, cautions, how to use, and where they fit in a Baptist historical position.

Principles for Healthy Oversight

Over the years of sending church planters, I've learned several lessons that often determine the health and longevity of a church plant. Consider these principles as you consider the task of sending governance.

Oversight Is Stewardship and not Ownership

The sending church is called to care for the plant with humility, not control. Its role is to guide the church toward maturity, not to hold it in permanent dependence.

Let the Relationship Shape Oversight

Healthy governance flows from a strong relational foundation. Trust, care, and regular communication are crucial to maintain this relationship. It is essential to have clear expectations about what this relationship entails.

Oversight Must Shift from Authority to Influence

Authority is usually necessary at the beginning, but it must give way to influence as the church plant matures. Wise sending churches plan for this transition from the beginning.

Healthy Plant Expectations and a Flexible Plan

A shared plan with defined expectations creates clarity and accountability. However, flexibility is key, as every plant will face unique challenges and exhibit distinct growth patterns.

Shepherding the Sent Demands Ongoing Soul Care

Pastoral care for the planter and his family is critical throughout the process. Regular encouragement and presence from the sending church can be the difference between burnout and endurance. Don't neglect to care for the souls of everyone sent, including single adults. Sending oversight is a gospel-shaped trust between churches. It is a step of faith that requires trust in God's power, not just our plans. As both churches move forward, let them do so with courage and joy, remembering Paul's words: "He who began a good work in you will carry it on to completion until the day of Christ Jesus" (Phil. 1:6).

CHAPTER 19

HOW DO I CONTINUE SHEPHERDING THOSE SENT?

Matt Rogers

We've all heard the adage "out of sight, out of mind." While we'd love to press against this reality, this language represents a truth that's common in church planting and mission sending. It's easy to give attention to the plant, the planting pastor, and the core group when those people are right in front of us and in our churches. We see them weekly, interact in the hallways, attend meetings together, show up at the same church events, and likely even rub shoulders in the community. This proximity makes it easy for a marginally intentional person to give care.

But as soon as that person is sent, everything changes, especially if they are sent to another city or around the world. In contrast to previous generations, we have it easy. Virtually anywhere in the world, people are only a text message or

FaceTime call away. We don't have to handwrite letters and wait months for them to arrive. Of course, such technological connectivity is a flimsy replacement for personal presence, but we are able to give intentional care to people literally around the world. Modern transportation also makes it accessible to get face-to-face with a planter in short order. Especially if the person is planting in the U.S., someone could receive an SOS call about a need one morning and be present with the planter by mid-afternoon. Our world makes connection and care easier. But sending churches still must consider how to avoid letting "out of sight, out of mind" be the reality in their planting efforts.

In this chapter, I'll aim to give guidance for how sending churches can cultivate ongoing, meaningful relationships with those they've sent. Chapter 9 by Clint Darst in this book aims to highlight how sending churches can help their *congregations* stay meaningfully invested in the plant. My intention in the present chapter is to focus on the *pastors* of these churches, especially the sending church, and to discuss how these pastors can continue to shepherd those they've sent.[1]

To accomplish this goal, I'll borrow the categories we use at the church I help to pastor in order to shepherd our members well. Early in the church, we adopted the terms "wounded," "wayward," and "walking faithfully." These categories refer to the general health of our members when we would talk about them and pray for them in elder meetings.

---

[1] See Phil A. Newton and Rich C. Shadden, *Shepherding the Pastor: Help for the Early Years of Ministry* (Greensboro, NC: New Growth Press, 2023) for an expanded view of how this kind of relationship might function.

The *wounded* are those members who've had something happen to them—some form of suffering—that created hardship. It might be a death in the family, a cancer scare, the loss of a job, or other byproducts of living in a fallen world. In contrast, those who are *wayward* have made intentional choices that have distanced them from God and his church. Many times, these are people we haven't seen in a while and seem to be isolating themselves from church life. Other times we know the issues and the sin that is prompting them to walk away. Finally, there sheep who are *walking faithfully*. They aren't perfect, but as much as we can tell they are seeking to honor God and live obediently to His ways. A wise shepherd attends to each of these sheep differently. The same is true for how we care for those we send to plant new churches.[2]

Sent Ones Who Are Wounded

Through my master's and doctoral studies, I read almost every book on church planting—both those with a focus on domestic missions and those with an international bent. There were various differences, but one of the starkest was the fact that almost every international church planting book had at least one chapter on spiritual warfare, whereas North American church planting books almost universally left that topic out entirely, or gave it a cursory mention among many

---

[2] For another approach used during the Reformation era, see Martin Bucer, *Concerning the True Care of Souls*, trans. by Peter Beale (Edinburgh: Banner of Truth Trust, 2009).

other topics.[3] I think the international missiologists are on to something important here because spiritual warfare is a defining factor for almost every church planter I've encountered, especially in the first few years of planting. Spiritual warfare has many faces, but it's common for planters to face opposition and endure wounds that aren't due to sin or poor choices. It's not universally true, but I've seen a large percentage of planters face grueling medical issues in the first five years. For some, emotional or mental health concerns show up, even among the planter's children.

Planters are often in their 30s or 40s, which means they are often caring for parents or other family members in failing health. Children may rebel as they enter teen years, or the demands of parenting young children exhaust the planter and wife's energy. Finances are also a huge variable—the pressure of bi-vocational work,[4] fears regarding support-rais-

---

[3] I am thankful for leaders like Chuck Lawless who focuses on this topic in much of his writing. See Chuck Lawless, *Spiritual Warfare in the Storyline of Scripture: A Biblical, Theological, and Practical Approach* (Nashville: B&H Academic, 2019). Dr. Lawless trains hundreds of missionaries with the International Mission Board of the Southern Baptist Convention and is therefore able to help future missionaries and church planters account for spiritual warfare in their work.

[4] Many prefer to speak of co-vocational planting now rather than bi-vocational because the prefix "co-" implies that the person is finding secular employment alongside, or with his planting efforts, rather than seeing secular employment merely as a means to the end of becoming employed solely by the church. In some contexts, such co-vocational work may be necessary, but my experience suggests that the best model is for a planter to attend to the church as his full-time vocation as much as possible, while having some type of side-hustle to support the work. There are exceptions, however. Those who do pursue long-term secular employment will need a robust

ing, or finding a home amid surging prices. This suffering compounds the fact that many planters are doing something really hard. Starting a church isn't for the faint-hearted, nor is it easy for planters to adjust to new roles and responsibilities, like preaching week to week. Every planter will take on his fair share of wounds.[5] And the same factors that wound the planter will also impact his wife, his children, and those on his core team in various ways.

How can sending church pastors help those who are wounded? First, they must *anticipate* these wounds. Rather than waiting for a hurting planter to stumble into the office and unburden several years of wounds, good pastors will expect these wounds and call them out ahead of time.[6] There's

---

team of pastors committed to the work in order to care for the church.

[5] One way a sending church could help would be to provide some type of ongoing counseling for the planting pastor. While much spiritual care can, and should, come from within the church, the planter will be somewhat isolated until a team is in place and there can be great wisdom in having someone outside of the local church where he pastors to talk to about current and past wounds. I've found great help in groups like Anchored Virtual who seek to provide biblically grounded, clinically informed care. See more at https://anchoredvirtual.com/.

[6] Admittedly, some of this requires pastoral instincts. Good pastors learn how to see and meet needs and they've disciplined themselves to seek out those who are hurting and minister the gospel in those situations. One reality I've seen in my own life as our church has become a sending church is my own limited bandwidth. Once someone is sent, I am often too quick to move on to the next-up leader and I've had to learn the hard way to fight this tendency. But I've also seen the value of having others on my pastoral staff who can care for sent ones also. It doesn't always have to be the lead sending pastor who reaches out and expresses care or concern. Instead, it's wise for a pastoral team to subdivide those who are sent from the church to various pastors for care so that no one is overlooked. Here's a good place to

a rough parallel to discipling men. Anytime I sit down with a young man who approaches me for discipleship, I assume that sexual sin and pornography are issues we will have to discuss. Rather than working through months of conversations before we get to that topic, I've learned to bring it up early and often. When I call out the elephant in the room, the man is often relieved of the pressure of having to figure out how to broach the topic himself. We can then make some strides toward help. Sending church pastors should do the same. Periodic check-ins in which the sending church pastor asks about their health, their emotional stability, the pressure of preaching, and other factors creates a context where the planter can be honest and open. One habit I've tried to cultivate over the years is to place the hard days of others on my calendar so I don't forget. Were you to look at my calendar you might see "Anniversary of _____'s dad's death" or "Day _____ had a miscarriage." Not only does this remind me to pray for the person, but it also gives me a chance to reach out at the start of the day and let them know I care.

Next, sending pastors should be *present.* This is the single most important factor in good pastoral ministry, whether you are caring for church members or other pastors. We must show up when life gets hard. I've found that it's best to consider the sending church pastor and core group as ongoing members of our church for a season. This doesn't mean they retain membership in two places—I'm simply saying that I

---

see elder plurality at work. See Dave Harvey, *The Plurality Principle: How to Build and Maintain a Thriving Church Leadership Team* (TGC BOOKS; Wheaton, IL: Crossway, 2021), for a thoughtful perspective.

try to approach them as if they haven't left. If I'd show up at the hospital during a surgery for a member, then I should strive to do the same for a pastor I've sent. Of course, this gets more complex if the plant is far away, but this distance can also be an opportunity to demonstrate an even greater level of care. I've often heard of the tremendous value of such prompt action on the part of the sending church pastor. Perhaps it's a death in the family, a tough medical diagnosis, or a dire situation in the marriage or with the children. The sending church pastor learns about it and promptly jumps on a plane to be there. The pastor may not be able to do anything about the situation, but the gift of presence shows the planter that he and his family are not forgotten.[7]

Finally, good pastors *pray* for the wounded. This should come as no surprise. The main way we fight spiritual battles on behalf of others is to pray for them. When we pray, we enter into the battle on behalf of those we love. Sending pastor, consider some rhythm that anchors these sent ones in your prayer. For me, it's Monday and missionaries. Each Monday I try to bring various sent ones to the Father in prayer. Some strategy like this trains me toward intentional intercession. But one other layer seems important. It has also proven profitable to let people know when I pray for them.

---

[7] The same level of care is critical to shepherd planters' wives. Often the wounds faced by planters involve children and this pressure impacts moms in unique ways that men may find difficult to understand. I know of countless stories of planters' wives grinding it out with little children and feeling exhausted and alone. A pastor's wife from the sending church who shows up to sit with this mom, pray with her, help her fold clothes, and make dinner can be a ray of sunlight in a dark season.

There's certainly a way to do this that's showboating: "Look at me and how I prayed for you!" We want to avoid that. You can simply take 60 seconds after your prayer time to send a short text message. You'll be surprised at how much this matters and how many doors it will open for people to share more about the wounds they are experiencing.

Sent Ones Who Are Wayward

Wayward sheep are tough, whether they are in your church or sent from your church. It's hard to help people who are hurting because of sinful things they've done. Again, there is a range of complexity here. The implications of some waywardness are different than others.

For example, some planters will drift due to fear of man.[8] They drive home on Sundays and give themselves a thumbs up or thumbs down based on how many people showed up, how well they preached, and if the people seemed happy. Fear of man plays a role in everyone's church planting experience; it takes years to outgrow people-pleasing. If fear of man lingers unaddressed, however, it can cripple the planter and lead to all sorts of sinful habits.

Marriage is another battleground. Many planters neglect their primary relationships with their wife and kids and give the best they have to the planting efforts. Over time, the

---

[8] Here I wanted to say "all pastors" instead of "some pastors" but you're taught never to say "all" in formal writing. It may not be all pastors but it sure is close. Every church planter that I've known has battled fear of man—the only difference is how that fear of man becomes evident.

unattended relationships suffer, pornography becomes an escape, and adultery is common.[9]

This area of waywardness is also a great danger for the core group in the plant. There, it's common to see people walk away into sin. As I mentioned in a prior chapter, it can be overwhelming to face issues that may necessitate church discipline when you are a young church and young church planter. Let's say the core team consists of twenty people and two of them have an affair. Such sin can be difficult for any church, but it's far easier to absorb this level of complexity if this occurs in an older, established church with many mature church members. It could cripple a young plant. Also, it's one thing for a church planter to have walked through something like this in a former ministerial role, but it's another thing altogether to lead a church through such pain. So how might a sending church pastor help care for a wayward pastor or core team member?

---

[9] I try to link a sending church pastor and wife with the planting pastor and wife for this very reason. Planting a church is extremely hard on a marriage and the planter and his wife need to have someone to talk to about the complexity they are facing. Rather than talking to different people, my experience suggests that it's ideal to have them linked with another husband and wife with whom they can have shared conversations through the planting journey. Sarah and I have actively sought this out in our city. Though not from our sending church, we've found a couple of couples from other churches whom we respect, and we've been intentional to ask them to double date with us so we can ask questions and allow them to poke around in our lives. We are doing this now with couples who are one step ahead of us in terms of sending their children off to college because we know this season will be tough. These couples have given us practical wisdom that would be hard to pick up simply from reading a book.

First, *help planters prepare*. You're likely familiar with Paul Tripp's book on marriage, *What Did You Expect?*[10] His premise is simple: Most marital discord, especially in the first few years, boils down to unmet expectations. I think he's right. The same can often be said for planters. Much of the angst in planting comes from the ill-fated assumption that they will either avoid such waywardness or that they will miraculously know how to navigate it when it happens. Then, when sin enters the mix, planters are underprepared to respond well, and it crushes them. We can serve planters well by talking about these issues ahead of time and giving them a backstage pass to go with us as we walk through hard things with others. Many people, even pastors, have never seen someone confront another person in sin. They've not sat in the room when a spouse confessed an affair. They've not been on the receiving end of the "Brother, we need to talk" phone call. But sending pastors have, and we serve future planters by allowing them to eavesdrop on our own efforts to give care in hard situations.

Next, sending pastors should *have hard conversations early*. You'll have to be doing a good job of staying connected for this to work, but if you are engaged with the planter then you'll likely pick up on concerns along the way. You might notice the planter cutting corners at home or see him speak harshly to or about his wife in public. You might notice that he's quick to despair when things go poorly or isolate himself

---

[10] Paul David Tripp, *What Did You Expect? Redeeming the Realities of Marriage* (Wheaton, IL: Crossway, 2015); now revised as *Marriage: 6 Gospel Commitments Every Couple Needs to Make* (Wheaton, IL: Crossway, 2021).

when he's having a bad day. Someone else close to the planter might tip you off to some concerning trends they observe. Should this happen, it's wise for the sending church pastor to preemptively have conversations about these concerns. One of the pastors on our team encourages us to have "I wonder…" conversations. By this he means to introduce potential issues gently and without accusation. "I wonder how you are doing at cultivating time with your wife," rather than, "You are not loving your wife the way you should." Or, "I wonder how you are responding to lower attendance at the church over the summer," rather than, "You care too much about attendance." These gentle but probing questions let the planter know you are aware of potential issues and want to give them a chance to talk freely.

Finally, a sending church pastor can *model repentance*. It's easy for planters to assume that they must have their act together now that they've started a new church. There's truth to this because planters and pastors should strive to be above reproach (1 Tim. 3:2; Titus 1:6–7). But all pastors will sin. Sending church pastors have a chance to model humility and repentance. There may be sin issues that disqualify the planter for a season or for good. But, if the sending pastor addresses issues quickly, it's more likely that he'll have a chance to talk about what form healthy repentance can take long before the sin becomes fully formed and leads to death or disqualification (James 1:15). It's wise for the sending pastor to share how he may have struggled with similar issues in the past—whether it was overworking, escaping through addictive behaviors, being harsh with his spouse, domineering with the children, anxious about money, or tossed to and fro by people's opinions. The sending pastor can model for the planter what he did to bring these issues into the light and, hopefully, set a model for the planter for the rest of his ministry.

Sent Ones Walking Faithfully

Finally, we'll end by discussing how we can care for those who are walking faithfully. I saved the best for last! In God's kindness, the joy of a pastor is to see many in his flock walking with Jesus and doing so with all of the fruit of His Spirit (Gal. 5:22–23; 3 John. 4). What a gift. The same is true for those we send. How blessed we are to see those we've invested in leave our churches to start other churches or support church-planting work. In many ways, these men and women are the lasting fruit of our ministry and proof that God was indeed faithful to do in and through our lives far more than we could ask or imagine (Eph. 3:20).

There are ways you'll know that a planter or team are walking faithfully. For one, you'll see them persevering. They'll stay at it. They'll preach sermons, share the gospel, plan God-honoring services, disciple others, and care for God's people. We should praise God as this happens. The supposedly "ordinary" work of a pastor is supernaturally extraordinary, so praise God if you have a brother still at it. You'll also see fruit in this ministry. We do have to be careful here because we don't want to communicate that faithfulness to the work means massive church growth or other forms of fruit that are easy to quantify on a chart.

But we'd also not want to swing the pendulum in the other direction. Fruit matters. We just want to make sure we are assessing the right kinds of fruit. We want to see a brother who is faithful to preach robust, expositional sermons that are faithful to the biblical author's intent.[11] We want to see a pastor who is intent to shepherd the flock of God that he does have, even if that flock is small (1 Pet. 5:2). We want to see someone laboring to evangelize the lost and disciple new converts, even if the soil is difficult and conversion is slow.

Lastly, faithfulness is measured by core team members giving their best to serve the church. When we planted, one of our core team members became dear to me. If you were picking a core team member out of a line up, this guy would not have been the one you'd pick. People weren't his thing and he struggled to engage in even basic conversation. His job? Show up at the storage unit at 6:00 a.m. each Sunday morning, hook his truck up to the trailer that had everything our church needed to set up in the elementary school, pull it to the school, and give instructions to a team of volunteers to get it in the right place. I truly don't know how our church would have navigated those early years had it not been for this faithful brother. The same story was shared recently by a planter friend in Alaska except his guy had to bring a blow torch each week to melt the ice on the trailer hitch. Praise God for faithful servants like these who are using their gifts to build up the church.

---

[11] Here again, "faithful" is the key word. For most of us, our first few years of weekly preaching will result in many sermons that are average at best. It takes time to develop the skills necessary to preach truly excellent sermons. So, better to look at a brother's faithfulness to the text and his commitment to proclaim the gospel early on. Get that right, and the skills needed to truly excel in the pulpit will come in time.

Once again, here are three ways a sending church pastor can care for those walking faithfully. First, the pastor can *encourage* faithfulness. We know that church planting takes faith, so any time we have a chance to stick courage into the heart of another person we want to do that. Technology can be your friend. As I was planting, I had an older pastor who would periodically text me that he had listened to one of my sermons. At first, I wanted to crawl in a hole for fear of what might come, but this older brother was able to speak to one or two things that I'd done in my sermon that he found particularly compelling. It wasn't the general "good sermon, preacher," but an actual note of appreciation tied to specific aspects of the sermon. I can't tell you how much those texts gave me courage, particularly when they came after I'd preached sermons that I thought were subpar.[12] You can do the same in an area where you see or hear of faithfulness on the part of someone on the planting team. And good news, pastor—if you develop the habit of calling out faithfulness when you see it, you'll be a better pastor to your people and a better husband and father. People thrive when they are affirmed.[13]

Sending churches can also find ways to *bless faithfulness*. Again, there's tension here. We don't want to simply

---

[12] If you ever read this, thanks Pastor Matt. You know who you are and I still have some of those texts saved because it meant so much to me to have a brother like you help me see the good in my fledgling efforts to become a preacher.

[13] For additional help in affirming others, see Sam Crabtree, *Practicing Affirmation: God-centered Praise of Those Who are Not God* (Wheaton, IL: Crossway, 2011).

reward people when they do a good job like a Pavlovian dog. But we can and should find ways to affirm those who are serving faithfully in the work. I've found that some of the best forms of blessing are linked to an area that the sending church knows the planter needs. For example, a sending pastor or his church can purchase a commentary series or Logos subscription for a new preacher. Or you could bless the pastor with a weekend away at an Airbnb with his wife. You might consider giving a scholarship to your annual men's or women's retreat for everyone serving on the core team. For most sending churches, this requires marginal financial investment, but it communicates to the planter and the team that you notice and value their work.

Finally, sending pastors can *celebrate faithfulness*. Here is a place where planting comes full circle and is a means of enhancing the health of the sending church. These sent ones are a steady source of examples and sermon illustrations of faithfulness to God's mission. Sunday services can highlight fruit from faithful church planters and core team members. Periodically, the sending church could have the planting pastor back to preach on a Sunday or lead a retreat in order to highlight the work being done. The church website, videos, or social media are other great ways to celebrate the good work being done through church planting. You'll be surprised at how this act of celebration encourages planters. Every Sunday in our weekly liturgy we have a time we call the "mission moment." We spotlight a church planter or missionary sent from our church, share some fruit of their work, and ask the church to pray for specific things. Sometimes those we've sent are there and able to give the report in person. Other times, one of our pastors does it on their behalf. Each Sunday during this moment I see people in the church holding up phones to take a picture of the prayer prompts from the slides. They text this picture to those we are praying for or post it on WhatsApp to let them know that their sending church is invested in their work. These moments encourage both the sending church who is seeking to raise up more men and women and the sent ones who feel the blessings that come through the prayers of God's people.

None of this is rocket science. And yet, "out of sight, out of mind" is the natural drift for those who are not attentive to care well for the sheep who are wounded, wayward, or walking faithfully. The guidance in this chapter assures that our sent ones are "out of sight, but always on our minds."

POSTLUDE

Phil A. Newton

A baker's dozen voices in one book speaking together on a singular subject may overwhelm the senses. As one of the editors, it's been a joy to hear each voice through writing, with each one's insights and experiences encouraging sending churches and those they plant. Knowing all the contributors, and having been in most of their churches, I felt intensely their passion to see churches in the nooks and crannies of the world become sending churches.

Yet with all the theological foundations, pastoral preparation, and church planting strategies, none of these things suffice to plant a church. No doubt, a church can do lots of good work, put together a planting team, supply the finances, secure a location, and see a new church rise from the dust into reality. But bricks and mortar, people and budgets, new members and ministries do not make a healthy church. More than anything, we need the gospel's power and the Spirit to direct our every step (Rom. 1:16–17; 1 Cor. 1:18–31; 2 Cor. 4:1–6; Gal. 5:16; Eph. 5:18). Church planting is hard work, as our writers have pointed out. It requires lots of attention to logistics and structures. But ministry to people is chiefly spiritual work. If that's the case, then pastors, elders, deacons, and members must be spiritually alive, Jesus-loving people.

I don't want to sound like a stick in the mud, but the hard work of church planting is not the structures, systems, and regimens we develop to keep the machinery running. It's living life together in Jesus Christ, mirroring the gospel in our relationships, walking in the fullness of the Spirit, and maintaining the unity of the Spirit in the bond of peace. Yes, the structures and systems can be gut-wrenching to put together. We desperately need people to serve in nursery, lead music, contact guests, show hospitality, and disciple new believers. More than that, we need them to do it all with skill and joy. But at the heart of it all are pastors and members who walk with Christ and by God's grace live out the gospel.

I had the opportunity to plant a church in 1987. That was before we had church planting networks, good theological emphases, and substantial ecclesiological and polity works to shape the process. I made so many mistakes! By the Lord's mercies, we made it—and I don't mean that as cliché. He showed mercy amid the stumbling and stammering of this planter and those joining him. I remained as lead pastor for thirty-five years before retiring to serve with The Pillar Network. Looking back, I see lots of things I could have done better. The chapters of this book would have saved me from countless missteps, relational blunders, and flawed structures. It would have helped me in subsequent years to be more engaged in church planting. And yet, the most important lesson I learned in those years of planting and pastoring is this: If we will serve Christ's church, then we must walk with Him.

So read these chapters. Learn from each writer's wealth of experience, study, and hard work. Discuss the details with your leadership team. Train the potential planting team with the insights found in these pages. But more than anything else, walk with the Lord Jesus. Model Christ-likeness to those you train and equip. Live in the fullness and power of the Spirit. Depend upon the Lord to build His church. Display the fruit of the gospel in the relationships formed in the church. Bear the joyful testimony of redeemed people into the community and across the globe. Do all that you do for the glory of God.

APPENDIX

CHURCH PLANT OVERSIGHT MODELS
COMPARISON TABLE

Model	Key Feature	Strengths
Elder Delegation	Sending church elders temporarily serve on plant's elder team	Doctrinal alignment, stability, elder plurality in early stages
Campus or Mission	Sending church fuctions as governing board	Legal and fiscal accountability, safeguards early integrity
Covenantal Partnership	Formal agreement outlines roles and phases	Clarity, mutual expectations, shared vision without authority confusion
Hybrid/ Phased	Oversight gradually decreases over time	Flexible, developmental, avoids indefinite control

Cautions	Best Used When	Baptist Conviction Fit
Risk of overreach; unclear roles if prolonged	Planter is called but not yet qualified; only one elder in place	Moderate— Valid sort-term; not sustainable after covenanting
Delays autonomy; undermines local authority	Very early stage with no qualified leaders	Low— Undermines local church autonomy and pastoral proximity
Needs a mature team; requires clear agreement	Qualified leaders in place; focus on collaboration, not control	High— Honors congregational authority and elder autonomy
Requires reassessment; timeline alone doesn't guarantee readiness	Plant has growing team, but needs gradual release	Moderate to High— As long as elder autonomy begins post-covenant

www.ingramcontent.com/pod-product-compliance
Lightning Source LLC
Jackson TN
JSHW021856230925
91531JS00012B/42